Metaphysics, Reference, and Language

Metaphysics, Reference, and Language

by James W. Cornman

New Haven and London • Yale University Press

TO BETTY

Whose loving encouragement was the greatest help.

Preface

This book has grown out of my first encounters with linguistic philosophy while I was a graduate student. Linguistic analysis seemed to be an incisive and important tool for approaching philosophy but I was not sure of its relevance to the traditional problems of philosophy. In one way or another I have been trying to become clear about the relationship between the two ever since. This book is an attempt to express the conclusions I have reached about this relationship and the consequences of it for philosophy. I am by no means certain that all these conclusions are true; my aim has been to argue that they are reasonable. Some of my arguments may fail, but I have tried to make each one at least a prolegomenon to a future sound argument.

I have benefited from the advice and criticism of many people and owe special thanks to John W. Lenz and Wesley C. Salmon for early help and encouragement, Richard Severens for many enlightening discussions during our three years as colleagues, Lewis W. Beck and Jerome Stolnitz for their comments on what would otherwise have been the final draft, and especially Keith Lehrer for his incisive comments and imaginative suggestions from beginning to end. Mrs. Jane Isay deserves not only my thanks but also that of the readers for making the book more readable.

JAMES W. CORNMAN

University of Rochester
January 1966

Contents

Preface   vii

Introduction   xi

PART I   The Mind–Body Problem   1

1. The Traditional Problem   3
    Reductive materialism, 4; mind–body dualism,
    8; the double aspect theory, 11
2. The Linguistic Problem   15
    Linguistic monism, 17; linguistic dualism, 25;
    the double language theory, 34
3. The Relation of the Linguistic Problem to the
    Traditional Problem   53
    Position 1—The solution of the linguistic prob-
    lem is the solution of the traditional problem,
    54; Position 2—The solution of the linguistic
    problem shows that there is no traditional prob-
    lem, 63; Position 3—The solution of the lin-
    guistic problem is evidence for the solution of
    the traditional problem, 70; Position 4—The
    solution of the linguistic problem has no re-
    lationship to the solution of the traditional
    problem, 78

PART II   Linguistic Reference and External Questions   81

4. Linguistic Reference   83
    The problem of finding the reference of an ex-
    pression, 83; reference is found by using a
    theory of reference, e.g. the theory of extension,
    86; designators and a problem for the theory of
    extension, 91; the picture theory of meaning as
    providing criteria of designators, 95; objections
    to the picture theory of meaning, 102; objec-

tions to theories of reference, 105; reference is
found by using the reference rule for each expression, 122; formal vs. nonformal reference
rules, 126; conclusion about reference rules and
the mind–body problem, 136

5. Internal and External Questions   139
A paradox about reference and ontological
questions, 139; five kinds of referring expressions, 142; referring expressions and ontological
commitment, 148; alternative criteria of ontological commitment, 151; ontological commitment and linguistic frameworks, 161; questions
internal and external to a linguistic framework,
166; external questions and resolution of the
paradox, 177; an objection to external ontological questions, 180; conclusion about external
ontological questions, 187

PART III   External Problems   195

6. External Problems and Philosophical Analysis   197
Meaning analysis, 200; the problem of synon-
ymy and ordinary language, 210; reconstruction
analysis, 216; the problem of justifying the
reconstruction of a linguistic framework, 224;
use analysis, 227; conclusion about the applicability of use analysis to external problems,
238

7. External Problems and Use Analysis   240
How use analysis is relevant to external prob-
lems, 240; the problem of justifying the application of use analysis to external problems,
244; attempts to justify the application of use
analysis to external problems, 253; conclusion
about use analysis and external problems, 255

Summary and Concluding Remarks   258
Summary, 258; a suggestion for a justifiable
approach to external problems, 262

Index   283

Introduction

Are there material objects or really only sense-data? Are there minds as well as bodies or only one or perhaps neither? Does God exist? Are there nonnatural ethical and aesthetic properties? Are there universals? Are free will and determinism compatible? These are some of the questions philosophers have tried to answer, questions about what there is, to be asked not by scientists, not the man in the street, but by philosophers who sit and ponder them. Currently, however, many philosophers no longer seem to be engaged in the attempt to answer these questions but consider what, at least at first glance, seem to be quite different questions. They no longer ponder problems about what there is; rather they try to establish the logical relationships among certain expressions of language, the very expressions philosophers have used to ponder about what there is. The questions these "linguistic" philosophers ask are something like: What is the logical analysis of 'There is a chair (material object) in the room'? Is this sentence logically equivalent to certain sentences about sense-data? What is the logical analysis of belief-sentences such as 'John believes that today is Tuesday'? Is this sentence logically equivalent to certain sentences about human behavior?

There does not seem to be any relationship between these two different kinds of philosophical questions because one kind seems to be about what there is, and the other about language. But it also seems that linguistic philosophers must think there is some relation between the two, because the problems that interest them, the linguistic problems, concern the language used to express the traditional problems. Some philosophers claim not only that there is a relation between the two sorts of questions but that they are really the same questions; the "traditional" philosophers are only pondering linguistic relationships although, perhaps, they do not realize it. Others, not so extreme, claim that a given answer to a linguistic question suggests a parallel answer to the corresponding traditional question. Still others claim that once we see the correct logic of the relevant expressions, we can see that we were misled in thinking there are any such things as the traditional problems. Those who think that there are such problems have misunderstood the logic of their language; seeing language correctly rids us of the perplexities that give rise to them.

At this point we may ask which, if any, of these views about the relationship between linguistic problems and traditional problems is correct. It may be that they are all wrong, that there is no important relationship between the two kinds of problems. In order to begin to answer this question, it seems best to concentrate on one specific problem. Because there has been much discussion of both the traditional and linguistic versions of the mind–body problem, we shall center our discussion upon it and examine different proposed views as to the relationship between the two versions.

One view about the relationship between the two is that the traditional mind–body problem is really only a linguistic problem. To see the difficulties of this view, let us look briefly at the views of two men, Herbert Feigl and Gilbert Ryle. Both men discuss language in their examination of the mind–body problem, but they do so in different ways. Feigl talks primarily about what certain linguistic expressions refer to and concludes that mind-expressions and body-expressions refer to the same things, in much the same way that morning-star expressions and evening-star expressions refer to the same thing, i.e. Venus. Feigl, then, is not merely talking about language but also about what language refers to, which in this case, he would claim, is nonlinguistic. In other words, it follows from Feigl's solution that there are not both minds and bodies but only one thing which we can talk about or refer to in two different ways. Feigl, then, is interested in the traditional problem rather than the linguistic problem, although he approaches the traditional problem by way of language.

But philosophers who claim that the traditional problem is really only the linguistic problem want to say more than this. They would claim that Feigl is wrong in thinking that he is talking about what there is, because the expressions he uses to state his position really refer to certain characteristics of mind-expressions and body-expressions. Feigl, although he thinks he is referring to the traditional problem, is really referring to the linguistic one. But it would seem that we can decide this issue only by considering what the relevant linguistic expressions refer to. Thus we must consider the problem of linguistic reference, a problem which, as we shall see, has far-reaching consequences for philosophy.

To return to Feigl and Ryle. Can they be discussing the same problem? They do not seem to be. Ryle, on one interpretation at least, discusses the logic of mind-expressions and the logic of body-expressions and concludes that their logic is quite different, but that together they make up the logic of person-talk. However nothing follows from this about what these expressions refer to, although Ryle sometimes seems to think that it does. It does not follow from Ryle's view that a view such as Feigl's is correct, because it does not follow that mind-expressions and body-expressions both refer to one kind of thing, i.e. a person. To get from the logic of person-talk to persons or minds and bodies we need a premise about the reference of the expressions, just as we need a premise to show Feigl is really talking about the linguistic problem. Because Feigl is concerned with the reference of language and Ryle with the logic of language, there seems to be no reason to think they are discussing the same subject. The only way to settle the issue, however, is to find out just what the expressions Feigl and Ryle use refer to.

It may be that Ryle's solution, although not a solution to
the same problem as Feigl's, provides evidence for the kind
of solution Feigl proposes. But why should anyone think that
because mind-expressions and body-expressions are logically different we have some evidence that these two kinds of
expressions really refer to the same thing? There is, then, a
question of whether a conclusion about the logic of certain
expressions is evidence for their reference. We can see that
this is a vital question by considering a contrasting position.
Roderick Chisholm claims that because mind-expressions are
intentional, and intentional expressions are not logically
equivalent to any set of body-expressions, this linguistic
dualism provides evidence for a traditional mind–body dualism. Thus the claim that there is a linguistic mind–body
dualism has been used in attempts to draw two entirely different conclusions about the reference of the expressions. To
choose between them, we must again consider the problem
of linguistic reference, because it is about the reference of
mind-expressions and body-expressions that Chisholm and
Feigl disagree.

The third view mentioned above seems to avoid all these
problems: philosophers with a tendency to search after and
ponder over what there is, the ultimate furniture of the universe, can be cured of this "disease" by being shown that
their perplexity arises because they misconstrue the logic of
their language. However, although this may well be true of
particular questions and answers stated by particular philosophers, it does not seem true in all cases. But even in
those cases where a philosopher is mistaken about language
he misconstrues not only the logic of the expressions but also
their reference. Supposedly, however, it is because a philosopher misconstrues the logic of certain expressions that he
becomes misled about the reference of the expressions. It is
held that Meinong's conclusion that golden mountains and
round squares "exist" is the result of such a mistake. The
logic of the sentences containing the relevant expressions is
different from what he supposed; therefore he was misled

into thinking that these expressions denote something. Russell's theory of descriptions supposedly shows that there is no good reason to think that these expressions denote.

Philosophy carried out in this way seems to be a method for curing people of the disease of doing philosophy. If everyone were cured there would be no philosophy to do, for no one would be misled by language to ponder philosophically about what there is. But this view, like the two mentioned above, involves assumptions about linguistic reference, because to substantiate this view we must at least be able to find a criterion for saying that someone is misled about linguistic reference. Could not Meinong, for example, fully agree with the logical features of the theory of descriptions and still make his claims that golden mountains exist? If an expression such as 'The golden mountain does not exist' is logically equivalent to Russell's translation, then if the one refers to a golden mountain the other does also. We seem again to be involved in the same problem. To understand what we can infer about the reference of linguistic expressions from conclusions about their logic, we must again consider the problem of linguistic reference.

Our conclusion, the conclusion of Part I of this book, is that we must establish some thesis about linguistic reference in order to infer justifiably anything about traditional problems from positions reached by a linguistic approach to philosophy, even if we infer that there are no traditional problems, or that philosophy is merely lexicography or games of logic. This leads us into Part II, an examination of certain proposed theories of linguistic reference, their problems and consequences for philosophy.

We can start the examination with the kind of theory of meaning proposed by Carnap, Quine, Church, and Lewis. Their theories are designed to provide us with tools for establishing both the intension (or meaning) and the extension (or reference) of certain linguistic expressions, in particular those linguistic expressions that, as Carnap puts it, are either cognitive sentences or parts of cognitive sentences.

Such theories must somehow distinguish between those expressions to which the tools apply and those to which they
do not. However, neither Carnap nor the others have done
this; their method and tools must be supplemented in some
way if they are to help us reach any decision about the
mind–body problem in particular, and the other philosophical problems like it.

To supplement such theories of meaning, we need a criterion for distinguishing expressions that refer from those
that do not and a criterion to find out what any specific referential expression refers to. The kind of theory that seems
to be needed is one like Wittgenstein's picture theory of
meaning, the theory that language pictures reality and that
certain essential features which language has in common
with pictures are the criteria by which we can establish
which expressions refer and what they refer to. However,
there are objections to this theory. One sort of objection is
that language is quite unlike a picture, and thus it is wrong
to claim that those features which a picture has—by means
of which it pictures—are also features of language. Another
is that even if language is pictorial, pictures are not what
Wittgenstein seems to think because there are no properties
of a picture which are essentially related to any particular
thing such that that thing *is* what the picture pictures. In
other words, the relation between a picture and what it pictures is not essential, but conventional, so that no features
of language are criteria of what it refers to. Rather we must
find out what linguistic expressions refer to in some other
way.

Even if these two kinds of objections aimed specifically
at the picture theory of meaning were to be rebutted, those
objections aimed at the enterprise as a whole remain. They
do not merely claim that the picture theory of meaning in
particular is wrong but also that any theory offered as an
alternative would be equally misguided. One such objection,
adapted from Wittgenstein himself, is aimed at showing that
any such attempt must fail, because to be successful it must

take us outside language in such a way that language cannot
be used to formulate the theory. A. J. Ayer raises another
criticism: it is not that the enterprise, although a legitimate
one, cannot be carried out, but that it is misguided from the
start because it presupposes that the reference of linguistic
expressions is some kind of relationship between language
and reality when actually it is not. We should not look for
some abstruse relation to find out what an expression refers
to, because we can find out merely by seeing how people use
the expression. For example, Ayer says that we can say that
'red' refers to red things because that is the way people who
speak the English language use the term 'red.'

However, aside from the fact that this method will not
help us in cases such as the mind–body problem, where we
are trying to find out just what mind-expressions and body-
expressions refer to, there is a question of the extent to
which it will help us in any case. Ayer admits that there must
be nonformal rules—rules which connect linguistic expressions not with other expressions but with states of affairs—
in addition to formal rules, because nonformal rules tell us
what it is that expressions refer to, and we need to know
this in order to know their meaning. But this brings us back
where we began, for it is just these nonformal rules we had
been hoping to find by examining the views of Carnap and
Wittgenstein. We turned to such views because it seemed
that we could not infer anything about what an expression
refers to merely from a conclusion about the logic of its use.
This became evident when we examined Ryle's approach to
the mind–body problem and concluded that we could infer
nothing about the traditional problem merely from his claims
about the logical features of mind-expressions and body-
expressions. Therefore it seems that this attempt by Ayer to
get around the problem of linguistic reference instead of
solving it will not work either. What rules we discover by
examining the use of expressions seem to be not nonformal
rules but formal rules—rules which connect linguistic ex-

pressions with other linguistic expressions. They will not help us.

It seems, then, that we can neither solve nor avoid the problem of finding some way to decide which expressions refer and what referring expressions refer to. This, however, does not hinder us in our everyday conversations; nonphilosophers seem to know or to be able to find out what they or others are talking about, which seems to imply that they know, or can easily find out, what the expressions of the language they use refer to. We seem, then, to have reached a conclusion which contradicts this fact. We have concluded that it appears to be impossible, or at best very difficult, to find out what linguistic expressions refer to, yet when we and others use language there is no such difficulty. How, then, can we resolve this paradox, that is, how can we reconcile our conclusion with this fact about people and their use of language?

I propose to resolve this paradox by utilizing the notion of a linguistic framework and by making a distinction between questions that can be answered within the framework and questions that take us outside the framework. The notions of a framework and of questions internal and external to it are characterized by comparing language with chess. Language is like chess in that certain moves are permitted or forbidden by rules. This network of permitted and forbidden moves is what I call the framework of language. Furthermore, there are two kinds of questions which language and chess have in common, the ones whose answers come under the jurisdiction of the rules and the ones whose answers do not. Using Carnap's terminology, but applying it a bit differently, I call the former internal questions and the second external questions.

This conception of language will allow us to resolve the paradox. Although nonphilosophers' questions about linguistic reference are internal questions, philosophers' questions are external ones; they are about what there is regardless of the linguistic framework employed. In this way not only can the paradox be resolved but also those philosophical problems which started us on this inquiry can be characterized: they are external problems.

Philosophical questions about the nature of the external world, about minds and bodies, about God's existence, about free will, about universals, and about ethical and aesthetic properties are external questions. They are questions about what the relevant expressions in each case refer to, if they refer at all. The nature of any particular linguistic framework has nothing to do with such questions. They are questions which can be answered only by "getting outside" any particular framework, for only in this way can we find out what it is that the expressions of the framework refer to. A nonphilosopher, however, who asks what an expression refers to is answered from within the framework by means of other expressions which refer to the same thing or which mean the same. Or, if these answers will not help, he can be *shown* what the expression refers to, that is, he can get ostensive answers. Such answers enable the nonphilosopher to understand how to use the expressions of a language without getting him involved in the external problem of just what it is these expressions refer to. In other words, the nonphilosopher need only know how his language allows him to talk about what there is. He need not consider what it is that the expressions of his language refer to nor what he is shown when given an ostensive answer. The philosopher, however, asks what it is that linguistic expressions refer to rather than what a particular language allows us to call something. For this question the answer which satisfies the nonphilosopher will not do.

Thus the seeming paradox is resolved because the nonphilosopher's question about what an expression refers to is not the same question the philosopher asks—what is an answer to one is not an answer to the other. However, although this resolves the paradox, it leaves the philosopher in a very precarious position: he is left with the problem of how to answer external questions. He cannot get outside linguistic frameworks to answer them, as it seems he must. Are we to conclude, then, with Wittgenstein that philosophy, at least a major part of it, is to be relegated to the realm of the mystical, the ineffable? It would seem that the only way to avoid this conclusion is to find some way to find clues to external questions from within some linguistic framework.

If we take this approach to external questions, and I see no other, all nonlinguistic approaches are ruled out because we shall be trying to find answers to questions about the reference of linguistic expressions. Thus we are left with linguistic approaches to philosophy, the three general kinds of which can be called meaning analysis, explication, and use analysis, each of which is examined in Part III.

In linguistic analysis we must at least start with ordinary language. Consequently meaning analysis fails; it requires a precise criterion of synonymy which is not applicable to ordinary language because of the vagueness of ordinary language. Thus in analyzing a term of ordinary language it seems that we must use explication, which is one species of what Stephan Körner calls replacement analysis. In replacement analysis, one linguistic expression is replaced by another which stands in some relationship to it (for meaning analysis but not for explication, the relationship must be synonymy), in order to correct some defect of the original expression when it is used for some purpose or other. Thus if an expression is not defective when used for a certain purpose we cannot use explication to correct that expression when it is used for that purpose. Explication, then, is justifiable for our purpose only if ordinary language is defective with respect to external questions. But ordinary language cannot be defective in this respect. Given a correct theory of meaning—and thus a criterion for the reference of the expressions of ordinary language—we could thereby find out what there is. If anything is defective in this respect, it is not ordinary language, but theories of meaning philosophers apply to it. Thus we cannot explicate ordinary language to help us discover truths about linguistic reference, and thereby answers to external questions. We must work within the framework of ordinary language when this is our purpose.

This leaves us with use analysis, the method of exhibiting the use of linguistic expressions, the method of discovering the way expressions are used within the framework of ordinary language by a comparison of the logical similarities and differences among expressions. This approach, then, is one which remains within the framework of ordinary language, as we have found any successful method must. These logical similarities and differences are to be considered the internal clues to external questions. From conclusions about the way an expression logically differs from or is similar to certain other expressions, conclusions are drawn about whether the expression refers. If it does not, then we have dissolved any external problem which assumes that the expression refers to something, and we have eliminated it as referring to an entity which might be a possible solution to any external problem. For example, G. A. Paul can be interpreted as showing that sense-data expressions are used in such a way that they do not refer, and thus sense-data are eliminated as a possible candidate for what constitutes the external world. It is this kind of clue that use analysis provides.

There are, however, problems for use analysis: expressions logically differ from and are logically similar to other expressions in many ways. Which of these logical features are the clues we seek that will help us solve, or dissolve, external problems? There seems to be no way to find out without going outside the linguistic framework, and we cannot do that. Because use analysis was the last possibility, we must finally conclude that there is no method that can solve or dissolve external problems. Must we as a consequence give up the pursuit of those problems I have characterized as external? I do not think that we must, but to understand why I think this, we must first examine in much greater detail the steps that have led us to conclude that external problems defy solution. This is the task of the rest of the book.

PART I

The Mind—Body Problem

1. The Traditional Problem

The mind–body problem is one facet of the larger philosophical problem about what there is. Other facets are the problems of the external world, free will, God's existence, and universals. In these and other such problems about what there is, the difficulty arises when we as philosophers try to justify sentences of the form, 'There are (are no) x's,' when for 'x' we substitute expressions such as 'material objects,' 'sense-data,' 'universals,' 'minds,' and 'bodies.' The problem that concerns us in this chapter is specified when we substitute 'mind' and 'body' for 'x.' We are interested, then, in the nature and justification of sentences such as: 'There are (are no) minds' and 'There are (are no) bodies,' especially when such sentences are uttered by philosophers. We are ultimately interested in finding a way to solve the mind–body problem, that is, in finding some way to decide among the four basic alternative solutions to the problem, and their many ramifications of the alternatives. Once we begin a search for the means to choose among these alternatives, we can quickly become engulfed in cognate problems such as the problems of interaction, free will and determinism, and phenomenalism. However, since my aim at this point is merely to present data for later investigation, here I shall only present three of the basic alternative solutions to the mind–body problem. I shall not consider the related problems, for they must await the results of the investigation of the data I shall now present.

First let us look at the basic alternatives open to us: Mind–Body Dualism—there are both minds and bodies; Materialism—there are only bodies; Idealism—there are

only minds; The Double Aspect Theory—there are neither
minds nor bodies, but rather some other kind of entity. I
will examine three specific views in some detail: (1) Materialism, (2) Mind–Body Dualism, and (3) The Double
Aspect Theory, because, as will become clearer later, it is
primarily these three views which have been mirrored in
the contemporary discussions of the linguistic mind–body
problem.

REDUCTIVE MATERIALISM

Reductive materialism is generally considered to be the
chief opponent of dualistic interactionism. According to
this theory whatever exists is material and what is taken to
be mental and thus immaterial either does not exist or is
really identical with something material. Hobbes presents
the classical exposition of this theory, although as we shall
see Hobbes, like many other materialists, has trouble being
completely consistent. At the center of Hobbes' materialism
is his conception of "sense," which he claims is the source
of all man's thoughts, imaginings, dreams, and remem-
brances "for there is no conception in a man's mind, which
hath not at first, totally or by parts, been begotten upon
the organs of sense. The rest are derived from that original." [1] His materialism becomes clear when he says that
sense is "some internal motion in the sentient, generated
by some internal motion of the parts of the object, and
propagated through all the media to the innermost part of
the organ." [2] Thus for Hobbes all that exists is either a material object or a physical event consisting of some material
objects in motion. Certain of these physical motions are
what constitute sense and consequently the whole realm of
the mental. Hobbes, then, does not deny the existence of
mental phenomena. Rather he appears to be reducing them
to motion and thus to material phenomena.

1. *Hobbes Selections,* F. J. E. Woodbridge, ed. (New York,
Scribner's 1930), p. 139.
2. Ibid., p. 107

Because of his reduction of the mental to physical motion, Hobbes can go beyond his claim of materialism to an assertion of mechanism. In his introduction to the *Leviathan* he says,

> For seeing life is but a motion of limbs, the beginning whereof is in some principle part within; why may we not say, that all *automata* (engines that move themselves by springs and wheels as doth a watch) have an artificial life? For what is the *heart,* but a *spring;* and the *nerves* but so many *strings,* and the *joints* but so many *wheels,* giving motion to the whole body such as was intended by the artificer?[3]

On this view living things, including man, are no different from nonliving things. In principle, they are just like a machine such as a watch, although perhaps much more complicated. Thus just as by using the laws of Newtonian mechanics and knowledge of the spatial location, velocity, and mass of the relevant material objects, we can explain and predict all the motions of machines and their parts, so by a like use of these laws we can explain all the behavior of living things. According to Hobbes then, not only is everything some kind of material object, but the science of mechanics is sufficient to explain and predict everything that happens. Hobbes, then, is not only a materialist but also a mechanist. However, Hobbes' mechanism is not essential to his materialism because, although mechanism implies materialism, materialism does not imply mechanism. It is possible that everything is material, and some events happen by chance and consequently are neither explainable nor predictable by the science of mechanics.

It follows from Hobbes' materialistic solution to the mind–body problem that the science of psychology is reducible to or replaceable by physics, but the converse is not true. If psychology is reducible to physics, it does not follow that living things are no different in principle from

3. Ibid., p. 136.

nonliving things. What follows is only that the data of psychology are no different from the data of physics. If, for example, it is claimed that the data of psychology are only behavior, that is overt motions and sounds of people, then psychology could be reducible to physics, in the sense that we could explain and predict with physical laws all the behavior that we could explain and predict with psychological laws. One view, clearly consistent with this behavioristic psychology but inconsistent with materialism, is epiphenomenalism which states that whereas certain material processes cause and indeed give rise to mental states and events, these states and events have no effect on any material processes or even on other mental processes. Consequently if epiphenomenalism is true, then a behavioristic psychology is sufficient to explain and predict all human behavior, but materialism is false. Other views consistent with a behavioristic psychology but not with materialism are the double aspect theory, which will be discussed later, and parallelism which, while dualistic, denies that there is any causal interaction so that behavior can be explained and predicted without reference to mental or nonmaterial causes.

However, although Hobbes is usually classed as a materialist (and we have seen textual reasons for this), there are other passages in his writings where he sounds more like a dualist of the epiphenomenalist variety or perhaps something closer to a double aspect theorist. This is apparent when he says, "sense, in all cases, is nothing else but original fancy, caused, as I have said, by the pressure, that is by the motion, of external things upon our eyes, ears, and other organs there unto ordained." [4] Sense, then, is fancy, and fancy is, according to Hobbes, the appearance of motion rather than motion itself, contrary to Hobbes' previous characterization of sense as motion. But if sense is appearance, then it would seem that there are not only material objects in motion or at rest but also appearances which are quite different. Hobbes is thus faced with the central prob-

4. Ibid., p. 140.

lem for materialists: how to incorporate into their theory what seem to be completely alien to it, i.e. appearances such as hallucinations, dreams, and mental images, and other phenomena such as sensations, thought, and emotions.

More recent and more sophisticated materialistic views have been expressed by men such as R. W. Sellars and Donald Williams. Williams defends his version of materialism, what he calls physical realism, as

> The doctrine that the whole of what exists is constituted of matter and its local motions, not Aristotelian 'prime matter' but physical matter, and is hence 'physical' in the literal sense that all its constituents are among the subject matter of physics. Every entity—stone or man, idea or essence,—is on this principle a vulnerable and effective denizen of the one continuum of action, and in the entire universe, including the knowing mind itself, there is nothing which could not be destroyed (or repaired) by a spatio-temporal redisposition of its components.[5]

Williams, like Hobbes, reduces mind to matter, but unlike Hobbes, does not subscribe to a mechanistic materialism. Although everything is the subject matter of physics, nothing follows from this about the truth or falsity of determinism.

Sellars also calls himself a physical realist. However, as we shall see, his version of that doctrine shades into one species of the third type of view to be discussed, i.e. the double aspect theory. Sellars' materialistic thesis is, "that everything which exists is spatial and temporal and is either a physical system or existentially inseparable from one. It will be one of my tasks to show that mind and consciousness are in a very real sense physical."[6] Later in the book

5. D. C. Williams, "Naturalism and the Nature of Things," *The Philosophical Review*, 53 (1944), 418.

6. R. W. Sellars, *The Philosophy of Physical Realism* (New York, Macmillan, 1932), p. 13.

he tries to show this for consciousness by trying to prove that consciousness "is in the brain as an event is in the brain, and is extended as the brain-event to which it is intrinsic." [7] In explaining the sense in which consciousness is *in* the brain, Sellars seems to qualify more as a double aspect theorist than a strict materialist. But let us wait for our discussion of the double aspect theory before we consider Sellars' position further.

MIND–BODY DUALISM

I shall consider only two dualistic positions: interactionism and parallelism. Both positions claim that there are both minds and bodies; however, interactionism claims that these two radically different kinds of things can each have causal efficacy with regard to the other; parallelism denies this causal interaction and postulates that there is merely a constant conjunction between certain mental events and certain physical events. The classical exposition of dualistic interactionism is given by Descartes. For Descartes, aside from God, there are two kinds of substances, both of which are such that we can have clear and distinct ideas of them: "we may thus easily have two clear and distinct notions or ideas, the one of created substance which thinks, the other of corporeal substance, provided we carefully separate all the attributes of thought from those of extension." [8]

However, although there are these two radically different substances, one which is extended and does not think, body, and one which thinks but is not extended, mind, Descartes finds that he (and therefore other men) is essentially a thinking substance. Yet it is also true that what he is—a mind—is "not only lodged in my body as a pilot in a vessel, but that I am very closely united to it, and so to speak so intermingled with it that I seem to compose with

7. Ibid., p. 415.
8. *The Philosophical Works of Descartes* (2 vols. New York, Dover, 1955), I, 241.

it one whole." [9] Thus a man, although essentially a thinking or mental substance, is also in part an extended substance.

These two kinds of substances which make up each person intermingle in such a way that they interact causally. But for Descartes, there is only one point of "contact" or immediate interaction between mind and body. Through this point of contact the causal effects of the mind are carried to all parts of the body by animal spirits, and the causal effects of all parts of the body are transmitted to the mind: "The part of the body in which the soul exercises its functions immediately is in nowise the heart, nor the whole of the brain, but merely the most inward of all its parts, to wit, a certain very small gland which is situated in the middle of its substance. . . ." [10] Again he adds:

> The small gland which is the main seat of the soul is so suspended between the cavities which contain the spirits that it can be moved by them in as many ways as there are sensible diversities in the object, but that it may also be moved in diverse ways by the soul, whose nature is such that it receives in itself as many diverse impressions, that is to say, that it possesses as many diverse perceptions, as there are diverse movements in this gland. Reciprocally, likewise, the machine of the body is so formed that from the simple fact that this gland is diversely moved by the soul, or by such other cause, whatever it is, it thrusts the spirits which surround it towards the pores of the brain, which conduct them by the nerves into muscles, by which means it causes them to move the limbs. [11]

Descartes' general position, somewhat refined and put in modern garb, has been held by C. D. Broad and C. J. Ducasse. As Ducasse states the position, the relation between mind and body "may be stated by saying that for

9. Ibid., p. 192
10. Ibid., p. 345
11. Ibid., p. 347.

each mind there is normally one and only one physical
object called its body which is such that it, or more specifically its brain, is *the immediate physical patient of that
mind, and the immediate physical agent upon that mind.*" [12]
Ducasse continues to talk about this relationship mentioning five points, the three most relevant of which are as follows:

> *First,* that, as we argued in the preceding chapter, a
> mind is a substance, and more specifically a psychical
> substance, and the brain is a physical substance.
> *Second,* that in each of these two substances various
> events occur.
> *Third,* that to say the brain is functioning at a given
> time as physical *patient* of the mind means that cer-
> tain mental events are then causing certain brain events;
> and to say the brain at a given time is functioning as
> physical *agent upon* the mind means that certain brain
> events then occurring are causing certain mental
> events.[13]

There are other dualistic positions. The parallelistic view
as put forth by Leibniz, for example, would accept the first
two points made by Ducasse but deny the third. There is
also a view which denies the first point but agrees essentially with the last two; it holds that there are no substances
whether physical or mental, there are only two kinds of
events, mental and physical, and that these can interact
causally. Another possible variation of the dualistic view
is an event theory of parallelism. This view would agree
with just Ducasse's second point, and that only after modifi-
cation. These last two views hold that things are merely
bundles of events in various relationships. They are not in
addition substances in which or to which these events happen. Dualism, then, can be either interactionistic or parallel-

12. C. J. Ducasse, *Nature, Mind and Death* (La Salle, Ill., Open
Court, 1951), pp. 431–32.
13. Ibid., p. 432.

istic, and either a substance theory or an event theory. All four possible variations of dualism share the thesis that there are two radically different kinds of events, mental events and physical events. It is this common thesis which entitles us to call all four views dualistic. When I talk of mind–body dualism from this point on, it will be to this common thesis that I refer.

Another version of this general dualistic thesis is the view that mind-expressions refer to mental events, not physical events, and that body-expressions refer to physical, not mental events. This is a theory about what certain linguistic expressions refer to. However, if someone is a dualist on this version, he is committed to two radically different kinds of events, just as the more traditional dualist is. Thus we can approach a dualistic conclusion in either of these two ways, one a nonlinguistic approach and the other a type of linguistic approach. The question of whether there are other linguistic approaches will arise in Chapter 3, after the linguistic mind–body problem is discussed in Chapter 2.

THE DOUBLE ASPECT THEORY

The two general views considered so far have by and large worked with Descartes' categories. These views assume that it is correct to use at least one of the two categories of mind and body to classify man. What I take to be the most characteristic version of the view now under discussion denies this assumption, claiming that neither mind nor body is an ontologically basic category, at least when applied to man. These categories characterize two different ways we can conceive of one basic reality which is neither mind nor body, or is (which comes to the same thing) both. Thus this one basic reality we call man has both physical attributes and mental attributes, and we get some knowledge of the basic reality by observing either or both of these aspects of man. But we must be careful not to think, as the dualists and the reductive materialists do, that either minds or bodies or both are *basic* realities. We should avoid being misled into thinking that mental events occur in mental substances and physical events occur in physical substances.

A classical example of such a view can be found in the writings of Spinoza. Although Spinoza might be classed as a parallelist because he claims that there is no interaction between mind and body, his is not like other parallelistic views which accept the categories of mind and body. One reason for calling Spinoza a parallelist comes from proposition II of the Third Part of the *Ethics: "The body cannot determine the mind to thought, neither can the mind determine the body to motion nor rest, nor to anything else, if there be anything else."* [14] However, from the scholium that follows this proposition, it becomes evident that the reason why there is no interaction is not that there are two distinct self-contained substances, but

> that the mind and the body are one and the same thing conceived at one time under the attribute of thought, and at another under that of extension. For this reason, the order or concatenation of things is one, whether nature be conceived under this or under that attribute, and consequently the order of the actions and passions of our body is coincident in nature with the order of the actions and passions of the mind.[15]

On Spinoza's interpretation, then, mind and body are not two different kinds of things but rather one and the same thing conceived of in two different ways. When we conceive of the basic reality in one way or under one attribute we conceive of it as mind, when in the other way, as body. These are the only ways in which we can conceive of this basic reality, we must always conceive of it from one aspect or the other, and never, as it were, directly. It is because of this, perhaps, that we can be misled into be-

14. *Spinoza Selections,* John Wild ed., (New York, Scribner's, 1930), p. 208.
15. Ibid., p. 209.

lieving that mind and body are ontologically basic categories.

The double aspect theory is one version of what has been called the identity theory. There are other possible modifications of this general view. One leads to idealism and the other to materialism. If one were to hold that the entity which we conceive of in two different ways is actually mind, then he would be denying that bodily events are anything but mental events conceived of in a certain way. He would be denying the reality of body. Similarly to claim that mental events are really only physical events, such as brain processes, conceived of in a certain way, would be to deny the reality of mind. For Sellars and perhaps Hobbes, although consciousness is a fact which cannot be denied, it is existentially inseparable from brain-events. Thus consciousness and brain-events go together to make up one basic entity: "Consciousness is the qualitative dimension of a brain event. It is the patterned brain-event as sentient. It is because of its status that we, as conscious, *participate in the being of brain-events.* Here, and here alone, are we, as conscious beings, on the inside of reality." [16]

For Sellars, I take it, brain-events, when viewed from "the inside of reality," appear as conscious activity; when viewed from "the outside of reality," they appear as physiological brain-events. Thus there are two ways of looking at the same thing, one through science such as physiology and the other through introspection. However, neither of these approaches gets us to the basic entity itself. Thus the categories of mind and body, of consciousness and of brain-events, are not ultimate ontological categories. It is for this reason that Sellars proposes that we must "achieve a new category," which applies to the brain as an entity with a qualitative dimension of consciousness.[17] Thus we can conclude that because Sellars is a proponent of one version of the double aspect theory, his version of physical realism is

16. Sellars, *Physical Realism,* p. 414.
17. Ibid.

not strictly materialistic, for a strict materialism would claim that the category of body or of physical object is the only category needed to describe humans; Sellars, unlike Hobbes, denies this.

In this chapter I have not discussed arguments for or against any of these views, for my purpose has been merely to present the views so that we can contrast them with comparable views concerning that other species of the mind–body problem, the linguistic mind–body problem. In the next chapter I shall put forth the three linguistic views which parallel the three views we have just discussed, and in the third chapter I shall investigate what relationship there might be between the linguistic problem and the traditional problem. Then, perhaps, we shall be ready to find out whether, as some philosophers have claimed, solving the linguistic problem will provide us with grounds for a solution to the traditional problem.

2. The Linguistic Problem

In the last chapter we discussed what I called the traditional mind–body problem; in this chapter I wish to discuss what I shall call the linguistic mind–body problem. Whereas the traditional views seem to consider mind and body and the relationship between them, the views that we shall discuss in this chapter seem to be about psychological and physical terms and the logical relationships between them. Carnap, who considers the linguistic problem, is interested in "the so-called problem of the 'relation between Body and Mind' (here also a non-metaphysical question, concerned not with the essential nature of two realms of being but with the logical relations between the terms or laws of Psychology and Physics respectively)." [1]

There are three linguistic views which parallel the three traditional views discussed in Chapter I. The view paralleling traditional dualism can be called the irreducibility theory, or linguistic dualism. This view claims a linguistic mind–body dualism: mind-expressions cannot be reduced to or translated into any kind of physical-expressions, i.e. into expressions containing only those terms needed to describe physical objects of all kinds adequately. The view paralleling reductive materialism can be called the reducibility theory, or linguistic mind–body monism. Its proponents claim that each mind-expression can be reduced or translated into some set of physical-expressions; they deny linguistic dualism and assert that physical-expressions are adequate to describe fully not only those things of which

1. Rudolf Carnap, *The Unity of Science* (London, K. Paul, French, Trubner, 1934), p. 25.

we do not predicate mind-expressions but also those things
of which we do. The third view to be discussed, which parallels the double aspect theory, can be called the double
language theory. It is a dualistic view like linguistic dualism
in that it asserts the irreducibility of mind-expressions to
physical-expressions. However, there are two different ways
in which a double language theory can go beyond linguistic
dualism. Whereas linguistic dualism merely affirms that the
class of mind-expressions is logically independent of the
class of physical-expressions, one kind of double language
theory also denies that the class of body-expressions (i.e.
certain physical-expressions which apply particularly to the
human body such as certain behavior-terms) and the class
of mind-expressions belong to the same logical category, the
category of reports, for example. Rather they belong to different logical categories and, in their logically quite different
ways, together make up one ultimately distinct or basic
linguistic category—what Ryle for example calls the category of our talk about persons. Physical-expressions which
are not body-expressions belong to a different basic linguistic category, the category of our talk about material objects. This view, then, parallels the double aspect theory. It
rejects the inference from talking about man using mind-
expressions and body-expressions to the conclusion that
there are two basic linguistic categories, the category of
mind-expressions and the category of body-expressions, just
as the double aspect theory rejects the inference from con-
ceiving man as mind and body to the conclusion that there
are two ultimately distinct or basic ontological categories,
the category of mind and the category of body.

A second kind of double language theorist goes beyond
talking merely of logical relations and logical categories,
inferring from conclusions about the logical categories that
both mind-expressions and body-expressions refer to the
same thing. J. J. C. Smart, for example, claims that both
kinds of expressions refer to certain bodily processes so that
we have two logically different ways of talking about one and

the same thing. This view, as we shall see, has obvious consequences for the traditional problem which none of the other linguistic views have. I shall now turn to a fuller discussion of these three linguistic views.

LINGUISTIC MONISM

One contemporary form of this view has been called by its proponents logical behaviorism. This view as stated by Hempel claims that "all psychological statements which are meaningful, that is to say, which are in principle verifiable, are translatable into propositions which do not involve psychological concepts, but only the concepts of physics. The propositions of psychology are consequently physicalistic propositions. Psychology is an integral part of physics." [2] An example of a psychological-sentence which Hempel claims to be verifiable, thus meaningful, and thus translatable into a physical-sentence is a statement that "Mr. Jones suffers from intense inferiority feelings of such and such kinds. . . ." [3] Since this sentence can only be confirmed or falsified by observing Jones' behavior, the sentence "means only this: such and such happenings take place in Mr. Jones' body in such and such circumstances." [4]

It is interesting to note that although a statement such as, 'Jones suffers from inferiority feelings a, b, and c' (call this sentence *J*) does not seem to mean or to be translatable into any kind of physical-sentence, there is nothing else such a sentence can mean, if it is to be considered a meaningful sentence, given Hempel's criterion of meaning. We can put Hempel's point into a deductive argument as follows:

1. The conditions of the verification of *J* are Jones' behavior under such and such conditions.

2. Carl Hempel, "The Logical Analysis of Psychology," in H. Feigl and W. Sellars, eds., *Readings in Philosophical Analysis* (New York, Appleton-Century-Crofts, 1949), p. 378.
3. Ibid.
4. Ibid.

2. The meaning of a sentence is the conditions of its verification.

Therefore

3. The meaning of *J* is Jones' behavior under such and such conditions.

Thus given the verifiability criterion of meaning, premise 2 in the above argument, it follows that if premise 1 is true, *J* has the same meaning as some statement about Jones' behavior. And, since statements about Jones' behavior are nonpsychological, physical-statements, this is an example of how a psychological-sentence, *J,* can be reduced to a physical-sentence. The thesis of logical behaviorism as put forward by Hempel is that all psychological-sentences which are meaningful can in a like manner be reduced to physical-sentences. There seems little doubt that this thesis can be substantiated, given premise 2, for all that Hempel need do for any particular psychological-sentences is find the correct first premise, and he has his translation.

Another philosopher who has attempted to arrange wholesale translations "by fiat," in much the same way as Hempel, rather than to provide specimen translations, is Rudolf Carnap. In *The Unity of Science* he sets forth the thesis of physicalism which is the claim that "every statement (whether true or false) can be translated into [the physical language]." [5] One specific problem for this view arises with regard to the status of sentences describing individuals' immediate experiences, such as my statements describing my present pains, joys, thirsts, and other sensations. If such statements, which Carnap calls statements of the protocol language, describe anything, they seem to describe not physical events but rather private mental events of one individual's experiences. Thus such statements seem to be evidence not only of a linguistic dualism but also of a mind–body dualism. To show that these statements are not of this

5. Carnap, *The Unity of Science*, p. 67.

kind but are merely a subclass of the physical language is one job Carnap sets for himself in defending physicalism.

Carnap's method of argumentation is a reductio ad absurdum of his opponent's view. Thus he assumes for the sake of the argument that the statements of someone's (say S_1) protocol language describe only the private experiences of S_1, and those of any other's (for example, S_2) protocol language describe only the private experiences of S_2. Thus, if

> by 'thirst of S_1' we understand not the physical state of S_1's body but his sensation of thirst, i.e., something non-material, then S_1's thirst is fundamentally beyond the reach of S_2's recognition [because all S_2] can verify when he asserts 'S_1 is thirsty' is that S_1's body is in such and such a state, and a statement asserts no more than can be verified.[6]

Here Carnap, like Hempel, depends upon the verifiability criterion of meaning. Given this, Carnap's argument seems plausible so far. Carnap continues by pointing out that the consequence of the above argument is that S_1's, as well as everyone else's, protocol language, "could therefore be applied only solipsistically; there would be no intersubjective protocol language," [7] because only S_1 can mean anything about his sensations of thirst. Others can only mean something about S_1's behavior and bodily states.

But this leads to problems. The physical language is supposed to be intersubjective—not a private language—in fact one not only verifiable but publicly verifiable. But, says Carnap, if the physical language is verifiable, there must be inferential relations between physical-statements and protocol statements, because only sentences which assert or imply something about experience are verifiable. Thus since we have assumed for the purposes of this argument that proto-

6. Ibid., p. 79.
7. Ibid., p. 80.

col statements describe private experiences, then physical-
statements must also describe private experiences because
"one statement can be deduced from another, if and only
if, the fact described by the first is contained in the fact described by the second." [8] Thus the intersubjective physical
language must describe the private experiences of S_1, S_2, etc.
But, as Carnap points out, this is impossible, "for the realms
of experience of two persons do not overlap. There is no
solution free from contradiction in this direction." [9]

In order, then, to avoid the contradiction that the physical
language is both intersubjective and describes private experiences, we must conclude that the physical language describes physical events. And furthermore, since the physical
language is verifiable and therefore has inferential relations
to the protocol language, protocol statements also describe
physical events. It is wrong, then, or at best misleading, to
claim that protocol statements describe the contents of an
individual's private experience, with the consequence that
each person's protocol is a private language. However, "that
the protocol languages of various persons are mutually exclusive, is still true in a certain definite sense: they are, respectively, non-overlapping subsections of the physical language." [10]

Carnap must take one more step to establish that protocol
statements do not constitute a counter-example to the thesis
of physicalism. Carnap has concluded that a protocol statement, p, asserts something about a physical event. Thus this
physical event, because it is physical, can be described also
by a physical statement, P. Thus, says Carnap, P and p both
describe the same physical state of affairs or, in other words,
can be logically inferred from each other. But if two sentences can each be inferred from the other, they are mutually translatable. Thus Carnap has reached his conclusion

8. Ibid., p. 87.
9. Ibid., p. 82.
10. Ibid., p. 88

that protocol statements are translatable into physical statements.

To examine some of the problems for this argument that Carnap has used to support his thesis of physicalism, let us put this complex argument into deductive form:

1. P-statements are intersubjective and verifiable.
2. A statement is verifiable if and only if it is logically related to some statement describing private experiences.

Therefore

3. P-statements are logically related to statements describing private experiences.   (1, 2)
4. p-statements describe private experiences.

Therefore

5. P-statements are logically related to p-statements.
                                                       (3, 4)
6. A statement describing private experiences describes only the private experiences of one person.

Therefore

7. A p-statement describes only the private experiences of one person.   (4, 6)
8. Statements which are logically related describe the same facts.

Therefore

9. A P-statement describes only the private experiences of one person.   (5, 7, 8)

Therefore

10. P-statements are not intersubjective.   (9)

Here 10 contradicts 1. But since the argument is valid, and according to Carnap premises 1, 2, 6, and 8 are true, then premise 4 must be false. Thus p-statements do not describe private experiences but, the only other possibility, physical events. Consequently P-statements also describe physical events (by 5 and 8). This leads to the final step.

Because *P*-statements and *p*-statements describe the same facts, they are mutually translatable.

Upon examining this argument we can see that a key move in it is establishing step 5, that *P*-statements are logically related to *p*-statements. It is by means of this step that Carnap reaches step 9 and thus step 10, which leads to the contradiction he desires. Furthermore, step 5 is needed to establish Carnap's final conclusion that *p*-statements are translatable into *P*-statements. Thus Carnap must establish step 5. But, strangely, he establishes 5 via step 4, which he later concludes is false. Furthermore, if 4 is false and 2 is true as Carnap maintains, then *P*-statements are not verifiable because in that case there would be no statements describing private experiences. What Carnap seems to want to say in 2 is that *P*-statements are verifiable if and only if they are logically related to statements of a certain form, those which *seem* to describe private experiences, i.e. *p*-statements. But Carnap cannot argue to the conclusion in 5 that *P*-statements are logically related to *p*-statements and also hold it as a premise in 2. It seems, then, that Carnap must either give up claiming that 4 is false, in which case he could not achieve his desired conclusion that *p*-statements describe physical events, or he must merely assert 5 without giving any reason for its acceptance, in which case he can give no reason for his conclusion that *p*-statements are translatable into *P*-statements.[11]

Another crucial step in Carnap's argument is the step from 9 to 10. Carnap assumes that if *P*-statements describe merely private experiences they are not intersubjective statements. But since they are intersubjective, they must describe not private experiences but physical events. However, it is not at all obvious that statements which describe private experiences must belong to a private, that is, in principle nonintersubjective language. Carnap holds, as seen above, that such a language must be private because all anyone can

11. See J. O. Urmson, *Philosophical Analysis* (Oxford, Clarendon Press, 1956), pp. 122–26, for a discussion of this point.

verify with regard to someone else's (say S_1) private experiences is his bodily behavior. Therefore only S_1 can describe his own private experiences, and thus the language which describes them is S_1's own private language. But why should we assume that because only S_1 can verify facts about his own private experiences that only S_1 can describe his own private experiences? Carnap does not answer this question, but it is easy to see what his answer would be. The meaning of an expression is the condition of its verification. Thus statements describing S_1's private experience, being only verifiable by S_1, are only meaningful for S_1 and thus are part of a language private to S_1.

Carnap's argument, then, depends upon the verifiability criterion of meaning, as does the less complex argument offered by Hempel. But this criterion of meaning is by no means obviously correct. Indeed it faces innumerable well-known problems which cast much doubt on its correctness and thus on the soundness of both Carnap's and Hempel's arguments.

There is one last dubious step in Carnap's argument that we might note before leaving the view of linguistic monism. It is the last move in the argument, the move from the premise that P-statements and p-statements describe the same facts to the conclusion that the two kinds of statements are mutually translatable, that is, logically imply each other. Carnap's claim is that to say "Statements A and B describe the same fact" in the material terminology is to say the same thing as "Statements A and B entail each other" in the formal terminology.[12] Leaving aside the mechanics of the technical notions of material and formal terminology (modes of speech) for now,[13] it would certainly seem that these two sentences can be at most materially equivalent, which is not sufficient for *saying the same thing*. It is, moreover, the thesis of the third linguistic view we are to ex-

12. Carnap, *The Unity of Science*, p. 89.

13. These technical concepts are discussed more fully on pp. 57–58.

amine, the double language theory, that although physical-statements and psychological-statements describe the same facts, they are not logically related. If Carnap's translation is correct, then this view is obviously wrong. Yet it does not seem to be. It certainly seems to make sense to talk of describing the same fact in two different ways, from two different points of view. This point can be made more clearly, if we talk of referring to the same fact in two logically unrelated ways rather than describing the same fact in two ways. Thus, for example, sentences about the morning star, although logically unrelated to sentences about the evening star, both refer to the same thing, Venus. Also, certain sentences about kinetic energy of certain molecules can be said to refer to the same thing as certain sentences about the degrees centigrade of some object. Both logically unrelated kinds of sentences refer to the temperature of the object. In both examples the two different kinds of sentences would in each particular case be materially equivalent, but certainly not translatable.

Carnap in his later writings acknowledges this problem of translatability and no longer tries to "arrange" translations in wholesale lots. In fact he acknowledges that psychological-sentences among others are neither translatable into observation-sentences—which, I take it, would amount to the protocol language—nor into a physicalistic language. This, of course, means he has given up physicalism in the strict sense. His later view is that

> terms like 'temperature' in physics, or 'anger' or 'belief' in psychology are introduced as theoretical constructs rather than as intervening variables of the observation language. This means that a sentence containing a term of this kind can neither be translated into a sentence of the language of observables nor deduced from such sentences, but at best inferred with high probability.[14]

14. Rudolf Carnap, "On Belief-Sentences," *Meaning and Necessity* (Chicago, University of Chicago Press, 1958), p. 230.

This revised physicalism, while avoiding all the problems connected with translatability, has some of its own, such as the problem of explaining the nature of theoretical constructs and the problem of finding in what sense belief-sentences, for example, are probable in relation to observation-sentences. This leads into the problem of other minds. How, for example, can we establish the probability of a sentence such as 'S believes that p' by observations of S's behavior?

These last remarks point to perhaps the central problem for linguistic monism, the problem of translating intentional sentences, such as belief-sentences, into a physicalistic language. This leads us directly back to the linguistic mind–body problem and one defense of the second view, linguistic dualism.

LINGUISTIC DUALISM

This view, unlike traditional mind–body dualism, is not so much a positive view as a negative one. Its thesis is that at least some psychological-sentences cannot be translated into a physicalistic language, and that thus the thesis of physicalism or any theory of linguistic monism is mistaken. The characteristic defense of this position is to challenge anyone to make translations and then to show that they do not work. The combat can begin at either of two points: first, at attempts to make psychological-statements extensional, and second, at attempts to make psychological-statements nonintentional which, it is claimed, physical-statements are.

We can use examples of Carnap's work to show the contest at the first point. Carnap at one time held the theses of physicalism and extensionality. Let us say, as Carnap does at one point, that the thesis of physicalism is the thesis that "the physical language is a universal language of science—that is to say, every language of any sub-domain of science can be equipollently translated into the physical language." [15] Our particular interest, of course, is to see

15. Rudolf Carnap, *The Logical Syntax of Language* (New York, Harcourt, Brace, 1937), p. 320.

whether the psychological language which contains sentences such as belief-sentences can be so translated.

The thesis of extensionality states that *"a universal language of science may be extensional;* or more exactly: for every given [nonextensional] language S_1, an extensional language S_2 may be constructed such that S_1 may be translated into S_2."[16] By an extensional language I shall mean a language such that each of its sentences is extensional. That is, each sentence of the language is extensional if and only if:

1. The truth-value of the sentence that results from the replacement of any substantive expression contained in the original sentence by an extensionally equivalent expression will not differ from that of the original sentence under any conditions, *and*

2. If the sentence is compound or complex, i.e. if it contains coordinate main clauses or at least one subordinate clause, then 1 is true of all the simple sentential elements which make up the compound or complex sentence, and the truth-value of the compound or complex sentence is a function of the truth-values of those simple sentential elements.

Taking together the thesis of physicalism and the thesis of extensionality, we arrive at the conclusion that psychological-expressions, like expressions of other sciences, can be made extensional, for if the thesis of physicalism is correct, such expressions are translatable into the physical language, and if the thesis of extensionality is correct, the physical language can be made extensional. Here, however, the problem of intensionality arises. Returning to belief-sentences, we seem to have a paradigm case of psychological-sentences which as they stand are not extensional, i.e. are intensional. For example, the sentence 'John believes that all humans are mortal' is not extensional because it fails to meet the first condition of extensionality. Let us assume that

16. Ibid., p. 245.

this sentence is true, and that John has a false anthropomorphic view of God. If this belief-sentence were extensional, then by replacing 'humans' by the materially equivalent expression 'featherless bipeds' the truth-value should not be changed. But in this case it would be changed because John believes that there is a featherless biped who is immortal, i.e. God. Thus the new sentence is false, and the original sentence is intensional.

However, that belief-sentences are not extensional is a problem for linguistic monism only if the physical language is considered extensional. But the truth of this is by no means evident. The physical language includes among other things physical laws, and these, it is widely claimed, warrant counterfactual inference. That is, the claim is that we can infer subjunctive conditionals which are of the form, 'If x were y, u would be z' from physical laws. Such sentences are plainly not extensional. They violate the second condition of extensionality because they are not sentences whose truth-value depends upon the truth-value of their sentential parts. Indeed some attempted translations of belief-sentences take this form using nonpsychological terms in place of the variables. Such translations, it could be argued, are all that is required for linguistic monism. The thesis of extensionality is not a requirement.

This brings us to the central problem, whether any translation which avoids all purely psychological-expressions can succeed, and thus to the second point of combat, the problem of intentionality. To see just what this problem is for the linguistic monist let us examine the defense of linguistic dualism as put forth by Chisholm. The central issue for him is intentionality. Chisholm states the thesis of intentionality:

Let us say (1) that we do not need to use intentional language when we describe non-psychological, or "physical", phenomena; we can express all that we know, or believe, about such phenomena in language which is not intentional. And let us say (2) that, when

we wish to describe certain psychological phenomena
—in particular, when we wish to describe thinking, believing, perceiving, seeing, knowing, wanting, hoping
and the like—either (a) we must use language which
is intentional or (b) we must use a vocabulary which
we do not need to use when we describe non-psychological, or "physical", phenomena.[17]

I must now explain what is meant by intentional language. According to Chisholm there are three individually
sufficient criteria of the intentionality of a sentence. The
first two, Chisholm claims, have to do with what has been
called intentional inexistence. The objects of intentional activity need not exist for the activity to be carried out,
whereas the object of a physical activity *must* exist if it is
to be carried out. Thus we can think about an object which
does not exist, but we can not weigh one unless it exists.
Chisholm's criteria, however, are not of intentional activity
but rather of intentional language. Whether we can infer
anything about the former from the latter is something we
shall discuss in Chapter 3.[18] The third criterion has to do
with Frege's concept of indirect reference. In this regard
Chisholm suggests that by adopting Frege's terminology we
could make the third criterion "do the work of the first
two." [19] In presenting these three criteria I shall use Frege's
terminology so that we can evaluate Chisholm's suggestion:

> 1. A simple declarative sentence is intentional if it uses
>   a substantive expression (a name or description)
>   in such a way that neither the sentence nor its con-
>   tradictory entails whether or not the expression has

17. Roderick Chisholm, "Sentences about Believing," *Proceedings of the Aristotelian Society, 56* (1955–56), 129. This point is
also discussed in Chisholm's book, *Perceiving* (Ithaca, Cornell University Press, 1957), pp. 168–73.

18. See pp. 71 ff.

19. Chisholm "Sentences about Believing," *PAS, 56* (1955–56),
128.

a nonnull extension, i.e. whether or not the expression truly applies to anything.

2. A complex declarative sentence, i.e. a sentence containing a subordinate clause or an equivalent phrase, is intentional if neither the sentence nor its contradictory entails anything about the truth-value of the subordinate clause.

3. A declarative sentence is intentional if it contains a substantive expression which is such that its replacement in the sentence by an expression with the same extension, i.e. by an extensionally equivalent expression, results in a sentence the truth-value of which will under certain conditions differ from that of the original sentence.[20]

Chisholm also says that a compound sentence is intentional "if and only if one or more of the component sentences of its indicative version is intentional." [21] And, although he does not say it, he uses the three criteria in such a way that any sentence which fails to meet all three criteria is nonintentional.

At this point let me give three examples, each of which proves to be intentional by at least one of the three criteria. First, the sentence 'John is thinking of Pegasus' is intentional by the first criterion, because neither the sentence nor its contradictory entails anything about the extension of the substantive expression 'Pegasus.' That is, neither the sentence nor its contradictory entails whether or not 'Pegasus' truly applies to anything. Second, the sentence, 'John believes that Pegasus once lived' is intentional by the second criterion, because neither this complex sentence nor its contradictory entails anything about the truth-value of 'Pegasus once lived.' Third, the sentence, 'John knows that Pegasus is a fictitious creature' is intentional by the third criterion, because if we replace the substantive expression 'Pegasus'

20. For the way Chisholm expresses these three criteria, see ibid., pp. 126–28.
21. Ibid., p. 129.

by the extensionally equivalent expression, 'the winged horse captured by Bellerophon,' the truth-value of the resulting sentence would differ from the original if, for example, John knew that Pegasus is a creature from Greek mythology but had never heard of Bellerophon.

It is important to notice that while there is an overlapping between nonextensional or intensional sentences and intentional sentences, the two classes are not coextensive. It is true that the third criterion of intentionality is the denial of the first condition of extensionality because the third criterion states that if the truth-value of a sentence changes under certain conditions when an expression in the sentence is replaced by an extensionally equivalent expression, then the sentence is intentional, and the first necessary condition of extensionality is that the truth-value of an extensional sentence will not change under any conditions when an expression in the sentence is replaced by an extensionally equivalent one. It is also true that sentences intentional by the second criterion are also intensional. The second criterion of intentionality states that if neither a sentence nor its contradictory entails anything about the truth-value of some subordinate clause in the sentence, then the sentence is intentional. In other words, a sufficient condition of intentionality is that the truth-value of a sentence is not a function of the truth-value of all the subordinate clauses in the sentence. If we look at the second necessary condition of extensionality and confine our attention to complex sentences, we can see that a necessary condition of the extensionality of a complex sentence is that the truth-value of a complex sentence is a function of the truth-values of all the simple sentential elements of which it is composed. But since a subordinate clause is either a simple sentential element or composed of simple sentential elements, a necessary condition of the extensionality of a complex sentence is that its truth-value is a function of the truth-values of all its subordinate clauses. This is the denial of the second criterion of intentionality.

However, some intentional sentences are extensional, and some intensional sentences are nonintentional. For example, the sentence, 'John is thinking of Alaska' is intentional by the first criterion because neither the sentence nor its contradictory entails whether or not the word 'Alaska' has a nonnull extension. But the sentence is extensional because it is a simple sentence in which any expression may be replaced by an extensionally equivalent one under any conditions without change of truth-value. The only expression in the sentence which might seem to violate this condition is 'Alaska.' But when we say that John is thinking of Alaska we are claiming that he is thinking of a particular place, and what name or description we use is limited only by the condition that it indeed applies to the place. This is true of those expressions extensionally equivalent to 'Alaska.' On the other hand, subjunctive conditionals are, as seen above, intensional, but not all of them are intentional. The sentence, 'If Lee had won the battle of Gettysburg, then he would have won the Civil War' is intensional but not intentional, because none of the three criteria of intentionality apply to it.

From the above discussion it can be seen that the problem a linguistic monist faces regarding intentional sentences is distinct from the problem he faces regarding intensional sentences. Neither problem is reducible to the other. This would not be true, incidentally, if, as Chisholm suggests, we could use the third criterion of intentionality to do the work of the first two because, as we have seen, the third criterion is the denial of the first condition of extensionality. Thus Chisholm's suggestion must be discarded.

We can now return to Chisholm's thesis of linguistic dualism. There are two main points to his thesis: first, no physical-sentences need be intentional, although perhaps some are nonextensional. Whether this point is correct will not be argued but assumed here. Second, many psychological-sentences are either intentional or, if they are made nonintentional, contain some expressions not needed in the physical language. For example, at one point Carnap translates the sentence, 'John believes that all humans are mortal' as "John has relation B to 'All humans are mortal' as a sentence in English." [22] The original sentence is both intentional and intensional, but as translated the sentence is extensional and nonintentional. It meets the first condition for extensionality and thus does not meet the third criterion of intentionality. It also does not meet the first two criteria of intentionality. Thus it is nonintentional. But it has been made nonintentional by means of a new technical term 'relation B,' which is an expression not needed in the physical language. It is an expression which functions only to make belief-sentences nonintentional, although it could also be used in psychology. But obviously this method of escaping the problem of intentionality will not help linguistic monism because there still remains the vocabulary dualism.

There is, however, an answer which could be given to this linguistic dualistic conclusion. This answer admits that there is a dualism which is not a physical language and psychological language, but a physical language and semantical language dualism. We need in addition to the vocabulary of the physical language a vocabulary to talk about language. We need, for example, expressions such as 'mean' and 'refer,' 'true' and 'false.' But these are expressions we need no matter which linguistic mind–body thesis is true. We need them because we use language. In this area we need expressions to talk of the relations of expressions to other expressions (syntactics), the relations of expressions to what they are about (semantics), and the relations of expressions to people who use them (pragmatics). The answer goes, given the above information, that the expression 'relation B' is a term of pragmatics because it concerns a relation between people and expressions of language. Thus sentences using this expression cannot be used as arguments in favor of a linguistic mind-body dualism.

Chisholm, however, has a counter-argument. In Carnap's

22. See Carnap, "On Belief-Sentences," pp. 230–31.

translation of 'John believes that all humans are mortal' into "John has the relation B to 'All humans are mortal' as a sentence in English," for example, we must unpack the phrase, 'as a sentence in English.' To spell this out we should first replace 'English' by 'the English language.' And to unpack it completely, says Chisholm, we cannot just talk of inkmarks and noises but of how certain people apply or interpret, that is, what they mean by these marks and sounds.[23] And, says Chisholm, "these references to the meaning of words and sentences—to their use, application, or interpretation—take us to the difficulty of principle involved in this linguistic interpretation of believing." [24]

Because we have to talk about what certain noises and marks mean, that is, about how certain people use those marks and noises, we get into the following problem when we try to analyze Carnap's translation of belief-sentences. In order to unpack the expression 'as a sentence in English' in the above translation we might try something like "as a sentence in the language used by those people who apply the marks 'human' to a thing if and only if it is a human being." But, as Chisholm points out, this analysis is not correct, because it implies that these people never mistakenly think that something is human when it is not, or that something is not human when it is. In other words we must expand 'as a sentence in English' to: "as a sentence in the language used by those people who apply the marks 'human' to a thing if and only if they take it to be, or believe it to be, a human being." But here once again we have a belief-sentence. Thus Carnap's translation and other linguistic ones like it either lead to an infinite regress of clauses if we always replace 'believe' by 'relation B' or some such expression, or they are stuck at some point with the belief vocabulary and thus intentionality.

One defense against this point admits that we must use phrases of the form 'in the language in which . . . means

---

23. Chisholm, "Sentences about Believing," pp. 141 f.
24. Ibid., p. 142.

y,' for the linguistic translation of belief-sentences, but not
those of the form 'in the language used by people who apply
the marks . . . to a thing if and only if they believe that it
is *y*.' For, it has been argued, the former, which talks of the
meanings of words, is not to be analyzed into the latter,
which talks of peoples' beliefs, as Chisholm seems to think.
However, discussion of this point must wait until Chapter
3.[25] We must now move on to the third linguistic thesis, the
double language theory.

THE DOUBLE LANGUAGE THEORY

There are two branches of this theory, both of which
agree on two basic points. First, they agree that psychological-sentences cannot be translated into the physical language; second, they agree that these two kinds of languages
are two different ways of talking about the same thing. However, they differ essentially in their views of the nature of
the psychological language. One species, whose represent-
atives include Feigl and Smart, assumes that psychological-
sentences and physical-sentences both belong to the same
logical category. As Smart says, both kinds of sentences are
reporting uses of language.[26] This assumption is common to
all the views we have examined so far. A report, roughly, is
a categorical sentence which is used to refer to something
or other and to tell us something about what it refers to, that
is, describe what it refers to by predicating something of it.
A report, then, can be called a descriptive sentence. Thus
'John is six feet tall' is used to refer to John and to tell us
something about his body, namely how tall it is (a physical
state of affairs). Likewise, it seems to many that 'John is
thinking' is used to refer to John and to tell us something
about his mind, namely that thinking is going on "there" (a
mental state of affairs). Thus we can be led to a mind–body
dualism.

25. See pp. 72 f.
26. See J. J. C. Smart, "Sensations and Brain Processes," *The
Philosophical Review, 68* (1959), 144–45.

However, Feigl, Smart, and others propose that a given psychological-sentence is a report of the same state of affairs or process of which some physical-sentence is a report. This is not to say that the psychological-sentence is translatable into the physical-sentence, but only that the two reports are reports of the same thing—refer to the same thing—although what they tell us about their common referent is different. Indeed Feigl claims that there are two nonpsychological ways of referring to the states of affairs or processes which psychological-sentences refer to. Both behavioral and neurophysiological reports have the same referents as psychological reports.[27] This does not mean, however, that Feigl should be construed as holding a triple language theory, because the first two classes of sentences are subclasses of the physical language. Furthermore, these three classes of reports are not mutually translatable but are merely correlated by empirical laws because, although they have the same referents, the three classes of sentences differ in that they have different evidential bases which are respectively behavioral, physiological, and introspective.[28]

Feigl's argument in favor of the double language theory, is, as I see it, briefly as follows. According to Feigl, once we sift all the objections to the various alternative solutions to the mind–body problem, there are only three plausible ones left: dualistic interactionism, parallelism, and the double language theory. Feigl claims that there is an empirically ascertainable difference between interactionism on the one hand, and parallelism and the double language theory on the other. Interactionism, Feigl claims, entails a many-one or many-many psycho-neurophysiological correspondence or correlation, while the other two views entail a one-to-one or at least a one-many correspondence. Which of

27. See Herbert Feigl, "The Mind-Body Problem in the Development of Logical Empiricism," in H. Feigl and Brodbeck, eds., *Readings in the Philosophy of Science* (New York, Appleton-Century-Crofts, 1953), p. 623.

28. Ibid., see p. 626.

these kinds of correspondence actually is the case is an empirically ascertainable matter. Feigl believes that the data at hand points towards a one-one or at least a one-many correspondence. Thus on the basis of empirical evidence he narrows down the alternatives. However, the final elimination is a philosophical, not a scientific, job because the difference between parallelism and the double language theory is not empirically ascertainable. Given that this is a philosophical matter, we can then employ Occam's razor to pick the simplest theory, the one which implies the least entities. This is the double language theory.[29]

I shall not criticize this argument here but merely mention two points at which the argument seems weak. First, although Feigl seems to claim that interactionism, parallelism, and the double language theory are the only plausible solutions, he does not give any reason for thinking that a reductive monism such as materialism is implausible. In fact Smart as we shall see, attempts to use the double language theory to help establish a materialistic view. The views that do seem false, as Feigl claims, are linguistic materialism and linguistic phenomenalism. However, it is not obvious as we shall see in Chapter 3, how this affects "traditional" materialism and phenomenalism. Second, it does not seem to be obvious, as Feigl claims, that interactionism is incompatible with a one-one or one-many psycho-neurophysiological correspondence. If it is compatible with such correspondence then one point in Feigl's argument is wrong, for we could not eliminate interactionism in the way Feigl suggests. We could still, however, select interactionism as the only possibility if a many-many or a many-one correspondence proved to be true. However, I am not sure what would count as proof of such correspondence, for it seems to me that the thesis of a one-to-one or at

29. See Feigl, "The Mind–Body Problem," and also "The 'Mental' and the 'Physical,' " in H. Feigl and M. Scriven, eds., *Minnesota Studies in the Philosophy of Science* (3 vols. Minneapolis, University of Minnesota Press, 1958), 2, esp. 374–87.

least a one-many correspondence is no more falsifiable than the thesis that every event has a cause. In either case it would seem that no empirical discoveries would be allowed to count against the thesis. If this is correct then the issue is not an empirical one as Feigl claims but a philosophical one. Furthermore, there are problems for the double language theory, which neither dualistic view has, as we shall see when we examine Smart's version. The use of Occam's razor does not seem appropriate unless the competing theories are equal in all other relevant respects. This "all else being equal" Feigl has not shown, and Smart runs into trouble trying to show.

Smart's thesis is much the same as Feigl's except that it is more restricted, dealing only with sensations and brain processes

> In so far as 'after-image' or 'ache' is a report of a process it is a report of a process that happens to be a brain process. It follows that the thesis does not claim that sensation statements can be translated into statements about brain processes. Nor does it claim that the logic of a sensation statement is the same as that of a brain-process statement. All it claims is that in so far as a sensation statement is a report of something, that something is in fact a brain process. Sensations are nothing over and above brain processes.[30]

Smart's thesis, then, is that sensation-statements refer to brain processes rather than to mental processes. Thus although we cannot translate sensation-statements into brain-process-statements they do refer to the same thing. Thus we have here a double language theory. Smart, like Feigl, supports the theory by showing it to be consistent with the results of science and by employing Occam's razor. However, he also attempts to answer in some detail what seem to be the key objections to his view. He thus

30. Smart, "Sensations and Brain Processes," pp. 144–45.

attempts to fulfill one prerequisite for the use of Occam's razor.

On one interpretation at least, Ryle's thesis, is, like Feigl's and Smart's, a double language theory. However, whereas both Feigl and Smart assume that psychological-sentences are reports or descriptive sentences, Ryle claims that they are of a different logical kind entirely; they belong to what he calls a different logical category. Sentences with certain logical features belong to the logical category of reports or descriptive sentences. Other categories delineated in a like manner would be those of exclamations, laws, mathematical sentences, and poetical sentences. The sentences of each of these categories have certain logical features in common which the sentences of no other category have.

According to Ryle, then, it is mistaken to think that when we use psychological-expressions we are talking in the same category as when we use physical-expressions, but we are talking about a radically different kind of substance, state of affairs, or process; nor are we talking in the same category about the same kind of thing, as Feigl and Smart claim. Rather we are talking in two different logical categories and, says Ryle, talking about one kind of thing—a person, not, incidentally, a physical object, state of affairs, or process as some have interpreted Ryle's view. As Ryle says:

> When we speak of a person's mind, we are not speaking of a second theatre of special status incidents, but of certain ways in which some of the incidents of his one life are ordered. His life is not a double series of events taking place in two different kinds of stuff; it is one concatenation of events, the differences between some and other classes of which largely consist in the applicability or inapplicability to them of logically different types of law-propositions and law-like propositions. Assertions about a person's mind are therefore assertions of special sorts about that person. So ques-

tions about the relations between a person and his mind, like those about the relations between a person's body and his mind are improper questions.[31]

An example of the technique Ryle uses to establish his thesis that psychological-sentences belong to a logical category different from the category of physical-sentences is the way he handles the sentence 'Jones is vain.' For Ryle it is not a shorthand version of a complicated description either of actual and possible behavior, or of neurophysiological processes. Thus he disagrees with a linguistic monist, such as Carnap, who claims some such translation is possible. Neither is it a sentence which refers to some kind of mental state or episode such as feelings or pricks of vanity, or to some behavioral or physiological process. Thus Ryle disagrees with Smart.

For Ryle, to say 'Jones is vain' is to say something like 'Whenever Jones finds a chance of securing the admiration and envy of others, he does whatever he thinks will produce this admiration and envy.'[32] According to Ryle this sentence is, first, neither a description nor report of a behavior pattern or a physiological process because it contains such nonphysical-terms as 'think,' 'find,' 'admiration,' and 'envy.' Nor does it refer to any such pattern or process, or to mental episodes or processes because it does not tell us any of these things about Jones. Nothing is predicated of Jones concerning such patterns, processes, or episodes because this sentence is not the kind of sentence that reports or describes something about Jones. It has a different use in language. It is, says Ryle, a law-like sentence about Jones. This is a sentence by means of which we neither describe Jones nor report something about him, but by means of which we both explain Jones' present behavior (in the sense of giving reasons, not causes) and also predict something about what he will probably do in the future. Thus

31. Gilbert Ryle, *The Concept of Mind* (New York, Barnes and Noble, 1949), pp. 167–68.
32. Ibid., see p. 89.

'Jones is vain' is quite unlike sentences like 'Jones is six feet tall' or 'Jones is blond,' which report about Jones by describing him in some way. It is in a different logical category, the category of law-like sentences.

We have seen how Ryle differs from linguistic monists such as Carnap and from double language theorists of the Smart-Feigl variety, but how does he differ from a linguistic dualist such as Chisholm? The dualist, unlike Ryle, takes psychological-sentences to be reports, just as physical-sentences are. As a consequence of this, the two also differ about what they consider to be the consequences of their linguistic views for the traditional mind–body problem. This will be discussed more fully in Chapter 3, but for now we can say that Chisholm takes the irreducibility of psycho-logical-expressions to be a mark of the mental and thus an argument in favor of a traditional dualism and against any form of monism. For Ryle, on the other hand, the tradi-tional problem is based on a confusion, brought about by a misunderstanding of the logic of the language. To talk about minds and bodies as two radically different kinds of entities or processes or bundles of events is to make a mis-take, a logical mistake, because mind-expressions and body-expressions do not belong in the same logical category. Rather our talk is about one kind of entity, a person, which we can talk about in expressions belonging to two different logical categories; these two categories go together in their logically different ways to constitute the category of person-talk. It is only because people, mainly philosophers, have thought that the two kinds of expressions belonged to the same category—the category of reports—that the problem arose. Those who are confused in this way argue that be-cause body-expressions refer to bodies, so mind-expressions must refer to something, presumably nonbodily entities. Thus a mind–body dualism is born.[33] But if we can resist

33. Ibid., see p. 19. See also pp. 63–70 of this book for a more complete discussion.

the temptation to place these two different kinds of expressions in this one logical category, there is no reason for us to investigate the ramifications and problems of such a dualism, nor, consequently, its chief adversary, reductive materialism. For mind-expressions go together in their logically different ways to make up the logic of our language about human beings, which is language about one kind of thing—persons—rather than two—minds and bodies.

We have seen here, then, two varieties of the double language theory. It is interesting to note that the Feigl-Smart species is faced with at least two problems that Ryle's thesis avoids. The second problem, moreover, is a problem for all the views we have considered, except Ryle's. This one then is particularly important because if it cannot be solved, a view such as Ryle's seems to be the only possibility left. Therefore I shall consider these two problems as Smart formulates them and briefly indicate what they are and the strength of Smart's reply to each.

The first problem is raised in the form of an objection which grants that "it may be possible to get out of asserting the existence of irreducibly psychic processes, but not out of asserting the existence of irreducibly psychic properties." [34] Thus, the objection goes, although sensations may be identical with brain processes, and thus there would be no irreducibly psychic processes, nevertheless these brain processes would have two quite different kinds of properties, physical and psychic. Thus even assuming, for example, that the sentence 'I see a yellowish-orange afterimage' is a report about some brain process, that brain process would have the property of "being a yellowish-orange afterimage." If this is a property, as Smart thinks, it is certainly a psychic property. And, as Smart says, it seems "that this property lies inevitably outside the physicalistic framework within which I am trying to work." [35] In other words, Smart seems

34. Smart, "Sensations and Brain Processes," p. 148.
35. Ibid.

still to be left with a dualism of sorts—a property dualism.[36] I am not sure that this kind of dualism need worry anyone except those who, like Smart, hold that we can explain everything, including all human properties and behavior, in purely physicalistic terms, i.e. without the need of psycho-physical laws—laws which involve psychological expressions. But since this is a widespread view, and since the double language theory has been utilized by men professing this view, mainly I suppose because a linguistic monism seems inadequate, the objection is important.

What Smart must do to answer the objection is to show that a sentence such as 'I see a yellowish-orange afterimage,' while being a report about a brain process, does not, as it seems, attribute some psychic property to that brain process. Smart must show, then, that this sentence either attributes some physical property to the brain process, or, while referring to the brain process, does not attribute any particular kind of property to it. Smart chooses the latter course and uses a translation to prove his point. He claims that when "a person says, 'I see a yellowish-orange after-image,' he is saying something like this: *'There is something going on which is like what is going on when* I have my eyes open, am awake, and there is an orange illuminated in good light in front of me, that is, when I really see an orange.' [37] According to Smart this translation shows that the sentence does not attribute any psychic property to a brain process because it does not attribute any kind of property at all. It merely refers to something going on that *in some unspecified way* is like other things that go on under certain physical conditions. Furthermore, claims Smart, because the translation uses nothing but physical-expressions it falls within the physicalistic framework.

However, there are problems for this translation. First,

36. For more on this point see J. T. Stevenson, "Sensations and Brain Processes: A Reply to J. J. C. Smart," *The Philosophical Review, 69* (1960), 505–10.
37. Smart, "Sensations and Brain Processes," p. 149.

whereas the original sentence, call it P_1, seems to specify in some respect what is going on, the translation, call it M, does not. The consequence of this is that although P_1 is a sufficient condition of M, it is not a necessary condition because there is a sentence which implies M but does not imply P_1. Such a sentence is:

P_2 I see a roughly spherical shape.

Thus M does not mean P_1. To avoid this problem we might try to translate P_1 into M′, which would refer not merely to an orange but to some *n* number of things which have only one thing in common, their yellowish-orange color. Thus since not all of the *n* things would be spherical or any other one specific shape, then P_2 would be eliminated. However, we would have a related problem because there is a sentence such as:

P_3 I see a colored afterimage

which implies M′, but does not imply P_1. Thus M′ does not mean P_1. I believe that any other emendations of M would fail in a similar manner because the crucial part of M, 'there is something going on,' is just too general.

There is also the problem of whether the translation is indeed within the physicalistic framework, as Smart thinks. It is within the physicalistic framework only if either the second "when" clause in his translation is equivalent to the first, as Smart implies, or, if it is not, the second clause is not necessary for the translation. However, the second "when" clause is not equivalent to the first clause because the former, unlike the latter, involves nonphysical terms and is necessary to the translation. Let me show this by making two translations, using one "when" clause for each:

M_1 There is something going on which is like what is going on when I have my eyes open, am awake, and there is an orange illuminated in good light in front of me.

> M₂   There is something going on which is like what
> is going on when I really see an orange.

If we start with M₁, then we can see that although it is
within the physicalistic framework it is not an adequate
translation of:

> P₁   I see a yellowish-orange afterimage

as it stands, even if we ignore the above-mentioned problem
of generality. For if M₁ were true, and I did not notice or
look at the orange, but at something else, such as a green
apple, or at nothing at all, then:

> P₄   I see a green afterimage

or:

> P₅   I do not see any afterimage

might well be true. But because if P₁ is true, then neither P₄
nor P₅ can be true, and if M₁ is true, P₄ or P₅ can be true,
then M₁ is not a translation of P₁. To avoid this problem we
would have to add some clause to M₁ to the effect I am
looking at or noticing the orange. But 'look at' must mean
more than 'focus on' or some such physicalistic expression
if P₄ and P₅ are to be impossible if M₁ is true. What more
is needed, I think, is expressed by 'notice.' But if I notice
something, then I see it. Thus the clause we must add to
correct M₁ turns out to be something like the "when" clause
of M₂.

Thus the "when" clause of M₂ is the kind of clause
needed for the translation. Is M₂ within the physicalistic
framework? The answer depends upon whether 'I really
see an x' can be brought within the framework. The sense
of 'see' which seems to be involved here is the sense which
implies my noticing something and consequently implies
that I believe that there is something here. But if the above
implication is correct (as it seems) then the translation implies a belief-sentence, which as Chisholm has pointed out,
lies outside the physicalistic framework. Thus if all the

above is true, then Smart has not escaped what certainly seems to be at least one psychic property, because his method of escape was to provide a translation that involved no psychological-terms, and his translation seems to have failed to do this.

Ryle does not face this problem. His view is that the concept of imaging or picturing or visualizing "is a proper and useful concept, but that its use does not entail the existence of pictures which we contemplate or the existence of a gallery in which such pictures are ephemerally suspended. Roughly, imaging occurs, but images are not seen." [38] The claim that the sentence 'I see an afterimage' entails that I am studying or observing or noticing some kind of image or picture gives rise to questions about this observing, whether or not it is really a brain process, and about the picture, whether or not it is a mental entity. Such a claim and the questions which stem from it are misguided according to Ryle. Thus the problem facing Smart of how to do away with the psychic property of being a yellowish-orange afterimage which (it seems on Smart's view) certain brain processes would have, is a pseudo problem. If Ryle is correct, nothing could have such a property because there being no images, there are no afterimages. Thus, Ryle would say, once we get clear about the concept of imaging we can see that there is no problem about psychic properties, as Smart believes. There is only a problem if a certain entailment holds, and it does not hold; Smart was misled by the logic of image-sentences into this problem.

Ryle's defense of his position that this entailment does not hold is, as we have seen earlier with a different example, to show that image-sentences are not reports, as Smart and others believe, and thus they do not describe some process or act, whether psychic or physical, which involves some kind of picture or image. Image-sentences belong to a different logical category.

38. Ryle, *The Concept of Mind*, p. 247.

The second objection to the Feigl-Smart species of the double language theory is concerned with the problem of how it is possible that sentences about private experiences such as sensations "if they are genuine reports, get a foothold in language: For any rule of language must have public criteria for its correct application." [39] This is the problem of private language, mentioned previously,[40] and can be generated as follows. For an expression to be meaningful there must be rules for its correct application. Thus we apply an expression correctly if and only if we obey its rules. Consequently it must be possible to distinguish between obeying a rule and merely thinking that we are obeying a rule because without this distinction no one could know whether he applied the expression correctly, and thus no one could know the meaning of the expression. But if no one could know the meaning of the expression, it would follow that it had no meaning and thus would not be part of any language.

If, for example, there were an expression, E, such that at most one person, A, could check its application, then only A could know the rules for the correct application of E. This expression, then, would be a private expression and part of a private language. But if only A could know these rules, then there could be no way for anyone including A to distinguish between A's obeying the rules and his merely thinking that he is. Thus A cannot know, and consequently no one can know, when E is correctly applied. Therefore E is meaningless and not part of any language. There are, then, no private expressions and no private languages.

If the above argument against the possibility of private languages were conclusive, then Smart and the others who consider sensation-sentences to be reports of private experiences would have the following problem: sensations are private in the sense that only one person can know whether any one of them occurs; thus if sensation-sentences are re-

39. Smart, "Sensations and Brain Processes," p. 153.
40. See pp. 19–23.

ports of sensations, i.e. refer to sensations (as Smart and others believe), then each sensation-sentence would be such that only one person, the person having the sensation, could check its application, and therefore only one person could know the rules for its correct application. It would follow, as above, that sensation-reports are meaningless and not part of any language.

The soundness of this argument has been debated. However this is too large a problem to delve into here.[41] I shall, therefore, merely present and criticize Smart's reply as an example of one attempt to handle the problem. Smart tries to show just how sensation-reports get into our language, thereby showing that the conclusion of the argument is false without considering the argument itself:

> the change from describing how things are to describing how we feel is just a change from uninhibitedly saying "this is so" to saying "this looks so". . . . Psychologically speaking the change from talking about the environment to talking about one's state of consciousness is simply a matter of inhibiting descriptive reactions not justified by appearances alone, and of disinhibiting descriptive reactions which are normally inhibited because the individual has learned that they are unlikely to provide a reliable guide to the state of the environment in the prevailing circumstances. To say that something looks green to me is to say that my experience is like the experience I get when I see something that really is green.[42]

Smart, then, seems to be saying that sentences such as 'x looks f' get into our language by our using them when we wish to refrain from saying 'x is f.' We use this language to

41. For a counter-argument see A. J. Ayer, "Can there be a Private Language?," *Supplementary Proceedings of the Aristotelian Society, 28* (1954), 63–76.

42. Smart, "Sensations and Brain Processes," pp. 153–54.

inhibit ourselves in this way. Thus there seems to be no problem about it being part of any language.

However, whereas this reply seems sufficient to get 'x looks f' into our language when it is used as a means to keep from committing ourselves in any way about what x is, it is not clear how it is relevant to sentences when used as a report about private experiences. This problem can be shown by distinguishing two senses of 'look.' If we use the first sense of 'look,' we mean by 'x looks f' something like 'x seems to be f' or 'apparently x is f,' with the implication perhaps, that x may not be f, or that we are not sure enough to go all out and say that x is f. This use is something like what Chisholm calls "the epistemic use of appear words." [43] That is, words such as 'appear,' 'look,' 'seem,' 'sound,' and 'feel,' when used in this way, are words "enabling us to say what we often say using such words as 'know,' 'evident,' 'unreasonable,' 'perceive,' 'see,' and 'probable.' " [44] In using 'look' in this way we are not reporting about our experiences but merely refusing or not daring to go all out in reporting something about x.

The second sense of 'look,' as used in 'x looks f,' what Chisholm calls the "non-epistemic" use, is, if it is a report at all, not a qualified one about x but an unqualified report about what experiences we have as a result of being sensibly stimulated by x. Smart's reply seems to overlook the distinction between these two senses of 'look' which I shall call 'look$_1$' and 'look$_2$' respectively. Smart wants to show that look$_2$-expressions are a part of language, i.e. there are such linguistic expressions. His proof is that we come to say 'x looks f' as we come to realize that we are not always justified in saying uninhibitedly 'x is f.' This gets one sense of 'look' into language, but this is surely 'look$_1$' because in refraining from saying 'x is f' we are being inhibited or cautious about what x is ('look$_1$'), rather than being uninhibited

43. Chisholm, *Perceiving,* pp. 43–44.
44. Ibid., p. vi.

about our experiences ('look$_2$'). Whether or not our grounds for caution or doubt, i.e. for using 'look$_1$,' can be said to be the peculiar ways things sometimes look$_2$ (appearances), as Smart seems to think, is, of course, a question which must await the results of the debate and not evidence either for or against the claim that there is such a sense of 'look' as 'look$_2$.' What Smart has done, then, is show that 'look$_1$' is a part of language. This was never in doubt. But he has not shown what *is* in doubt: that 'look$_2$' is part of language. Thus the problem of private language remains for Smart as it does for the others we have considered, with the exception of Ryle. Smart and the others must face the problem because they all consider many psychological-sentences to be reports and thus, prima facie at least, reports about private experiences. Ryle has no such problem because he does not consider such sentences to be reports about private experiences or anything else. They are not reports but sentences of a different logical kind.

While Ryle does not have to face the above two problems, there is one he must face that the others do not. Since this problem will be discussed more fully in Chapters 6 and 7, I shall indicate it here only briefly. Central to Ryle's view, and the way in which he avoids the above two problems, is his contention that psychological-sentences belong to a logical category different from the category of factual reports. However, his unique problem arises in his attempts to establish criteria for deciding to which logical category a given sentence belongs or does not belong. His method, briefly, is to point out certain logical differences between a sentence or a kind of sentence in question and sentences of a generally agreed-upon category and to point out certain logical similarities between the sentence and sentences of other agreed-upon logical categories. By means of this procedure Ryle concludes that the sentence does not belong to a particular category, as others have thought, but to an entirely different one. The problem arises when he tries to justify his conclusion because he must establish just those logical features of a language which mark off a certain logical category.

Before concluding this chapter, I should like to compare briefly the views of Feigl, Smart, and Ryle about what kind of entity the common referents of mind-expressions and body-expressions are. This foreshadows the subject of the next chapter, the relevance of the linguistic problem to the traditional problem, as well as the subject of the second part of the book, the problem of linguistic reference. Feigl, who in his earlier work ventures no opinion about the nature of the referents, later talks of them as being what we are directly aware of—"raw feels." [45] Smart claims the common referents are brain processes, while Ryle can be interpreted to imply that they are neither physical events nor mental events, but what might be called person-events.

In so far as Feigl's primary interest is in the philosophy of the language of science, in investigating the relations among the sentences of the various sciences and of the various "levels" of each science (observation-sentences, law-sentences, theory-sentences), there is no reason for him to discuss the referent of such sentences. Indeed, there does not seem to be any reason for him to discuss linguistic reference at all because whether or not a linguistic dualism or a double language theory is correct, and whether what is referred to is mind, body, or something else, are irrelevant questions for science. What is important for science is Feigl's claim that mind-sentences are not translatable into any kind of body-sentences but are merely correlated with them as a result of empirical discoveries. Thus the implications of Feigl's and Smart's view for science seem to be no different from those of linguistic dualism. It is only for the traditional philosophical mind–body problem that, as we

45. See Feigl, "The 'Mental' and the 'Physical'," pp. 446–53; and "Mind-Body, Not a Pseudoproblem," in Sidney Hook, ed., *Dimensions of Mind* (New York, Colliers Books, 1961), pp. 33–38.

shall see, the reference of psychological-sentences is important.

Thus linguistic reference is important for Smart, who seems to be interested in the philosophical problem. He argues that sensations are really brain processes by showing that there are no objections to the view that sensation-expressions refer to brain processes, and therefore no objections to the double language theory. Thus, given no objections to the theory,[46] we can employ Occam's razor to eliminate unnecessary entities and conclude that there is "nothing in the world but physico-chemical mechanisms," that is, sensation-sentences, like all others, refer to some physico-chemical process or state.[47] Smart offers, therefore, not only a solution to the linguistic problem but to the traditional problem as well. He is a reductive materialist. However, two objections to Smart's reasoning can be raised at this point. First, Smart's argument, depending as it does on Occam's razor, assumes what we are setting out to examine and what others have denied: that there is no way to discover what the referents of sensation-expressions and brain-process expressions are. If we can find out what these referents are, then the use of the razor is out of place. Second, Occam's razor cuts two ways: Smart assumes that nonpsychological reports refer to physico-chemical mechanisms. But what reason is there for this? Science offers none because, as we have seen, whether we conclude a dualism or some form of monism consistent with the double language theory makes no difference for science. This is purely a philosophical problem. Why then could we not use Occam's razor and the double language theory to con-

46. In my article, "The Identity of Mind and Body," *The Journal of Philosophy, 59* (1962) 486–92, I have considered objections not mentioned here and briefly explained what may be one way to avoid them.

47. See Smart, "Sensations and Brain Processes," pp. 142, 143, 156.

clude a reductive idealism or a neutral monism? Given
Smart's argument, these views are as plausible as reductive
materialism.

Ryle, in fact, can be interpreted as concluding that both
idealism and materialism are wrong because they are based
on confusions about the categories of language. We refer,
rather, to persons, a "neutral" kind of entity. However, since
Ryle does not talk explicitly about linguistic reference there
is an interpretation of his thesis such that we can conclude
that he is interested solely in the linguistic problem. On
this interpretation he is concerned only with certain logical
and linguistic categories, and nothing more. Thus his point
would be that it is wrong to speak of the linguistic categories of mind-expressions and body-expressions as being
ultimately distinct categories. Both of these categories belong, rather, to the basic linguistic category of persons.
Whether we can get from claims about distinct logical categories and basic linguistic categories to a conclusion about
the traditional mind–body problem, as Ryle sometimes
seems to imply, will be one of the central issues of the next
chapter and will lead to the problems discussed in the subse-
quent parts of the book.

3. The Relation of the Linguistic Problem to the Traditional Problem

In the last two chapters I discussed what I have called the traditional mind–body problem, and the linguistic mind–body problem. In the present chapter I wish to discuss what consequences the solution of the linguistic problem has for the traditional problem: assuming a given conclusion to the linguistic problem, does this commit us to or give us any grounds for any particular conclusion about the traditional problem? Aside from whatever intrinsic value such a discussion might have, there are at least three other reasons for conducting such an investigation.

First, such an investigation will clarify the relationship, if there is any, between the currently popular linguistic conception of philosophy and philosophy as it has been done by those who consider linguistic considerations at best necessary conditions, but certainly not sufficient conditions for solutions of philosophical problems. Second, some philosophers have merged the two problems and assumed there is only one mind–body problem. Our investigation will, among other things, examine this assumption and the assumption held by other philosophers that a solution to the linguistic problem provides a basis for handling the traditional problem. The third and most important reason is that, as I see it, there is no way to solve the traditional problem other than by a linguistic approach. I shall try to show this in Chapters 5, 6, and 7. For now, I shall assume that some kind of linguistic approach is at least necessary to a solution of the traditional problem, so that it becomes of the utmost importance to understand the relation of the linguistic problem to it, or better, to understand what must be the case if there is any relationship at all.

In conducting this investigation I will examine four possible positions regarding the relationship between the linguistic and traditional mind–body problem in order to discover and examine critically the kind of premise needed to establish each position. We shall see that for each of the first three there is an important suppressed or missing premise. The four positions are:

1. The solution of the linguistic problem is the solution of the traditional problem because the traditional problem is really the linguistic problem talked about in a misleading way.
2. The solution of the linguistic problem shows that there is no traditional problem. People have thought that there is a traditional problem because they misconstrued language.
3. The solution of the linguistic problem is evidence for the solution of the traditional problem.
4. The solution of the linguistic problem has no relationship to the solution of the traditional problem.

POSITION I

This seems at first glance to be obviously false. In the previous discussion of traditional dualism I spoke of two approaches: One, the classical approach, involves minds, bodies, and the relations between them; the other considers the linguistic reference of mind- and body-expressions as well. That is, there have been two basic ways of arguing for a mind–body dualism: first, by taking scientific, introspective, and common-sense evidence for it and by answering points raised against it; second, by arguing in addition from the reference of key expressions and replying to any new objections which arise because of the discussion of reference.

We have seen the same two kinds of approaches taken to reductive materialism. Both Hobbes and Smart, for example, are reductive materialists. While Smart must face all the objections that Hobbes must face, unlike Hobbes he includes in his defense of the view a discussion of linguistic reference. However, it should be noted that Smart can, by means of his use of modern linguistic apparatus, handle these objections more easily than Hobbes, who did not have such apparatus available. For example, one objection raised to Smart's view, which if suitably phrased could be altered to apply to Hobbes as well, is that "it is only a contingent fact (if it is a fact) that when we have a certain kind of sensation there is a certain process in our brain." [1] But if a sensation were identical with some brain process, it would seem that the fact would not merely be contingent but necessary. It certainly seems true that if A and B are identical then it is not a contingent fact that when A occurs, B occurs because when A occurs B must occur.

This objection seems well taken, but we can dispose of it if we use the distinction between reference and meaning as Smart did. To say that it is a contingent fact that when A occurs B occurs is to say, in this case, that it is logically possible that B not occur when A occurs. But this amounts to saying that the sentence 'When A occurs B occurs' is not analytic but synthetic. There is nothing incompatible between that sentence being synthetic, and 'A' and 'B' referring to the same thing, i.e. A and B being identical. It is important here to distinguish between identity of meaning and identity of reference. The distinction is easily missed unless the distinction between reference and meaning is made explicit. Although this is an example of how a linguistic approach to a traditional problem can be helpful in disposing of otherwise difficult objections, it does not fol-

1. J. J. C. Smart, "Sensations and Brain Processes," 147.

low that there is any connection between the traditional problem and the linguistic problem. All that follows from what we have said so far is that at least one objection is based on a linguistic confusion.

To return to the main point, we have seen that there can be a linguistic approach to the traditional problem. We have also seen that this approach involves some discussion of linguistic reference to get from a consideration of language to a consideration of minds and bodies. But a solution of the linguistic problem need not involve any discussion of linguistic reference. As we have seen in discussing the views of men such as Hempel, Carnap, and Chisholm, a solution of the linguistic problem involves only a discussion of certain sentences and the logical relationships among them. And, furthermore, no matter what is established about the logical relationships of such sentences, it seems that nothing follows about what it is that the sentences refer to. But this is just what some philosophers deny. They would claim that when we discuss the mind–body problem we are really discussing the linguistic problem, although we may be confused and think that we are discussing something entirely different—the traditional problem. Thus Carnap says:

> The so-called *psycho-physical problem* is usually formulated as a question concerning the relation of two object-domains: the domain of the psychical processes and the domain of the parallel physical processes in the central nervous system. But this formulation in the material mode of speech leads into a morass of pseudo-problems (for instance: 'Are the parallel processes merely functionally correlated, or are they connected by a causal relation? Or is it the same process seen from two different sides?'). With the use of the formal mode of speech it becomes clear that we are here concerned only with the relation between two sub-languages, namely, the psychological and the physical

language; the question is whether two parallel sentences are always, or only in certain cases equipollent with one another, and, if so, whether they are L- or P-equipollent. This important problem can only be grappled with at all if it is formulated correctly, namely, as a syntactical problem—whether in the manner indicated or in some other.[2]

To be able to understand and examine critically Carnap's view, we must first see what he means by his two technical terms 'material mode of speech' and 'formal mode of speech.' In order to do this we must explain Carnap's distinction among three kinds of sentences. There are, first, *syntactical sentences:*

> They concern the form of linguistic expressions. With these there are to be contrasted those sentences which concern not linguistic expressions but extra-linguistic objects; they may be called *real object-sentences.* There is also a third, an intermediary kind of sentence. Sentences of this kind are, so to speak, amphibious, being like object-sentences as to their form but like syntactical sentences as to their content. They may be called *pseudo-object sentences.*[3]

More specifically, says Carnap, pseudo-object sentences are:

> Sentences which are formulated as though they refer (either partially or exclusively) to objects, while in reality they refer to syntactical forms, and, specifically, to the forms of the designations of those objects with which they appear to deal. Thus these sentences are syntactical sentences in virtue of content, though they are disguised as object-sentences.[4]

2. Rudolf Carnap, *The Logical Syntax of Language,* p. 324.
3. Carnap, *Philosophy and Logical Syntax* (London, K. Paul, French, Trubner, 1935), p. 60. For more detail see *The Logical Syntax of Language,* p. 287
4. Carnap, *The Logical Syntax of Language,* p. 285.

These pseudo-object sentences, which Carnap also calls "quasi-syntactical" sentences, are sentences in the material mode of speech. Syntactical sentences are sentences in the formal mode of speech.

Carnap goes on to say that any pseudo-object sentence can be translated into the syntactical sentence which is equipollent to it, that is, into that sentence which has the same content or consequences that it has. Thus we can translate any sentence in the material mode of speech, any pseudo-object sentence, into the syntactical sentence in the formal mode of speech that parallels it. In this way we can avoid being misled by expressions in the material mode into thinking that they refer to extralinguistic objects, because we know that the parallel expressions in the formal mode refer to syntactical forms of language.

Before we move on we must give Carnap's criterion of a pseudo-object sentence and his criterion for translating such sentences into the formal mode. He begins by defining the phrase 'parallel syntactical quality':

> A syntactical quality Q_2 is called *parallel* to the quality Q_1 if it is the case that when, and only when, an object possesses the quality Q_1 does a designation of this (i.e., an expression which designates or refers to this object) possess the quality Q_2. And the criterion of a pseudo-object sentence can now be stated as follows (if we regard only sentences of the simplest form): such a sentence attributes to an object (say a) a quality Q_1 to which a parallel syntactical quality Q_2 can be found. Such a sentence '$Q_1(a)$' can then be translated into the syntactical sentence '$Q_2('a')$' which attributes the quality Q_2 to a designation of that object.[5]

We are now ready to examine Carnap's argument to show that the traditional mind–body problem is really the linguistic problem. To begin let us call (T) the class of all

5. Carnap, *Philosophy and Logical Syntax,* p. 63.

sentences which refer to the data of the traditional problem, supposedly the domain of psychological processes and the domain of physical processes and the relations between them. And let us call (L) the class of all sentences which refer to the data of the linguistic problem, the syntactical forms of psychological-sentences and physical-sentences, and the syntactical relations among them. Carnap's argument can be construed in the following way:

1. Sentences of (L) refer to the syntactical forms of psychological- and physical-sentences.
2. Sentences of (T) are pseudo-object sentences.
3. Pseudo-object sentences refer to the syntactical forms of those expressions which refer to those objects to which the pseudo-object sentences appear to refer (see p. 57).

Therefore

4. Sentences of (T) refer to the syntactical forms of psychological-sentences or physical-sentences.

Therefore

5. Sentences of (T) and sentences of (L) refer to the same thing; i.e. the data of the linguistic mind–body problem.

Therefore

6. The traditional mind–body problem and the linguistic mind–body problem are identical—both are really the linguistic problem.

Premises 1 and 3 are true by definition. Thus if premise 2 can be established, Carnap's conclusion, 6, follows. The problem, then, is to establish premise 2. To see whether this can be done, let us apply Carnap's criterion for a pseudo-object sentence to some sentence of the class (T). Let us pick a sentence that Smart might use, 'Sensation-sentences refer to brain processes,' which we can symbolize as '$Q_1(S)$' to fit Carnap's model. Here we can let 'Q_1' designate the quality of referring to brain processes and

'S' designate sensation-sentences. Thus if we are to establish that '$Q_1(S)$' is a pseudo-object sentence we must find some syntactical property, Q_2, such that S possesses Q_1 if and only if 'S' possesses Q_2. In other words, $Q_1(S)$, if and only if, $Q_2($'S'$)$. Carnap claims that the syntactical quality parallel to 'referring to x' is "being equipollent to 'x'." [6] Given this it follows, according to Carnap, that '$Q_1(S)$' is a pseudo-object sentence and thus refers to the data of the linguistic problem, i.e. certain syntactical forms, rather than to the supposed data of the traditional problem, i.e. mental and physical processes.

There are two steps in this argument to establish premise 2. First, there is the translation step for which sentences of the form " 'x' is equipollent to 'y' " are taken as equivalent to sentences of the form " 'x' refers to y." The problem involved in this step is that the equivalence does not seem to hold. Second, there is the step which, given the translation, concludes that sentences of the form " 'x' refers to y" are in the material mode, they are pseudo-object sentences. The problem here is how to establish the conclusion merely on the basis of the translation. It is true that Carnap's criterion for pseudo-object sentences states as its sole requirement just such a translation. However, it is this very criterion that seems questionable.

Let us consider the first step. I shall take as an example of a refer-sentence (a sentence using the term 'refer') Carnap's own definition or characterization of pseudo-object sentences as I have paraphrased it in premise 3 of the above argument. Premise 3 reads as follows: "Pseudo-object sentences refer to the syntactical forms of those expressions which refer to those objects to which the pseudo-object sentences appear to refer." I shall show that this is one refer-sentence for which Carnap's translation will not work and thus that his translation fails. It follows from this that Carnap has not established the first step in his argument to establish premise 2. Carnap's translation runs into this

6. See Carnap, *The Logical Syntax of Language,* pp. 288–90.

trouble: either we cannot eliminate 'refer,' or in order to do so we must make the translation so general that the result is an implied contradiction. We can see this by examining two specimen translations:

> TRANSLATION (I): Pseudo-object sentences are equipollent to those expressions which refer to the syntactical forms of those expressions to which the pseudo-object sentences appear to be (but are not) equipollent.

> TRANSLATION (II): Pseudo-object sentences are equipollent to those expressions to which the pseudo-object sentences appear to be (but are not) equipollent.

Obviously the first translation will not do because it involves the word 'refer.' We might try to avoid 'refer' by eliminating the clause in which it appears. But if we do that, we arrive at the second translation and the implied contradiction that pseudo-object sentences are both equipollent to and not equipollent to the same expressions. Thus this translation is inadequate. We need, it seems, the expression 'syntactical forms.' But when we reintroduce that expression and try to avoid 'refer,' we arrive at a longer, more complicated version of either (I) or (II), neither one of which will do. Thus Carnap's translation of refer-sentences will not work, and thus he has not established premise 2. Neither has he shown that 'refer' is a quasi-syntactical term. That he has not is important, for if 'refer' were a quasi-syntactical term, then among other things it would seem that all the rules necessary to characterize a language would be formal rules—rules connecting linguistic expressions to linguistic expressions. If this were true, it would seem that we could learn language without relating it to the world at all. It might also lead us to a coherence theory of truth and other "oddities" of formalism.

That Carnap does not establish the second step in his

argument to establish premise 2 can be easily shown. Suppose that the required translations could be made of all
sentences of (T): each sentence of (T) when symbolized
in the form '$Q_1(S)$' is equivalent to one of the form
'$Q_2('S')$.' It follows from this, given Carnap's criterion of
a pseudo-object sentence, that the sentences of (T) are
pseudo-object sentences. But must we accept Carnap's criterion? The most that could be said to follow without the
criterion is that '$Q_1(S)$' and '$Q_2('S')$' refer to the same
thing, or given Carnap's translation, are equipollent. But
we saw in the discussion of the views of Feigl and Smart,
nothing follows from this about what it is that sentences
which refer to the same thing refer to. Furthermore, if we
use the translation and 'equipollent' rather than 'refer,' we
are no better off because the relation of equipollence is
symmetrical. (This is, perhaps, one reason the translation
fails. What is needed is a nonsymmetrical relation.) Thus
on the basis of the translation alone we have as much right
to call the sentences of (L) pseudo-syntactical sentences,
i.e. sentences which refer to psychological and physical
processes rather than what they appear to refer to, i.e. syntactical forms, as to call the sentences of (T) pseudo-object
sentences. If we accept Carnap's criterion of a pseudo-object
sentence, however, the issue is no longer in doubt. But why
should we accept his criterion rather than another which,
for example, makes the sentences of (L) pseudo-syntactical sentences? Carnap gives us no reason.

What Carnap must do, then, to establish premise 2 seems
to be more than merely examining the logical syntax of certain sentences. He must also consider what it is that the
sentences of (T) and (L) refer to.[7] More specifically, to

7. At present Carnap would, I believe, agree that establishing Position 1 or any other such position is a semantical problem involving
linguistic reference, rather than a syntactical problem. In Chapter
4 I shall examine Carnap's semantical method of handling linguistic reference, partly to see whether such a method can help us
decide among the positions discussed in this chapter.

establish his conclusion, 6, Carnap must show that the sentences of (T) refer to the syntactical forms of psychological- and physical-sentences. This is the missing premise in Carnap's version of Position 1, the premise he must establish but has not established, to justify Position 1. What he in effect must do is establish statement 4 without relying on his criterion of a pseudo-object sentence. And this task of deciding what expressions refer to, as we have seen in our examination of the two steps of Carnap's argument to establish 2, does not seem to be a syntactical task. What kind of task it is and how to go about it will be the central topic of parts two and three of this book.

POSITION 2

This is much like the first position: both claim that we are misled if we think that there is some mind–body problem other than the linguistic problem. However, whereas the first position claims that the traditional problem is just the linguistic problem, Position 2 claims that once we get clear about the logic of the relevant linguistic expressions, i.e. solve the linguistic problem, we can see that there is no traditional problem. We are misled into thinking that there is one only if we are confused about the logic of the relevant expressions. Once we see the logic of our language correctly, the traditional problem dissolves. This is the general kind of approach to philosophy taken by many of the so-called Oxford philosophers. Ryle, for example, at least on one interpretation, seems to hold this position.

Ryle argues that mind-expressions belong to a different logical category from body-expressions, that is, they are logically different types of sentences. As Ryle says in *The Concept of Mind:* "The logical type or category to which a concept belongs is the set of ways in which it is logically legitimate to operate with it. The key arguments employed in this book are therefore intended to show why certain sorts of operations with the concepts of mental powers and processes are breaches of logical rules." [8] Such breaches of logical rules Ryle calls "category mistakes." He goes on to say that while it is legitimate to conjoin two expressions which belong to the same logical category, it is a category mistake to conjoin two expressions from two different categories. Thus, to use Ryle's example, it is legitimate to say, "I am wearing a left-hand glove and a right-hand glove," but it is a category mistake to say, "I am wearing a left-hand glove, a right-hand glove, and a pair of gloves." Here the expressions 'left-hand glove' and 'right-hand glove' belong to one category, while 'pair of gloves' belongs to another.

On this interpretation, Ryle's thesis regarding the mind–body problem is that expressions such as 'there occur mental processes' belong to a different category from others such as 'there occur physical processes,' and thus it is a category mistake to conjoin the two expressions. But if we cannot conjoin them it is also a category mistake to say things such as "There are no mental (physical) processes, only physical (mental) ones." It follows, then, according to Ryle, that the traditional views of dualism, materialism, and idealism involve category mistakes and thus the question to which these views are answers is an improper question. Thus the question "Are there both mental processes and physical processes, or only one and if so which one?" is an improper question because it conjoins expressions from two different logical categories; it is improper because it embodies a category mistake. But we use just such a question to formulate the traditional mind–body problem. Therefore it is logically improper to formulate the traditional problem. Once we understand this, we are cured of the tendency of trying to solve this "problem," which is as it should be because if it is illegitimate to formulate a problem there is no problem, although there may be some sort of perplexity or feeling of puzzlement which stands in need of curing.

We have already seen in Chapter 2 an example of Ryle's

8. Ryle, *The Concept of Mind*, p. 8.

method of showing that mental-expressions and physical-expressions belong to two different logical categories. I shall not examine his arguments for this conclusion for they and others like them will be dealt with in Chapters 6 and 7. We shall assume for now that Ryle has proved that mental- and physical-expressions belong to two different categories. Our task, then, is to see whether Ryle's conclusion—a solution to the traditional mind–body problem is an answer to an improper question—follows as Ryle seems to think.

In order to facilitate matters let us call (M) the class of all mental-expressions and (B) the class of all physical-expressions relevant to bodily processes. Thus if Ryle is correct, the expression, 'There occur mental processes' M_1 of (M) cannot be conjoined with another, 'There are physical processes' B_1 of (B) because this would be a category mistake. But given this, can we not still properly say sentences of the form, 'B_1 refers to x,' and 'M_1 refers to y'? And if so can we not substitute for 'x,' 'bodies' or 'bodily processes,' and for 'y,' 'minds' or 'mental processes'? Or perhaps claim that x and y are really identical, and thus M_1 and B_1 refer to the same thing? If we can do all this, we can provide solutions to the traditional problem, and Ryle is wrong to claim that to try to solve the traditional problem is to be confused because it involves a category mistake.

Indeed Ryle himself seems at certain places to talk about what certain expressions refer to. Thus when he says: "Assertions about a person's mind are therefore assertions of a special sort about that person" (see p. 38), he seems to be at least implying that assertions which *seem* to refer to a person's mind are really assertions of a special kind that refer not to a mind, but to that person, or, as Ryle says elsewhere, to certain events in the *single* series of events which constitute the *single* rather than dual life of that person. Similarly, I believe, he would say that assertions which *seem* to refer to a person's body are really assertions of a different special sort which refer not to a body but to that person, or, more specifically, to certain events in the *single* life of that person. He seems to be saying, therefore, that it is wrong to say that expressions such as M_1 refer to minds and that expressions such as B_1 refer to bodies, but that it is correct to say that B_1 and M_1 refer to persons, or rather to certain events in the single lives of persons.

However, in saying this does not Ryle seem to be offering a solution to the traditional problem rather than showing that any solution involves an answer to an improper question? In other words, has not Ryle found a way to formulate the traditional problem and to express a solution of it without committing a category mistake? Thus when Ryle says that B_1 and M_1 both refer to events in the one life of a person he is not committing a category mistake because he is not conjoining expressions of two different categories but is rather conjoining the names of these expressions. But he is at the same time offering a solution of the traditional mind–body problem because he is answering the question, "What is it that mental-expressions and physical-expressions refer to?"—one way of formulating the traditional problem.

It seems, then, that Ryle himself offers proof that Position 2 is mistaken. But perhaps we have interpreted his thesis incorrectly. He might escape this predicament if his thesis is that there is no traditional problem, not because we cannot formulate a question expressing the problem without committing a category mistake, but rather because once we become clear about the logical features of the relevant expressions, we will see the only answer possible and will realize that there is no problem. Our perplexities will dissolve, and we will be cured of looking for a solution to a problem which does not exist. Once we fight our way through the complexities of language the answer to the questions expressing the problem will be so evident there will be no reason to ask the question.

This interpretation of Ryle raises a new question. It is the question of whether, as Ryle seems to think, once the logic of our language is clear, there is no excuse for being unclear about the proper view concerning the mind–body problem, in other words, whether the correct view of the logic of language constitutes grounds on the basis of which Ryle's thesis about the mind–body problem becomes obvious. Ryle seems to think that it does constitute such grounds and tries to establish this point by showing that the sentences of (M) belong to a different category from those of (B). The first, says Ryle, belong to the category of law-like sentences, and the second to the category of reports. But what claims about the traditional mind–body problem are made obvious by this? It would seem that no claim is even made probable unless we are able to find out whether the expressions of (M) and (B) are referential, and if so, what they refer to, because it is only in this way that we can get from conclusions about language to conclusions about the world. Thus if this interpretation of Ryle's thesis is to be acceptable it must be the case that once we get an expression into a particular logical category, the correct inference about the reference of the expression becomes obvious.

What would give us the right to make such inferences must either be the criterion we use to put expressions into categories or the definitions of the categories. If it is the criterion which gives us the right to make inferences from categories to reference, we have the problem of finding whether any sentences meet the criterion. Examining the logical features of sentences, as Ryle does, is not enough unless we can infer from statements about logic to conclusions about reference. But this is the very question at issue. If, on the other hand, the definitions of the categories justify this inference, and the criterion requires us to consider only certain logical features (as Ryle's criterion seems to do), then, as with Carnap's criterion for pseudo-object sentences, we must see whether the criterion is adequate to the task. But we can establish that such a criterion is adequate only if we take expressions that meet the criterion and examine them independently of the criterion in order to see what we can find out about their reference. In either case we must be able to establish something about the reference of the relevant expressions in some way other than by merely examining their logic. But if we must do this to justify the inference from logic to reference, then merely putting expressions into their proper logical categories will not provide irrefutable evidence for the correct view concerning the traditional mind–body problem unless once we have done this we just see, not infer, what we need to know about their reference. However, barring such "intuitions," which I for one do not have, it would seem that this version of Ryle's argument for Position 2 will not work. For if we have to establish something about the reference of the expressions of (M) and (B) there would seem to be more than one kind of thing to which they might refer and thus more than one possible solution to the traditional problem, even given all the proper conclusions about the logic of the relevant expressions.

It seems, then, that we have not been able to interpret Ryle's arguments so that they establish Position 2. But might there not be another, more fruitful interpretation? I think that there is none unless we attribute "intuitionism" to Ryle. For nothing seems to follow about the traditional problem from a solution to the linguistic problem, i.e. from a conclusion about the logical features of the expressions of (M) and (B), unless we establish something about the reference of those expressions. For Ryle to establish Position 2 he must establish the suppressed premise that the expressions of (M) and (B) all refer in different ways to events in the single life of persons. Thus Ryle has a different suppressed premise from that of Carnap. Furthermore, if Ryle were to establish this premise he would thereby establish an answer to the traditional problem which, because it had to be established, was by no means evident. But if Ryle were to establish such a premise in his argument for Position 2 he would thereby refute the position by providing an answer to the traditional problem, and, furthermore, an answer which, given all the proper conclusions about the logic of the expressions, is by no means evident at that. Thus on no interpretation does it seem that Ryle can establish Position 2.

Although it seems that Ryle cannot establish Position 2, there is a weaker thesis he might establish which may perhaps be the thesis he actually holds. Although a discussion of this thesis is not relevant to Position 2, it is of interest both because it will indicate a possible way to interpret an important and influential book, and also because it will present a possible way of pointing out confusions which have trapped philosophers concerned with the mind–body problem. We can interpret Ryle's purpose in *The Concept of Mind* as an attempt to show that certain confusions about logical features of language are the basis upon which one argument for traditional dualism is built, the very argument which leads to the central issue over which most dualists and their opponents, the materialists and idealists, come to blows. We can formulate this "spurious" argument for dualism as follows:

1. Sentences of (M) and (B) belong to the same logical category.
2. Sentences of (B) are reports of bodily processes.

Therefore

3. Sentences of (M) are reports.
4. Sentences of (M) are not reports of bodily processes.

Therefore

5. Sentences of (M) are reports of a different kind of processes, i.e. nonmaterial or mental processes.

Therefore

6. There are two different kinds of processes: mental processes and physical processes.

As we are here interpreting Ryle's thesis, it states that premise 1 is false, and therefore the dualistic conclusion 6 is not warranted on the basis of this argument. However, many dualists and their opponents assume premise 1 and debate 4 or 5. A materialist such as Smart, for example, would deny 4, and therefore 5, and try to establish the denial of 5. The dualist would try to refute his arguments and propose a defense of 5. But, according to Ryle, this is a fruitless debate because to argue about 5 and its denial is to assume the truth of 1, which is a mistake. Thus to argue about the truth or falsity of 5 in order to prove or disprove traditional dualism, or any other traditional view, is to be confused by the logic of expressions of (M) and (B). Once we see the logic of these expressions, we can see that the argument is not sound because its first premise is false.

This version of Ryle's thesis, then, shows us, if we accept his denial of 1, that in so far as the traditional mind–body problem is a problem involving the truth-value of 5, it is a problem based on a confusion. Ryle, then, if his contention is correct, cures us of the tendency of trying to solve the traditional problem by arguing about the truth of 5. However, it does not follow from this that the reason that we are mistaken in trying to solve the traditional problem in this way is that there really is no problem. It only follows that we are mistaken if we try to solve it in this particular way. There may be other, legitimate ways. On this interpretation of Ryle's thesis, he is not arguing for Position 2.

We have seen that Ryle's arguments, construed as attempts to establish Position 2, do not succeed; nor, I think, will any such attempts. We have also previously seen that to establish Position 1 we must ascertain certain things about linguistic reference. Let us turn, then, to Position 3—that the solution to the linguistic problem is in some way evidence for the solution to the traditional problem—in order to see what kind of suppressed premise is needed to establish it.

POSITION 3

This position, while not claiming that once we have solved the linguistic problem we have thereby either solved or dissolved the traditional problem, does claim that a particular solution to the linguistic problem gives weight to or is some reason in favor of a particular solution to the traditional problem. Chisholm, who, as we have seen, defends linguistic dualism, is inclined to think that such a solution to the linguistic problem gives weight to some kind of traditional dualism.

To see better Chisholm's version of Position 3, let us distinguish between two theses of intentionality, what I shall call "the linguistic thesis" and the nonlinguistic, or "traditional thesis." According to Chisholm, Brentano held the nonlinguistic thesis that certain activities are intentional, that is, they may take as objects things that do not exist. This "intentional inexistence" of the object is "peculiar to what is psychical; things which are merely physical show nothing like it." [9] Thus we can think about something which does not exist but we cannot lift something which does not exist. There are, then, two radically different kinds of activities: psychical, characterized by or marked off by intentionality; and physical, marked off by the lack of intentionality. If this interpretation of Brentano's thesis is correct, we can conclude that he is some kind of a traditional dualist. Regardless of Brentano's own views, however, we can say that the nonlinguistic thesis implies traditional dualism.

Chisholm holds the linguistic thesis that we must employ what he calls the "intentional use" of language when we use psychological-sentences, but we can avoid this when we use nonpsychological- or physical-sentences. Thus the intentional use of language is, according to Chisholm, a mark of psychological-sentences, and the nonintentional use of language is a mark of physical-sentences. Chisholm's linguistic thesis thus implies a linguistic dualism.

Chisholm, however, goes beyond this. He says that the fact that we cannot avoid using intentional language "may provide some reason for saying, with Brentano, that 'intentionality' is a mark of what is psychological." [10] Or, as

9. Roderick Chisholm, *Perceiving,* p. 168.
10. Chisholm, "Sentences about Believing," 125.

he says in another passage, "I think that, if our linguistic thesis about intentionality is true, then the followers of Brentano would have a right to take some comfort in this fact." [11] Thus Chisholm seems to think (although he is not sure) that if the linguistic thesis of intentionality is true, then this gives some weight to the traditional thesis. But it follows from this that linguistic dualism, if true, gives weight to traditional dualism—a specific case of Position 3. Thus Chisholm seems to hold Position 3. However, all he may be claiming is that one condition necessary for the truth of the traditional thesis is that the linguistic thesis be true. This would surely afford the followers of Brentano some comfort, although I should think not much, but it certainly would not provide them with some reason *for* their thesis as someone who holds Position 3 would claim.

Another reason for claiming that Chisholm holds Position 3 can be found by examining the main point at issue in an exchange of letters between him and Wilfrid Sellars. In our previous discussion of Chisholm's defense of linguistic dualism, one objection to this position mentioned was that although there is a dualism, it is not physical–psychological language dualism but rather physical-semantical language dualism (see pp. 32 f.). It is this point that Chisholm and Sellars debate. If we can analyze psychological-sentences into sentences using only physical expressions and semantical expressions such as " 'p' means p," this seems sufficient to show that linguistic mind–body dualism is false. However, says Chisholm, this will not do because a semantical expression such as " 'p' means p" is analyzable into " 'p' expresses t, and t is about p," where 't' stands for some thought. And this reference to thoughts, implicit in semantical expressions, implies, says Chisholm, that "living things have a funny characteristic that ordinary physical things don't have." [12] Thus, Chisholm concludes, if we can-

11. Ibid., p. 147.

12. Chisholm, in *Minnesota Studies in the Philosophy of Science,* 2, 524.

not analyze expressions such as " '*p*' means *p*" without using intentional terms or some primitive term of semantics which "if it means anything at all, will refer to what you call thoughts," [13] then this is a reason to believe that living things have this "funny characteristic." Here again Chisholm is affirming Position 3 by claiming that the funny linguistic characteristic gives us reason to infer that there is a funny characteristic of living things.

Sellars agrees with Chisholm that " '*p*' means *p*" cannot be analyzed in behavioristic terms alone. Some primitive semantical term is needed. However, Sellars asks why the primitive term "must stand for a *characteristic,* even if a 'funny' one?" [14] In other words, why should we think that semantical terms are names of or refer to some kind of characteristic; thus why should we conclude from the fact that such terms are used that intentional sentences involving such terms are a sign of the mental? Sellars is, then, denying Position 3: he sees no right to infer from a linguistic dualism to a traditional mind–body dualism.

How are we to decide whether Chisholm or Sellars is right? One way to find out is to see first what is needed to establish Chisholm's position. The minimal interpretation of Position 3 is that on the basis of the linguistic thesis of intentionality, it is more reasonable to believe the traditional thesis than its denial. The most plausible way that I can find to establish this, again barring intuition, is to argue somewhat as follows:

1. No sentence of (M) is translatable into (is entailed by and entails) any sentence of (B).

Therefore it is more reasonable than not to believe:

2. Sentences of (M) refer to things different from the things sentences of (B) refer to.

Therefore it is more reasonable than not to believe:

3. There are two kinds of things, minds and bodies.

13. Ibid., p. 523.
14. Wilfrid Sellars in *Minnesota Studies,* 2, 525.

Here we have an inductive argument in which 1 is claimed
to provide grounds sufficient for making 2, and consequently
3, more reasonable than not. But does 1 provide such
grounds for 2? We know that some pairs of sentences do
not mutually entail each other but refer to the same things.
'The morning star is a planet' and 'The evening star is a
planet' refer to the same thing but do not mutually entail
each other. Can we assume, then, that there is something
special about these particular two classes of sentences so
that in this case, although not in many other cases, we can
agree that 1 provides grounds for 3? I do not think so.
Indeed Feigl, Smart, and others like them who hold the
double language theory claim that although 1 is true, it
provides no reason against their thesis that there are certain pairs of sentences, one member from (M) and one
from (B)—what I shall call *M-B* pairs—that refer to the
same thing. They, as I, would agree that from 1 we can
infer that it is *not* more reasonable to believe the denial of
2 than it is to believe 2. But, although this might provide an
embattled dualist some minimal comfort, he cannot infer
from this that it is more reasonable to believe 3 than its
denial. Premise 1 by itself seems to provide no grounds for
making either 3 or its denial more reasonable than not.
Thus a defender of Position 3 such as Chisholm requires an
additional premise if he is to arrive at 3 via 1. Position 3,
then, is in the same situation as Positions 1 and 2. It requires an additional premise.

The sentence 'No two sentences that do not mutually
entail each other refer to the same thing' will not do for an
additional premise because we have seen that it is false. We
might try instead, 'Most pairs of sentences that do not mutually entail each other do not refer to the same thing.' However, there is reason to think that this is false, because there
are an infinite number of pairs of sentences that can be constructed from 'The morning star is x miles from the earth'
and 'The evening star is x miles from the earth' such that
the members of each pair do not mutually entail each other

but do refer to the same thing. What we must do to find a suitable premise is to restrict the kinds of pairs of sentences mentioned so that it might be true, but also so that, with 1, it makes 3 more reasonable than not. Because we are interested in pairs of sentences that are materially equivalent but do not mutually entail each other, and because, as discussed above, *M-B* pairs seem to have the characteristic of their members coming from different logical categories, we might try limiting the additional premise to a consideration of all or most of what can be called cross-category pairs of equivalent sentences. However, this premise does not seem promising either. If, for example, we consider the class of equivalent pairs which are such that one member is a material object-sentence and the other is the corresponding sentence of atomic physics, then we would seem to have cross-category pairs. But such pairs again provide grounds for concluding that the additional premise is false, because when certain expressions of atomic physics are found to be or are postulated as being materially equivalent to certain material object-expressions, these expressions from different categories are claimed to refer to the same things. Such cases of identity are classed as theoretical identities. Indeed it has been claimed that, because *M-B* pairs are relevantly similar to material object-atomic particle sentence pairs, the latter provide sufficient grounds for concluding that corresponding *M-B* pairs refer to the same things rather than different things. Thus the denial of Chisholm's thesis would be more reasonable than his thesis. Furthermore, there are some people who go beyond using theoretical identities as the basis for an inductive argument against Chisholm's thesis. Hilary Putnam, for example, has claimed that every argument for and against identification would apply equally in the mind–body case and in the accepted cases of theoretical identity.[15] Thus if we accept theoretical identities, as has

15. See Hilary Putnam, "Minds and Machines," in Sidney Hook, ed., *Dimensions of Mind,* p. 157.

been done in many areas of science, then we should also accept mind–body identity.

However, not everyone agrees with Putnam's claim. Richard Brandt suggests that there are reasons to identify material objects with aggregates of micro-objects which do not apply in the mind–body case.[16] The atomic theory is "all-encompassing in the physical world; it leaves no room for micro-objects *and* correlated macro-objects." [17] But there is no analogous theoretical compulsion to identify the mental world with the physical world. Correlation of the two is compatible with all theoretical requirements. It might be argued, in addition, that mind–body identity, although it would be a cross-category identity, is significantly unlike theoretical identities because neither expressions of (M) nor of (B) are theoretical. They are expressions used to report experiences, not expressions that function as parts of a theoretical explanatory system. We experience mental events and bodily events in the sense that we can be sensibly aware of both kinds of events, but we do not, in the same sense, experience both physical events and microevents.

As a result of such a view, someone might claim that the additional premise should be further restricted in order to exclude the cases involving theoretical identity. If we include this restriction we have, I believe, arrived at a premise that may well be true—'All (or most) cross-category pairs of equivalent sentences that do not entail each other and do not involve theoretical terms do not refer to the same thing.' Unfortunately, we have restricted the class of sentence-pairs so drastically that the only sure candidates for membership in the class of which I am aware are *M-B* pairs. Consequently, it seems that we cannot find a premise which might be true and would allow us to apply our knowledge of the reference of some other sentence pairs to *M-B* pairs in order to render 3 more reasonable than not. It seems that we are

16. See Richard Brandt, "Doubts about the Identity Theory," *Dimensions of Mind*, p. 69.
17. Ibid.

forced to work directly with *M-B* pairs. But this means that, in order to avoid begging the question against identity theorists such as Feigl and Smart, we must investigate the reference of the expressions of (M) and (B). We can conclude from this that not only does 1 by itself not provide grounds which make 3 more reasonable than its denial, but also that there seems to be no premise we can add to 1 to provide such grounds. All those premises considered seem either to be false or so restricted that they apply only to *M-B* pairs and thus make 3 no more reasonable than 1 does by itself.

Position 3 is faced with a dilemma: if no additional premise can be established, then the position cannot be established; if an additional premise can be established, then there is no need to establish Position 3, because what we must do to establish the one additional premise that avoids objections is to consider the reference of sentences of (M) and (B). Thus either Position 3 cannot be established or there is no need to establish it. In other words, there is no need to consider Position 3.

Position 3, then, like Position 1, can be established only if we can establish something about the reference of certain linguistic expressions, specifically in the case of Position 3, a premise about whether all or at least most sentences of a certain kind which are materially equivalent but which do not entail each other, refer to different things. However there is a major difference between Positions 1 and 3. If we can establish Position 3 by establishing the above additional premise, as it seems that we must, then, we can establish an answer to the traditional mind–body problem without considering Position 3. But if we can establish Position 1 by establishing its suppressed premise, the premise that the sentences of (T), i.e. sentences which refer to the data of the traditional problem, refer to the syntactical forms of psychological-sentences or physical-sentences, we have only shown that *if* we solve the linguistic problem we thereby solve the traditional problem. Thus, Position 1, unlike Position 3, is perhaps worth trying to establish because it has nontrivial consequences for the traditional problem.

POSITION 4

Position 4, which states that the solution of the linguistic problem has no relationship to the solution of the traditional problem, remains to be considered. We have seen that if we have solved the linguistic problem we have not thereby either solved or dissolved the traditional problem. Furthermore, it seems that a solution of the linguistic problem provides no basis for an inductive justification for a solution of the traditional problem. Should we conclude, then, that Position 4 is correct? There are several reasons why we should not. The first is that there seems to be an *inferential* relationship between certain possible solutions of the two problems in spite of the above conclusions. If linguistic monism is true, that is, if each mind-sentence is analyzable into some physical-sentence, then it seems we should be able to infer that traditional dualism is false because if two sentences are synonymous then they refer to the same thing. As we shall discover in Chapter 6, however, the matter is considerably more complicated. Furthermore to establish which monistic theory is true—materialism, idealism, or neutral monism—requires in addition a premise about the reference of the relevant linguistic expressions. Nevertheless, because linguistic monism may have consequences for traditional dualism, we should accept Position 4 only if it is understood in the limited sense that neither a solution nor a dissolution of the traditional problem follows inductively or deductively from any solution of the linguistic problem. In each case an additional premise about the reference of linguistic expressions is needed.[18]

18. In this chapter I have not examined every attempt to move from premises about linguistic facts to conclusions about the traditional mind–body problem, but I know of none which fares any better than those I have examined. Another attempt is the one made by P. F. Strawson in *Individuals* (London, Methuen, 1959),

We have found one good reason for considering the linguistic problem when we are interested in the traditional problem. There are at least three others. First, it is important to consider the linguistic problem if only to point out certain problems for philosophers who overlook or try to argue away the deductive and inductive independence of the two problems. Second, it is important to consider the linguistic problem because seeing it as part of a linguistic approach to the traditional problem can help us discover how to handle certain arguments and objections which are based on linguistic confusions. We have seen two examples of this use of the linguistic approach to the traditional problem, one by Smart (see pp. 34–38) and one by Ryle (his "weak" thesis, see pp. 69–70). Third, considering the linguistic problem points out the importance of linguistic reference to a linguistic approach to the traditional problem. It is this last reason which I find most important because, as I shall try to establish in Part II, it is only by a linguistic approach to the traditional problem that we have any chance of solving it. Given this, linguistic reference takes on added importance. In any case, it seems appropriate to turn attention to linguistic reference at this point, not only because it is essential for those who take a linguistic approach to the traditional problem, but also because if we find out what certain expressions refer to we thereby solve the problem.

chap. 3, where he concludes from premises about the logic of language that "the word 'I' never refers to this, the pure subject" (p. 103), and that "there is no mind–body problem, as traditionally conceived" (p. 115). I have criticized Strawson's argument in "Strawson's 'Person'," *Theoria, 30* (1964), 145–56, where I show that Strawson, like the men examined here, requires additional premises about the relationship of language to ontology in order to establish his conclusions.

PART II

*Linguistic Reference and
External Questions*

4. Linguistic Reference

We have concluded that it is necessary to consider the reference of certain linguistic expressions in order to be able to choose among certain views about the relationship of the linguistic mind–body problem to the traditional problem. Furthermore it seems that such a discussion is necessary for anyone taking any sort of linguistic approach to the traditional problem. For both these reasons and because a linguistic approach to philosophy in general is both a widespread and, as I hope to show, necessary approach to that group of problems of which the mind–body problem is a prime example, it is important to consider linguistic reference in some detail. More specifically, there are two questions about linguistic reference that, because of the results of Part I, we are interested in:

1. What does the linguistic expression, 'p' refer to?
2. How can we find what 'p' refers to?

In order to justify an answer to 1 we must, of course be able to answer 2. We found out in Part I that, barring intuitions, it is not at all evident in certain cases what an answer to 1 is. This is because we did not know the answer to 2. For this reason I propose to concentrate on trying to find an answer to 2, an answer which, perhaps, will help us to answer 1 not only for expressions relevant to the mind–body problem but also for expressions involved in other philosophical problems.

However, before we begin to consider question 2 it seems that I should first go into some detail about how I am using the key term 'refer' in sentences such as "The linguistic expression '*p*' refers to something." This sentence as I shall use it is taken to be equivalent to "The linguistic expression '*p*' is a referring expression." It should be noted that I am here, as throughout the discussion, talking of linguistic expressions, i.e. entities that are expressions of some language. In the next chapter I shall distinguish among five different kinds of referring expressions and will show how I am using the phrase 'referring expression.' But in so doing I shall be using the expression 'refer to,' so that understanding it is vital for understanding what I am talking about when I talk of referring. But a problem crops up here. We want to keep any analysis of what is meant by 'refer to' clear of any implications for any particular theory of reference, because any such theory provides criteria for deciding which linguistic expressions are referring expressions and what any particular referring expression refers to. We want to define 'refer to' so as not to exclude any possible solutions to problems such as the mind–body problem; and because it seems that we can solve such a problem by finding out what the relevant expressions refer to, we want to leave open the question of which theory of reference is correct and not beg the question by definition.

If we look around for terms to help us define 'refer to,' we find either that they imply some theory of reference—'name' or 'stand for'—or they are no clearer than 'refer to'—'denote' or 'designate.' It may be that 'refer to' is a primitive, unanalyzable expression. We found earlier that Carnap could not analyze it away. If this is the case then the best I can do is to indicate that I am using it in a very broad sense. Any theory concerning the relation of any linguistic expression (or expressions) to what it is about is to be called a theory of reference. This well may be an extension of the term, but I think that any term I might use would also have to be extended. Some people would even claim that my talking of linguistic expressions referring to things is a distorted extension of 'refer' because it is people who refer to things by using words rather than words that refer to things.[1] But, even if this is an extension I do not see any harmful consequences. Futhermore, I think that I can show the relationship between the sense in which people refer to things and the sense in which words refer to things. I shall say that a linguistic expression 'p' refers to q if and only if it is correct to use the linguistic expression 'p' to refer to or talk about q. Thus, for example, we should say that 'Pegasus' refers to the winged horse captured by Bellerophon if and only if it is correct to use 'Pegasus' to refer to the winged horse captured by Bellerophon. And we should say that 'red' refers to certain physical objects if and only if it is correct to use 'red' to refer to those physical objects.

However, the above examples may seem to be of little help because the problem is merely transferred from what it means to say that expressions refer to things to what it means to say that people refer to things. Futhermore, I have used the word 'correct,' and until it is clear how this word is being used, it does not seem we have advanced much in trying to understand 'refer to.' For example, it seems that there is a sense in which it is correct—grammatically correct—to use 'green' to refer to red things, but we do not want it to follow from this that 'green' refers to red things. Thus we must be able to exclude that sense of 'correct.' However, it is not essential to do it at this point, for here we shall be primarily interested in examining certain attempts to answer question 2. We shall do it, however, in the next chapter where it will be not only appropriate but necessary. Let us therefore proceed to consider question 2: How can we find what 'p' refers to?

One way to begin is to divide linguistic expressions into different kinds and then investigate what kind of thing each kind of expression refers to, that is, to try to answer the question:

1. Leonard Linsky, "Reference and Referents," in Charles E. Caton, ed., *Philosophy and Ordinary Language* (Urbana, University of Illinois Press, 1963), pp. 74–89.

3. What kind of thing does each kind of linguistic expression refer to?

Once this is answered, we can go on to answer 1 by first seeing what kind of linguistic expression 'p' is. Then we can infer what kind of thing it refers to, and from there we can find out what in particular it refers to. Those who approach 1 in this way generally consider answering 3 to be one half of the larger task, trying to answer the more general question:

4. What do linguistic expressions mean?

Thus if someone asks what an expression means, he may be asking either or both of two questions. One way to distinguish between them is to construe one as asking what the expression refers to (or designates or denotes), and the other as asking what other expression has the same meaning as (or is synonymous with) the expression in question. I shall call a proposed answer to question 4 a theory of meaning. What I wish to do as the first step in our attempt to answer question 2, and thereby 1, by means of 3, is to consider the relevant features of a particular theory of meaning in order to see if it can provide an answer to 3—which it must do to be useful for our purposes. If it cannot, we shall see whether it might be supplemented somehow or indicate some other way to find an answer.

To begin, I propose to examine the relevant features of the theories of meaning of men such as Frege, Carnap, Quine, Lewis, and Church. Carnap states that the chief task of his book, *Meaning and Necessity,* "will be to find a suitable method for the semantical analysis of meaning, that is, to find concepts suitable as tools for this analysis." [2] Our present task, then, is to examine these tools and, so far as necessary, those employed in other theories of meaning in order to see how they might help us answer question 1: What does the linguistic expression, 'p' refer to?

2. Rudolf Carnap, *Meaning and Necessity,* p. 2.

It is generally agreed that there are two parts of a theory of meaning, one part for each of the two kinds of answers to question 4. Thus one part deals with sentences such as: " 'p' means (refers to) q," and the other with those such as: " 'p' means (is synonymous with) 'q'." We need, then, a different concept for the analysis of each part. There have been several different names given to such a pair of concepts: denotation and connotation, nominatum and sense, reference and meaning, extension and intension. As Carnap says:

> The theory of the relation between a language—either a natural language or a language system—and what language is about may be divided into two parts which I call the theory of extension and the theory of intension, respectively. The first deals with concepts like denoting, naming, extension, truth, and related ones. The theory of intension deals with concepts like intension, synonymy, analyticity, and related ones.[3]

While those interested in a theory of meaning agree that such a theory must have two parts, they disagree about which concept should be taken as the tool to analyze each part. Their disagreement concerns what is to be taken as the extension (denotation, etc.) and the intension (connotation, etc.) of a linguistic expression. However they generally agree that the criterion for deciding the disagreement is: Which proposed pair of concepts is the most efficient and productive tool for the job? It is on these grounds, for example, that Carnap argues for what he proposes as the extensions and intensions of linguistic expressions. When talking of the tools Frege proposes he says his view and Frege's are not incompatible because choosing between two pairs of concepts is analogous to choosing between two different methods of classifying animals:

> Since the two classifications and the assertions made on their bases are not incompatible, it would be theo-

3. Ibid., p. 233.

retically possible to use both simultaneously. However, if the simultaneous use of both seems unnecessarily complicated, there is a kind of practical incompatibility or competition. In this case the decisive question is this: which of the two [sets] of concepts is more fruitful for the purpose for which both are proposed, namely, a classification of animals? [4]

Given that this is a disagreement over which particular set of tools is best suited for the agreed-upon task, then for the purposes of our discussion we need examine, at least at first, only one of these theories. What we are interested in is discovering how helpful the approach common to all these theories is for finding an answer to question 1. If the general approach is found helpful, we can then look more closely at the individual differences. If not, we are interested only in what else is needed. At this point, then, I shall discuss Carnap's theory exclusively, using it as an example of the general approach.

In *Meaning and Necessity,* Carnap proposes

to use the term 'designator' for all those expressions to which a semantical analysis of meaning is applied, the class of designators thus being narrower and or wider according to the method of analysis used. [The word 'meaning' is here always understood in the sense of 'designative meaning', sometimes also called 'cognitive', 'theoretical', 'referential', or 'informative', as distinguished from other meaning components, e.g., emotive or motivating meaning. Thus here we have to do only with declarative sentences and their parts.][5]

Since the proposed method is concerned with declarative sentences and their parts, we must find—or propose—the extensions and intensions of such sentences and their parts. As Carnap says, his method must take as designators at

4. Ibid., p. 128.
5. Ibid., p. 6.

least declarative sentences, predicators (predicate expressions), functors (expressions for functions), and individual expressions (expressions which refer to individuals).[6] Carnap proposes extensions and intensions for all of these kinds of designators and defends his proposal by showing how it avoids many problems which complicate other theories. For our purposes, however, we need only give an indication of his method for picking a pair of concepts for each kind of designator.

He begins his discussion by defining two sentences: (1) Two designators have the same extension $=_{df.}$ they are equivalent. (2) Two designators have the same intension $=_{df.}$ they are L-equivalent. Without going further into the mechanics of Carnap's discussion we can say that by 'x is equivalent to y' he means '$x \equiv y$ is true,' and by 'x is L-equivalent to y' he means '$x \equiv y$ is L-true (roughly, logically true).'[7] He then proposes to find the extension and intension of each kind of designator by means of these two definitions of 'same extension' and 'same intension.' The extension of any designator must be something such that if two designators were equivalent they would have the same extension. A similar criterion holds for intensions. Using these criteria, he proposes the following pairs of concepts:[8]

DESIGNATORS	EXTENSIONS	INTENSIONS
Predicators	**Corresponding class**	**Corresponding property**
Sentences	**Truth-value**	**Proposition**
Individual expressions	**Individual**	**Individual concept**

Without going further into each concept we can say that for Carnap these extensions and intensions are all to be

6. Ibid.
7. Ibid.; see pp. 14, 23.
8. Ibid.; see p. 19.

taken as nonmental, nonlinguistic, objective entities, which he says "may or may not be exemplified in nature." [9] They are, I take it, what language is related to, what it is about— at least what that part of language which comprises declarative sentences and their parts is about. Thus Carnap, using these entities for what certain kinds of linguistic expressions are related to, proposes to be able to give the meaning analysis of the expressions. That is, he proposes to use these entities which he takes as the extensions and intensions of different kinds of linguistic expressions to answer question 4—What do linguistic expressions mean?—and thereby question 3—What kind of thing does each linguistic expression refer to?

Keeping in mind this brief sketch of Carnap's purpose and the kinds of tools with which he proposes to achieve it, we can now turn to two criticisms of both Carnap and the others mentioned above. The first objection is based on the fact that, since in stating the extension or intension of any particular designator we must use a metalanguage, all semantical theories of meaning must be formulated in a metalanguage. For example, Carnap says that the extension of the sentence 'Hs' (in language S_1) is the truth-value that Scott is human.[10] According to this objection, methods of meaning analysis like that of Carnap can give us analyses only if we already know the meanings of a different language, the one we choose for a metalanguage. But it seems that we must either analyze the metalanguage also in order to do what we want with the object-language, a process which leads to an infinite regress; or we need not make such an analysis—in which case there seems to be no reason for analyzing the object-language in the first place. The reason cannot be to get clear about the meanings, since we are only as clear about these as we are clear about those of the metalanguage. But if we are clear about those of the metalanguage without analysis, why not also in the object-lan-

9. Ibid.; see pp. 27–28.
10. Ibid.; see p. 27.

guage? Or, if we are in no case clear without analysis, then we are led into an infinite regress and to the conclusion that we never can be clear about the meaning of linguistic expressions. I will not pursue this objection and proposed answers to it here, for a similar and more forceful one will arise when we consider attempts to avoid the second kind of criticism to Wittgenstein's theory of meaning. I shall examine such objections more fully at that time.

The second point is not so much an objection to the method as a claim that the method and the others like it, even if unobjectionable, can by themselves do neither the job for which we wish to use them, to answer question 1—What does 'p' refer to?—nor the job for which they are designed, to analyze and describe the meanings of linguistic expressions. Carnap's theory again gives us an example. His concepts are proposed as tools for analyzing only a certain segment of the linguistic expressions of a given language. Carnap claims to be interested only in "designators," by which he means expressions having "cognitive" or "referential" meaning.[11] Because of this, his method has only to do "with declarative sentences and their parts."[12] There is, however, a problem. The class of expressions usually called "declarative sentences" is a class determined in one of two ways: either syntactically, by means of formation rules for a constructed language or grammatical rules for a natural language, or semantically, by deciding which of such syntactical expressions have truth-values. But a question arises in both cases about which of the sentences of this syntactical form have truth-values. On the first interpretation, expressions of a certain form are called "declarative sentences," regardless of their interpretation or meaning. The question would then arise whether Carnap wants to apply his method to all expressions of this syntactical form or not. His answer, it seems, would be that he wishes to apply it only to those which have truth-values, because he

11. Ibid.; see p. 6.
12. Ibid.; p. 6.

takes the extension of the class of sentences in which he is interested to be their truth-values. We can now rephrase the question and ask which declarative sentences have truth-values. Unless one wished to claim that all sentences of this specific form have truth-values—a position most philosophers, including Carnap, wish to reject and for which there seems to be no good reason—then we face the problem of how to delimit this class. A similar problem arises for the second interpretation. On this interpretation we must ask which sentences of this syntactical form are declarative sentences. Since the problem arises on both interpretations, let us use the first. Then, assuming that this is a problem for Carnap and the others, our question becomes, "Which declarative sentences have truth-values?"

One answer that comes immediately to mind is the claim that only those sentences which fit the verifiability criterion of meaning have truth-values. But (as has often been brought out quite clearly) there seem to be insuperable difficulties connected with this criterion. First, no formulation of the criterion seems to work. Any given formulation is either too broad—it allows *all* declarative sentences to have truth-values—or too narrow—it does not allow enough declarative sentences to have truth-values. Second, even if some formulation avoided this problem, there does not seem to be any reason for asserting that there is an isomorphism between those sentences which have truth-values and those which are verifiable—roughly, those for which empirical evidence somehow relevant to establishing their truth-values can be found. In other words, there is a question about what reason there could possibly be for claiming that this is indeed the criterion to use in deciding which declarative sentences have truth-values. The reason could not be that the criterion is analytic, for it is not. Nor could it be an empirical generalization about the way people use the words 'true' and 'false,' for if it were it would seem more likely to be false than true. It must then be either a metaphysical statement or a rule of language, a rule which is not itself verifiable. Indeed, if it is anything at all it would seem to be a rule of language, for it implies something about the relation between language and reality, namely, that all sentences having truth-values are in some way related to certain nonlinguistic elements of reality which we can experience.

But the only reason for accepting this claim would seem to be that this is indeed the way language is related to reality. Thus if we propose the verifiability criterion of meaning as the solution to the problem we have raised for Carnap and the rest, then it seems we are driven to a consideration of the relation between language (actually, the particular language in question) and reality. Therefore, there seems to be no reason to consider the verifiability criterion, because to justify it we must do exactly what we must do when we do not use it. In both cases we appear to be driven to a consideration of the relationship between language and reality if we are to find any solution at all, because picking any criterion for deciding which declarative sentences have truth-values seems to involve some reference to the relationship. Nonanalytic sentences which are true or false are so because of their relations to some nonlinguistic elements of reality. None of these is true or false just because of certain merely linguistic facts, because their truth-value depends upon what there is besides language. But it depends on more than this. For if I were to know everything about a language except its relation to reality and everything about reality independent of language, I still could not decide which sentences had truth-values unless I also knew in what way that language was related to reality.

Another way of putting my point is briefly this: Carnap and the others wish to answer questions like, "What is the extension of this designator 'p'?" But this is a complex question in that it presupposes an affirmative answer to a previous one: "Is the linguistic expression, 'p,' a designator?" Since an affirmative answer to this question is presupposed, it is surely reasonable to ask for a justification of this implied answer. It is certainly not enough to say, as we have seen, that 'p' has a certain syntactical form or certain linguistic relationships or meets some formulation of the verifiability criterion of meaning. Unless it is obvious which sentences are designators—and this does not seem to be the case— the kind of reason that seems to be needed would, when put in a deductive argument form, go somewhat as follows:

1. Sentences (in language L) have referential meaning, are designators, if and only if they are in relation R to reality.
2. Sentences (in L) are in relation R to reality if and only if they have the additional characteristics a, b, c, . . . , e.g. verifiability.
3. 'p' has (does not have) characteristics a, b, c, . . .
Therefore
4. 'p' is (is not) in relation R to reality.
Therefore
5. 'p' is (is not) a designator.

We might be able to establish one of the premises of this argument, 3, by investigating the logical features of the expression, 'p,' but the other two are of a different kind. Carnap and others like him have not considered what might be relevant to these two premises. Their proposed methods do not concern these premises because the tools of their methods are applicable only after an expression has been found to be a designator. Thus their tools cannot alone do the job for which they were designed, since these premises must be established in order to know where to apply those tools. Consequently we must first investigate the problem of establishing such premises if we are to continue our discussion of the method of meaning analysis proposed by Carnap, for if there is no basis for these premises, then there is a genuine doubt whether there is any basis for such methods. The easiest way to proceed is to begin by examining what has been said that is relevant to these two premises. For this purpose I believe we can find no better source than the views of Wittgenstein in the *Tractatus,* because it is just these two premises (among other things) that Wittgenstein discusses there. On his view, the relation R is one of picturing, and the characteristics $a, b, c, \ldots$ are just those which a picture would have. Let us then look at Wittgenstein's attempt to talk about the relationship between language and reality and consider the way he interprets the concepts of a picture and of picturing. Then we shall see how he applies these concepts to sentences.

To begin I shall list for comment some of the passages of the *Tractatus* most relevant to Wittgenstein's interpretation of pictures:

2.12 The picture is a model of reality.

2.13 To the objects correspond in the picture the elements of the picture.

2.14 The picture consists in the fact that its elements are combined with one another in a definite way.

2.15 This connexion of the elements of the picture is called its structure, and the possibility of this structure is called the form of representation of the picture.

2.151 The form of representation is the possibility that the things are combined with one another as are the elements of the picture.

2.1511 Thus the picture is linked with reality; it reaches up to it.

2.16 In order to be a picture a fact must have something in common with what it pictures.

2.17 What the picture must have in common with reality in order to be able to represent it after its manner—rightly or falsely—is its form of representation.[13]

13. Ludwig Wittgenstein, *Tractatus Logico-Philosophicus,* Eng. trans. C. K. Ogden (London, Routledge and Kegan Paul, 1958).

The first thing to notice is that Wittgenstein is talking only about representational pictures or pictures which are attempted likenesses of things. Thus for Wittgenstein a picture represents something, and to represent something is not only to stand for something as a proxy but also to show or present what it stands for. Not all things which stand for other things show what they stand for, as in the case of some nonrepresentational cubist paintings. Likewise, not all things which show certain other things stand as proxies for the things they show, e.g. directional arrows. In picturing, however, one thing not only stands for another but also shows the viewer what it stands for. This is perhaps one reason why Wittgenstein took picturing as the genus of which linguistic representation is a species.

The question immediately arises: What enables a picture both to stand for something and to show what it stands for? To answer this we must interpret the passages from the *Tractatus*. First, a picture is something made up of certain elements which are combined in a definite way (2.14) and stand in the picture for the objects which make up what is represented (see 2.131). The way in which those elements are combined is the structure of the picture (2.15). But to be a picture and thus to picture something, a thing must be more than just elements in a structure. It must also be linked with reality (2.1511) and with what it pictures (2.16), because without these links a thing could not represent anything. Thus we must examine these links in order to answer our question.

A picture is linked with what it pictures in that it has something in common with what it pictures (2.16). This common element is structure. The structure of the picture is identical with the structure of what is pictured, that is, the elements of the picture are combined in the same way as are the elements of what is pictured. This is what enables a picture to show—and thus *represent*—what it stands for. We can begin to understand this by seeing that we need not go beyond or outside a picture in order to understand it. Because of this there must be something in the picture essential to our understanding it, that is, knowing what it represents. This essential factor cannot be the particular elements of the picture, because there is no set of elements essential to representing something. For example, it is not essential that a picture representing something be in color. It can, then, only be the structure of the picture, the combination of its elements that is somehow essential to our understanding the picture. But then the structure of the picture must be essentially related in some way to what is pictured. How? By identity. We see the structure of the picture which, by being identical with the structure of what is pictured, shows us what is pictured. This point, as we shall see, is important for explaining how we can understand a sentence we have never encountered before without having it explained to us.

We must be clear about what it is for a picture to have the same structure as what it pictures, and how this identity of structure enables a picture to show what it pictures. For Wittgenstein the structure of a picture stands to the structure of what it pictures as the structure of a musical score stands to the structure of its music. That is, given the musical score, we could read the music out of the score by means of the law of projection, "connecting" the score and the music (see 4.011, 4.014, and 4.0141). We can say, then, that the structure of a picture (a musical score) is identical with the structure of what is pictured (the music) if and only if the structure of what is pictured (the music) is derivable from the structure of the picture (the score) by means of the law of projection which applies to pictures (musical scores). Thus if we know the law of projection for representational pictures, then a picture shows us what is pictured just as a score shows the music to someone who knows how to read it.

It is also necessary that a picture be linked with reality.

This link is what Wittgenstein calls the logical form of representation of the picture (2.17). Although it is not easy to understand what this form is, we can begin by saying that the form of representation is the possibility that the structure of things is the same as that of the picture (2.151 construing "the way things are combined" as "the structure of things"—see 2.15). We can go on to say that what a picture has in common with reality is the possibility that the structure of something other than the picture is the same as the structure of the picture. In other words, something P is a picture only if it is logically possible that its structure is identical with the structure of some other part of reality.

But why must a picture have *this* link with reality? Why is a link with what it represents not link enough? The answer is, I think, as follows. If something P is a picture, then it represents either "rightly or falsely" (2.17), it either represents some part of reality or it does not represent any part of reality. Because all pictures have their structure identical with the structure of what they represent, they show what they represent. Consequently, those pictures that represent rightly, that is, truly, show some part of reality. But whether a picture represents truly or falsely is a factual problem, and therefore it cannot be settled completely by the resources of logic alone. Consequently it is not logically impossible that any picture represents truly. That is, if P is a picture, then it must be logically possible that P represents truly. And it is logically possible that P represents truly only if it is logically possible that the structure of P is identical with the structure of some part of reality. Consequently this link with reality is a necessary condition for anything being a picture. This may seem to be a trivial link, but it is most important for our purposes because although it may seem that we have represented it, we shall find that if something else Wittgenstein says is correct we cannot represent it.

With this sketch of a picture in mind let us now turn to Wittgenstein's discussion of sentences to see in what sense he takes a sentence to be a picture:

3.21 To the configuration of the simple signs in the propositional sign corresponds the configuration of the objects in the state of affairs.

3.34 A proposition possesses essential and accidental features. Accidental are the features which are due to a particular way of producing the propositional sign. Essential are those which alone enable the proposition to express its sense.

4.001 The totality of propositions is the language.

4.01 The proposition is a picture of reality.

4.021 The proposition is a picture of reality, for I know the state of affairs presented by it, if I understand the proposition. And I understand the proposition, without its sense having been explained to me.

4.022 The proposition *shows* its sense. The proposition *shows* how things stand, *if* it is true. And it *says,* that they do so stand.

4.03 The proposition communicates to us a state of affairs, therefore it must be *essentially* connected with the state of affairs. And the connection is, in fact, that it is its logical picture. The proposition only asserts something, in so far as it is a picture.

4.04 In the proposition there must be exactly as many things distinguishable as there are in the state of affairs, which it represents.

4.12 Propositions can represent the whole reality, but they cannot represent what they must have in common with reality in order to be able to represent it—the logical form.

Wittgenstein (4.01) says explicitly that propositions are pictures of reality. Propositions or sentences,[14] like pictures, consist of simple elements in a configuration or structure (3.21) and have something in common with reality, their

14. Although the English translation I have used translates *Satz* as 'proposition,' I shall use 'sentence' instead. One reason for this is 4.001.

logical form of representation (4.12). Furthermore, sentences are essentially connected to what they represent (4.03); the structures are identical. This essential connection is what enables a sentence to show its sense or what it pictures or represents (3.34, 4.022). It is because of this that we are able to understand a sentence without needing to have what it represents explained to us first (4.021). I believe that this common property of sentences and pictures is one of the main reasons why Wittgenstein calls sentences pictures. In the case of representational pictures he thinks that we can get some idea of the reason why we understand them without going "outside" them. The reason is that they have something in common with what they picture, their structure. Sentences, like pictures, not only stand for things but also show what they stand for and do so because, like pictures, they share a common structure with what they stand for. That is, the structure of what a sentence represents is derivable from the structure of the sentence by means of its law of projection. Once we have learned a language we thereby know its laws of projection, and consequently each sentence of the language shows us what it stands for in the way that a musical score shows music to a knowing musician.

Sentences are like pictures not only in this respect. Just as there are good and bad representational pictures so, for the same reason, we can speak of good and bad sentences. In fact, just as we can imagine an ideal or "best" picture of, say, a particular man, so can we imagine an ideal or best sentence for each state of affairs, and therefore an ideal or best language, because the totality of sentences is the language (4.001). Using what Wittgenstein says about pictures as our guide, we can say what the properties of an ideal language would be like. An ideal representational picture of a man is one such that when we look at it, the very man seems to be presented to us. In the case of a bad one we are not sure which man is represented by the picture. Indeed, we may not be sure what kind of thing is supposed to be represented. So it is with language. In ordinary language it may be unclear which state of affairs a sentence represents because one of its terms is ambiguous and signifies or represents in several different ways (see 3.323). It may also be unclear what is supposed to be represented because the sentence itself is vague (4.002). An ideal language, like an ideal picture, would avoid features such as these. And this is important, believes Wittgenstein, because from such features of language arise fundamental philosophical confusions.

An ideal language, then, is clear and precise, not vague and ambiguous. It would avoid ambiguity by avoiding ambiguous terms; how would it avoid vagueness? We can construct an answer from Wittgenstein's claim that in a sentence "there must be exactly as many things distinguishable as there are in the state of affairs which it represents" (4.04). This is usually interpreted as meaning that there must be an isomorphism between a sentence and what it represents. However, this does not seem to be true of nonideal languages, and we do not want to conclude that the expressions of such languages are not sentences, that is, not expressions which represent reality. This conclusion can be avoided because I think it is reasonable to assume that Wittgenstein is only talking about those features of a sentence which are what he calls essential. On this interpretation we can find a reason why many sentences are vague and thus not ideal. It is because it *seems* that this isomorphism does not hold. There are many nonessential (accidental) features of such sentences, and when we use them we are not sure which features are essential (which alone allow the sentence to express its sense—3.34) and which are accidental (which are due to the peculiar way of producing sentences in that language—3.34). We can conclude, then, that for a language to be ideal all the features of its sentences must be essential, so that what is shown or represented by the sentences is clearly and distinctly shown and not disguised (see 4.002).

I have tried to show that Wittgenstein considers the relation R between language and reality to be the relation of picturing. I have also tried to explain in what picturing consists and the characteristics an expression must have to picture something: its structure must be identical with the structure of what it pictures, and it must be possible that its structure is identical with the structure of some other part of reality. These are the data needed to fill in the first two premises of the argument that Carnap and others need to supplement their method of meaning analysis. We might now state the argument somewhat as follows:

    1'. A sentence (in language L) has referential meaning, is a designator, if and only if it can picture reality.

    2'. A sentence (in L) can picture reality if and only if it has its structure identical with the structure of what it pictures and possibly identical with some part of reality other than itself.

    3'. Expression P has (does not have) its structure identical with the structure of something and possibly identical with some part of reality other than itself.

Therefore

    4'. P can (cannot) picture reality.

Therefore

    5'. P is (is not) a designator.

If, then, Wittgenstein's picture theory is correct, it would be just what is needed to supplement Carnap's theory of meaning. There are, however, objections to examine before we can justify using this theory—or indeed any theory of this kind—to supplement Carnap's theory.

These objections can be divided into two kinds: the ones aimed specifically at the picture theory of meaning, and the ones rejecting the whole enterprise of trying to find the relation between language and reality. I shall mention the first kind only briefly but will spend more time on the second which, if sound, will rule out not only Wittgenstein's theory but all like it and thus eliminate any basis for Carnap's kind of approach to question 1.

Those objections aimed specifically at the picture theory can themselves be divided into two kinds. The first kind grants that sentences may be pictures but holds that Wittgenstein was mistaken about pictures. The second denies that sentences are pictures or even enough like them to use pictures as a model for sentences. Objections of the first kind were made by Wittgenstein, himself, in his later book *Philosophical Investigations* and by Urmson in *Philosophical Analysis*. Both reject the view that pictures, and therefore sentences, show their sense or what they represent. Wittgenstein attacks this in the *Investigations* by saying that even if something is a picture we do not know what it is a picture *of* unless we know how to apply the picture, and it can be applied in many ways.[15] Urmson says that on Wittgenstein's interpretation of a picture, any picture can picture any state of affairs. For Wittgenstein says, as we have seen, that two things have the same structure if by means of the law of projection or translation we can move from one to the other. But although there must be some rule of projection, it is possible for a picture to be combined with innumerable rules so that it is not evident which one of all the possible rules is *the* rule. This is not shown us; we must figure it out. If this is true, then as Urmson says:

> If a law of projection is all that we require for similarity of structure, then the fact that we can find a law of projection connecting any drawing with any object reduces the significance of the demand for identity of structure almost to vanishing point.[16]

15. Ludwig Wittgenstein, *Philosophical Investigations,* Eng. trans. G. E. M. Anscombe (New York, Macmillan, 1953), paras. 139–41.
16. J. O. Urmson, *Philosophical Analysis,* p. 90.

Thus, given a picture, we can pick a rule of projection so that the picture is a picture of whatever we choose. What is essential to a picture, and therefore to a sentence, is that it have some rule of projection, but not any rule in particular. Consequently, according to this objection, no picture shows what it stands for because what a picture stands for depends on which rule of projection it has, and this is not evident. There is, then, no ideal picture or language in the sense of a picture or language which, because all its features are essential, shows clearly and precisely what it stands for. However, this does not rule out the possibility of an ideal language in another sense. Such an ideal language would be the one with the simplest, most straightforward, and least misleading rules of projection. But because no sentence shows what it stands for, this language would not be ideal in the first sense.

The second kind of objection aimed specifically at the picture theory claims that sentences are neither pictures nor even significantly like them. Such an objection has been raised by Elizabeth Daitz in her "The Picture Theory of Meaning." Miss Daitz tries to bring out all the ways in which sentences differ from pictures, the implication being that the differences are so many and so great that it is more misleading than helpful to take pictures even as a model for sentences. For example, she says that representational pictures are icons and as such show something, but sentences state something: an iconic picture of a girl standing shows a girl standing, while a sentence about a girl standing states that the girl is standing.[17] But showing and stating are quite different because "showing consists in representing and arranging, stating in referring and describing." [18] These and other differences are, she thinks, sufficient for refuting the picture theory of meaning.

17. Elizabeth Daitz, "The Picture Theory of Meaning," in Anthony Flew, ed., *Essays in Conceptual Analysis* (London, Macmillan, 1956), p. 60.
18. Ibid.

I think that neither of these objections is sufficient to refute the picture theory. Let me briefly indicate my reasons. First, the examples of the disanalogies offered by Miss Daitz do not show that sentences are not pictures. They merely show that some pictures are not sentences—which never was in doubt. Wittgenstein's point is not that all representational pictures are sentences which state, but that all sentences which state also represent. Miss Daitz would have to admit that sentences of some languages are literally representational pictures, so that at least some sentences represent. She must be denying, then, that *all* sentences which state also represent. She implies that a sentence about a girl standing does not show a girl standing so it does not represent a girl standing. But this point has force only if 'show' is taken to mean 'present iconicly' rather than merely 'present,' and surely Wittgenstein meant the latter. Furthermore, most sentences about a girl standing present a state of affairs involving the girl rather than the girl, although a skillful writer can often present, virtually iconicly, a girl standing. I think that similar doubts can be raised concerning her other disanalogies.

The objection which stems from Urmson and the later Wittgenstein also seems to lack force. It must be granted that for any sentence there are innumerable rules of projection possible, and that everyone must learn how to apply a language because which rules are correct is not evident to someone who does not understand the language. But nothing essential to the *Tractatus* is refuted by this. There the claim is that a sentence is like a musical score: both show what they stand for to one who *understands* the language, whether or not he has ever seen this sentence or this score before. In learning the language we implicitly learn its rules of projection, and this is what enables a new sentence to show us what it stands for.

I do not know of any compelling objections aimed specifically at the picture theory of meaning. However, there have been serious objections leveled at the whole enterprise of trying to find the relationship between language and reality. Once again Wittgenstein provides the source of one of these objections. This one is stated in the *Tractatus* and gives that book its paradoxical character. He expresses his objection as follows:

> 4.12 Propositions can represent the whole of reality, but they cannot represent what they must have in common with reality in order to be able to represent it—the logical form. To be able to represent the logical form, we should have to be able to put ourselves with the propositions outside logic, that is, outside the world.

Although Wittgenstein did not make explicit the line of reasoning he used to arrive at this conclusion, one common interpretation is as follows.[19] Language pictures reality. Thus the relation between language and reality is one of picturing, and what language has in common with reality is what a picture has in common with reality, the logical form of representation. In order to represent the logical form we must be able to represent structure. But we cannot make a picture nor, therefore, a sentence which will represent or picture structure. The structure of a picture or sentence is the way in which its elements are combined, their combination. But I can not "draw" merely *this* combination because the picture I "draw" must have elements in combination. Therefore, although the elements in my picture may be in the same combination as that of the picture in question, I will not have "drawn" merely the combination of that picture, but a picture with the same combination of elements.

The reply usually given to the above objection is formulated by Russell in his introduction to the *Tractatus*. He, as others since, grants that within any given language nothing can be said about the structure of that language, but claims

19. See Urmson, *Philosophical Analysis*, p. 91, and Bertrand Russell in his introduction to the *Tractatus*, p. 21.

"that there may be another language dealing with the structure of the first language, and having itself a new structure, and that to this hierarchy of languages there may be no limit." [20]

Although it is true that no language can represent its own structure and thus its relation to reality, it is not required that we be able to represent what a language has in common with reality in the language itself. We just have to be able to deal with it somehow in some language, and this, according to Russell's reply, we can do. Consequently, Wittgenstein's objection is unsound. The reply seems at first glance well taken because there is reason to believe, first, that any language which expresses the whole of its semantics (which is semantically closed), is a language in which paradoxes arise;[21] and, second, that we can express the semantics of a language and avoid the paradoxes by using a different language. In other words, it seems that the way to avoid semantical paradoxes is to use two languages, one the object-language (the language whose semantics is being discussed) and the other the metalanguage (the language used to talk about the semantics of the object-language). According to the reply under discussion, Wittgenstein, although correct in maintaining that a certain semantical problem could not be expressed in the language in question, failed to realize that by employing a metalanguage we can discuss all semantical problems of the object-language without falling into contradiction or paradoxes. More specifically this reply is that we can represent the relation between a language and reality by means of a metalanguage. Wittgenstein's objection appeared sound only because he did not employ a metalanguage in formulating it.

20. Russell, *Tractatus* p. 23. This position seems to be taken also by Paul Feyerabend in "Wittgenstein's *Philosophical Investigations,*" *The Philosophical Review, 64* (1955), 482–83.

21. See Alfred Tarski, "The Semantic Conception of Truth," in Feigl and Sellars, eds., *Readings in Philosophical Analysis,* pp. 52–84 for a more detailed discussion of this.

Let us examine whether this reply avoids objections similar to the one Wittgenstein raised concerning his own picture theory of meaning. We shall consider the two parts of this reply separately: (1) We cannot represent the relation between a language and a reality using the language itself; (2) We can represent it using a metalanguage.

To see the trouble we would get into if we tried to talk about the relationship between a sentence and reality in the object-language itself, let us first examine a different kind of relationship between two things. Take the sentence, 'John loves Mary.' Here we are talking about two people by using words which refer to them. More generally, if we wish to use a sentence to talk about something, we have to use in the sentence not the thing talked about but a name or description of it; we cannot use the two people as part of the sentence but must use words which refer to them. Similarly, if we want to talk about a sentence as we do in talking of its relationship to reality, we must use a name for it rather than the sentence itself. However, in a language made semantically adequate by utilizing a hierarchy of languages there are no names of, nor anything which refers to, the linguistic expressions of the language. These occur only in the metalanguages of that language. Thus any attempt to express in some language what relationship a sentence of that language has to reality is bound to fail, just as Wittgenstein claimed in his objection.

The first part of this reply to Wittgenstein's objection seems reasonable. Let us turn to the second part. Russell says that the force of Wittgenstein's objection is based on the impossibility of representing the structure of a given language in that very language. But, says Russell, we need not worry about this because we can deal with the structure of any given language by using a metalanguage to talk about that structure. This certainly seems true. We can deal with the structure of a given language by using a metalanguage which employs a syntactical or formal calculus. In such a calculus we use uninterpreted symbols and operators to lay out the structure of the language in question. It is true that we are using elements—the symbols—but because they are not interpreted, they represent at most a structure when they are connected in a certain way. Thus they are not elements of a language which represents something with that structure. That is, to get a picture or representation of reality, and thus a language about reality, we must give some interpretation to the elements. So long as all languages are thought to be like representational pictures, Wittgenstein's objection is good. But if we consider that some can be more like an abstract picture we can see better how one language could deal merely with the structure of another.

Perhaps, then, by using a metalanguage we can avoid Wittgenstein's objection, if we interpret his objection to be that we can in no way deal with the structure of language by means of language. However, as I have interpreted Wittgenstein, this is not his point. His claim is that no sentence can represent what another sentence must have in common with reality in order to be able to represent reality, and this common element is not structure, as Russell and others[22] seem to think, but the possibility that the structure of the sentence is identical with the structure of reality. Thus even if we can deal with the structure of a language, it may still be the case that we cannot deal with the link between language and reality.

That the above interpretation rather than Russell's is correct is bolstered by the fact that whereas Wittgenstein can

22. See Russell, *Tractatus,* p. 21. John Passmore, *A Hundred Years of Philosophy* (London, Duckworth, 1957), pp. 360–61. Urmson, *Philosophical Analysis,* p. 90. This confusion between logical form and structure may result from a failure to distinguish between 'state of affairs' (*Sachlage,* see 2.11) and 'fact' (*Tatsache,* see 1.11). Eric Stenius, *Wittgenstein's Tractatus* (Ithaca, Cornell University Press, 1960), pp. 99–102, also identifies logical form and structure, but he does it in a way that avoids Russell's problem. Max Black, *A Companion to Wittgenstein's 'Tractatus'* (Ithaca, Cornell University Press, 1964), pp. 66, 81, points out the difference between logical form and structure.

give a plausible account of false sentences with it, he cannot as Russell interprets him. If Russell is correct then a sentence, i.e. a picture, whether true or false has its structure in common with reality. However it also has its structure in common with what it pictures. Furthermore, a picture shows what it pictures by virtue of having its structure in common with what it pictures. Consequently sentences or pictures, whether true or false, would on Russell's interpretation of Wittgenstein show some part of reality—something which exists—by virtue of having its structure in common with the structure of that part of reality. Thus all pictures on Russell's interpretation would picture something existing. This would lead us to say either that, contrary to appearances, there are no false sentences, or that, although what a false sentence represents does not exist in any usual sense, it does exist (subsist) in some Meinongian sense. Both of these alternatives seem to lead to unhappy consequences, consequences which can be avoided if we use the interpretation I have proposed.

Using the above interpretation let us see if it is possible to represent the link that sentences have with reality. How might this be done? As we have previously seen, Wittgenstein claims that for something to be a sentence and thereby to picture something, its structure must be identical with the structure of what it represents; the structure of what is represented is derivable from the structure of the sentence by use of the applicable law of projection. Because of this a sentence is able to show what it stands for. But it makes no sense to talk of the structure of a structure, let alone the structure of the identity of two structures, or the structure of the possibility of the identity of two structures. Consequently, nothing which might be said to stand for these three things can show what it stands for. Thus no sentence can be used to represent them. Not only can no sentence represent the links a language has to reality and to what it pictures, it cannot, in spite of what Russell claims, even represent the structure of a language. This is as we might have expected because, according to Wittgenstein, it is by virtue of the nonrepresentational showing of the structure of something that what has that structure is representationally shown. "That which expresses *itself* in language, *we* cannot express by language" (4.121). "What *can* be [nonrepresentationally] shown *cannot* be said" (4.1212).

Thus this reply to Wittgenstein's objection that we cannot represent what a sentence has in common with reality if it is to be able to represent does not seem justified. We have further concluded that we cannot represent the structure of a sentence nor, consequently, the structure of a language. This latter conclusion, however, may seem to conflict with the previously discussed claim that it is possible to deal with the structure of a language by using a formal calculus, but I think that it does not. Although a formal calculus can be used to deal in some way with the structure of a language, it does not show what it deals with in the way that a sentence shows what it represents. Given a calculus, to find out whether or not it stands for the structure of a particular language, we must interpret the symbols of the calculus in such a way that we thereby construct the language. But if we must discover whether or not the calculus applies to the language, it does not show what it stands for and therefore does not represent what it stands for. This can be emphasized by stressing that while languages are like representational pictures, formal calculi are more like abstract pictures. Abstract pictures if they can be said to stand for anything at all do not show us what they stand for; we must interpret them.

We cannot, then, represent the structure of a language. However, it seems that there are ways we can deal with it linguistically, and since we can deal with the structure of a language by means of a calculus, the fact that we cannot represent it seems to be of little consequence. Perhaps, in some like manner, we can deal with the links a sentence has with what it represents and with reality, even though the links cannot be represented. If this can be done, then

it matters very little whether or not Wittgenstein's claim
about what cannot be represented is correct. Thus we must
consider whether or not we can in some nonrepresentational way deal linguistically with these two links.

A necessary condition of dealing with them linguistically
is the ability to deal linguistically with the two structures
that are so linked: the structure of language and the structure of reality. Thus if we cannot do this, then when we
claim to be dealing linguistically with the identity of the
structures of language and reality, or of the possibility of
such an identity, we are talking nonsense. We have seen
that we cannot represent either structure, but we can deal
linguistically with the structure of language. We use a formal
calculus to stand for the structure, and because we can
deal with such a structure only if we can establish that the
calculus actually stands for it, we must also be able to construct the language from the calculus by substituting the
elements of the language for the uninterpreted symbols of
the calculus. Similarly, if we are able to deal linguistically
with the structure of reality, the only possible way, it seems,
would be to use such a calculus. Thus we must be able to
substitute for the uninterpreted symbols what in reality
corresponds to the elements of a language; we would have
to substitute the objects of reality in the calculus. But this
cannot be done because only elements of a language are
appropriate. Thus in order to deal linguistically with the
structure of reality we would have to do it without the aid
of a calculus. We would put ourselves and the sentence
standing for the structure outside any calculus, that is, outside logic (see 4.12). This, obviously, cannot be done.

We can, therefore, in no way deal linguistically with
whatever it is we have been calling "the structure of reality,"
and consequently we can in no way deal linguistically with
what we have been calling "the link a sentence must have
in common with reality in order to be able to represent it."
As a result, any time we attempt to use language to do what
cannot be done, we fail to talk sensibly—whether we use a

metalanguage or not. It seems, then, that using a metalanguage will not avoid Wittgenstein's objections which, regardless of how we interpret Wittgenstein's claims about
what language and reality have in common, is surely that
in order to express in language a fully adequate theory of
meaning we must but cannot get outside or beyond language. In other words, because we cannot express in language what language has in common with reality, and,
therefore, cannot express in language those features which
a language and only a language in relation R to reality has,
we cannot express what is needed to justify premise 2
[Sentences (in L) are in relation R to reality if and only if
they have the additional characteristics $a, b, c, \ldots$ e.g.
verifiability] of the argument needed to supplement the
kind of theory Carnap proposes. It follows from this that
we cannot establish an answer to question 3—What kind
of thing does each linguistic expression refer to?—and,
therefore, cannot answer question 1—What does the linguistic expression 'p' refer to?—using the approach of Carnap and the others.

Should we accept the conclusion that we cannot justify
premise 2 because we cannot express it in language? Perhaps we should not, because the conclusion is based on two
assumed, and thus unjustified, premises. The first assumption is that Wittgenstein's argument against his own picture
theory of meaning applies mutatis mutandis to any theory
that tries to express in language those features a linguistic
expression must have in common with reality if and only
if it is to be in relation R to reality. Perhaps there is another
theory of this kind that not only can be expressed, but also
can be justifiably used to supplement Carnap's theory. It is
true that this has been assumed, but this is because the
only way that I know to justify the general claim that no
theory of meaning which attempts to incorporate such features can be adequately expressed is by induction from an
examination of particular theories. But I know of no theory
other than Wittgenstein's, and can conceive of none that

would differ sufficiently from Wittgenstein's to avoid the above objections. Thus I think that the assumption is justified.

The second assumption, however, is more dubious. It seems that, like Wittgenstein, I have assumed that the features of language that must be expressed in premise 2 are features a sentence must have in common with reality. It can be claimed that there are many other features of language that not only are readily knowable, but also may be sufficient for premise 2. Let us examine this claim. We can divide the features of a linguistic expression into two exclusive and exhaustive kinds: what I shall call formal characteristics, the grammatical properties of the expression and its relationships with other linguistic expressions; and nonformal characteristics, the relationships of the expression with anything nonlinguistic. A linguistic expression has grammatical properties—'John is a bachelor' is an indicative sentence. It has relationships with other expressions in its language—'All humans are mortal' is materially equivalent to 'All featherless bipeds are mortal.' It has relationships with expressions in a different language—'John is a bachelor' (in English) means the same as 'Jean est un célibataire' (in French); and with expressions in its meta- or object-language—Carnap's designation rules for his semantical system S_1 such as: 'RAx' (in S_1) designates 'x is a rational animal' (in English). A linguistic expression can also have relationships with nonlinguistic things. A linguistic expression may have some relationship with what it is used to talk about—'John is a bachelor' pictures a fact —and with certain situations or contexts in which it might be used—when someone's overt behavior is pain-behavior, it is correct to say of him, 'He is in pain.'

Can any of these available features of language replace those ineffable features we had been attempting to use in premise 2? Consider the nonformal features first. The nonformal relationship an expression has with what it is used to talk about is obviously of no help because although premise 2 would be true if this were the characteristic mentioned in the premise, it is just the relationship we would be trying to establish by means of a more available characteristic. The relationships an expression has to the conditions or contexts of its correct and incorrect use avoid this problem but face others. If we try the characteristic of having some contexts of correct use and some contexts of incorrect use, then premise 2 becomes false. For example, 'Hurrah!' which is surely not a designator would turn out to be one if we used this characteristic in premise 2, because 'Hurrah!' has contexts of correct and of incorrect use just as do 'He is in pain' and 'He is in school.' Someone might propose that instead of this we need the characteristic of having specific kinds of contexts of correct and of incorrect use. If this proposal is satisfactory then we might be able to show, for example, that 'He is in pain' is not a designator by showing that the contexts of the correct and incorrect use of 'He is in pain' are in some ways more like those of 'Hurrah!' than like those of a known designator such as 'He is in school.' Although arguments such as this will be more fully discussed in Chapter 7, we can conclude here that such a characteristic does not seem to be suitable for premise 2 because we would have to show first that 'He is in pain' lacks certain contextual characteristics that 'He is in school' has, and then that these characteristics—contextual or otherwise—are relevant to the sentence being a designator. Someone might claim that the fact that both sentences are of the form 'He is in P' is relevant to 'He is in pain' being a designator, but this cannot be discovered by examination of contexts. Thus neither the characteristic of having some contexts of correct and incorrect use nor the characteristic of having certain kinds of contexts of correct and incorrect use seem to be what is required in premise 2. We can, for now at least, conclude that neither of the nonformal relationships will do.

Let us turn to the formal characteristics. I have already stated grounds for rejecting the grammatical properties that are sufficient for a linguistic expression being an indicative sentence. Similarly, whatever grammatical properties qualify an expression as a noun or an adjective, or a subject or predicate of a sentence, they are not sufficient for deciding whether an expression is what Carnap calls an individual expression or a predicator. Given agreement about all the grammatical properties of 'The Absolute' and 'beautiful,' there is still room for disagreement about whether they are designators. We can dismiss nonentailment formal relationships equally fast. Using the relationships of material equivalence, implication, and other truth-functional relationships in premise 2 either begs the question (if it is assumed that what are related have truth-values), or (if this is not assumed) then deciding that two sentences, p and q, are materially equivalent is not sufficient for deciding whether p has a truth-value even if q has one. For example, it may be that the Mona Lisa is a beautiful painting if and only if the painting has certain empirically discoverable characteristics. But, even given this material equivalence with a designator, it may be, as some philosophers claim, that 'The Mona Lisa is a beautiful picture' has no truth-value.

There is, however, one and I think only one formal relationship which might help produce a justifiable premise 2. If p and q are synonymous, and we know that q is a designator, then we can conclude that p is a designator. An immediate objection to this proposal is that if there is doubt about whether p is a designator and p is synonymous with q, then there are doubts about whether q is a designator. Although this is correct in some cases, e.g. 'You ought to do x' and 'You have an obligation to do x,' there are other cases in which it seems to be false. It is possible that, although there are among the components of p some expressions that might be designators but seem not to be, there are in q, synonymous with p, only obvious designators. This is, in part at least, the motive behind meaning analysis. Attempts have been made to analyze sentences containing expressions such as 'the average man' and 'the English na-

tion' by means of sentences containing only obvious designators such as 'men' and 'Englishmen.' The programs of
logical behaviorism (which we have already examined)
and logical phenomenalism have at their base meaning
analyses. It may be, then, that the relationship of synonymy
with a known designator may be the characteristic for which
we are looking in premise 2.

There are, however, objections to using this. First, although it seems to be true that if p is synonymous with a
known designator, then p is a designator, there is no reason
to believe that if p is not synonymous with a known designator, then it is not a designator. Therefore this relationship is not by itself all that is needed in premise 2. Any
other characteristics would seem to be the ineffable ones,
because no other available ones will do. Another objection
is aimed at the assumption that this synonymy relationship
is available. As will be brought out much more fully in
Chapter 6, in which a detailed examination of meaning
analysis is carried out, reasons have been given to establish, first, that no two expressions are synonymous, and,
second, that even if some expressions are synonymous, there
is no way to establish this. That such claims may be true,
at least in the cases in which q is supposed to be an analysis
of p, is bolstered by the inability of anyone to produce any
but the most trivial examples of meaning analysis, as wit-
nessed by the failures of logical behaviorism and logical
phenomenalism.

We have been unable to find any characteristics of linguistic expressions, whether they be formal or nonformal,
that we can justify using in premise 2. Where does this
leave us? One thing to note at this point is that we have
been talking of characteristics an expression has if and only
if it is a designator, rather than if and only if it is in relation
R to reality. Perhaps we can collapse premises 1 and 2
into: A sentence is a designator if and only if it has characteristics $a, b, c, \ldots$ Relation R was brought into the
argument in order to help establish which sentences are or

are not designators. However, we have concluded that the kind of characteristics obviously relevant to such a relation, i.e. the features a sentence has in common with reality, do not seem to be available for inquiry. Once we began to examine available characteristics, we began to check their relevance to the argument by considering their relevance to designators rather than to relation R. We may, then, be able to avoid considering relation R. This would be quite helpful not only because it would simplify what we must consider, but also because it would allow us to avoid having to examine the following argument directed at showing that even if we can express what the relation R is, we cannot justify any claim about what it is.

We are interested in whether or not we can justify the sentence: 'The relationship between sentences of L and reality is R.' Let us call this sentence p_1. Is p_1 true? It is true only if it has a truth-value, and, consequently, only if 'p_1 is in relation R to reality,' a sentence we can abbreviate as p_1Rq, is true. But p_1Rq is a sentence of L also, call it p_2. Thus p_2 is true only if p_2 has a truth-value, that is, only if p_2Rq is true. Thus we can justify that p_1 is true only if we can justify that p_2Rq is true. But how can we justify that p_2Rq is true? Once again we can do so only if we can justify that p_2Rq has a truth-value. But p_2Rq is a sentence of L, call it p_3. Thus we must justify that p_3Rq is true. Generalizing, we can say that we can justify that a sentence of the form p_nRq is true only if we can justify that one of the form $p_{n+1}Rq$ is true, and this goes on ad infinitum. And, so goes the argument, this infinite regress is vicious because justifying that $p_{n+1}Rq$ is true is not only a necessary condition of justifying that p_nRq is true, it is also an epistemologically independent task. That is, no evidence sufficient for justifying that p_nRq is true is sufficient for justifying that $p_{n+1}Rq$ is true, so that justifying $p_{n+1}Rq$ requires some evidence not required for justifying p_nRq. Thus we have two premises: (i) p_nRq is justifiable only if $p_{n+1}Rq$ is justifiable, and (ii) justifying $p_{n+1}Rq$ is epistemologically independent from justifying p_nRq. From these it follows that for the justification of any claim of the form p_nRq, there are an infinite number of epistemologically independent tasks to be accomplished, and this is obviously impossible. Thus there is no evidence sufficient to justify a claim of the form p_nRq.

Is this argument sound? The most obvious way to attack it is to claim that premise (ii) is false because, although p_nRq is justifiable only if $p_{n+1}Rq$ is justifiable, it may well be that there is some evidence justifying p_nRq from which it follows that all claims of the form p_iRq, where i is greater than n, are justified. There surely are many sentences we can justify as true without independently investigating whether or not they have a truth-value. Why can we not claim that at least some sentences of the form p_nRq are of this kind? If at least one is, then the regress is not vicious, and the argument fails. The reply to this objection is that, although in many cases we can justifiably assume that a sentence has a truth-value, there are many other cases, as we have already seen, in which this is not so. There is enough doubt about whether any sentence of the form p_nRq even makes sense to provide reason for doubting whether it has a truth-value. And if p_nRq belongs in this doubtful category, then because we are trying to justify that sentences of the form p_nRq are true in order to establish whether or not sentences that belong in this doubtful category have a truth-value, we cannot without circularity also claim that, in justifying that a sentence of the form p_nRq is true, we need not be concerned with whether p_nRq has a truth-value, i.e. with whether $p_{n+1}Rq$ is true.

I have not, however, used a metalanguage in formulating this argument. To see if either the regress or its viciousness can be avoided, let us say that the object-language in question, which we shall now call L_1, is in relation R_1 to reality, the metalanguage L_2 is in relation R_2 to reality, and so on. Once again we are interested in establishing the relationship between sentences of L_1 that are designators and reality.

We are interested, then, in establishing the truth-value of p_2, i.e. $p_1 R_1 q$. But because p_2 is a sentence about the relation of sentences of L_1 to reality, it is a sentence in the metalanguage L_2. Thus if we can find the truth-value of a certain sentence in L_2, we will have established the nature of the relation between L_1 and reality. We are not, then, as in the previous case, faced with an infinite regress involving the relation language L_1 has to reality. However, a related problem arises: if we are to justify that p_2 is true, we must justify that p_2 has a truth-value, i.e. that $p_2 R_2 q$ is true. What is necessary to establish a claim about R_1, then, is to establish one about R_2, but this merely sets us back a level, because L_2 is a language also. Therefore unless we can find out which sentences of L_2 have truth-values in some way different from the way we must use for L_1, we seem to be no better off than before. But there does not seem to be any reason to believe that there is any relevant difference between L_1 and L_2. We have a regress again. For $p_2 R_2 q$ is a sentence of L_3, call it p_3. Thus in order to justify that p_3 has a truth-value, we must justify that $p_3 R_3 q$ is true. Thus to establish a claim of the form $p_n R_n q$ we must justify one of the form $p_{n+1} R_{n+1} q$, and this goes on ad infinitum. Metalanguages will not help us avoid the regress. Neither will they help us avoid its viciousness because once again we are faced with an infinite number of epistemologically independent tasks in order to justify that $p_n R_n q$ is true. We cannot justify that a sentence of a language L_{n+1} has some particular relation to reality merely by showing that the sentences of its object language L_n have some, perhaps different, relation to reality. The task of establishing this relation for each language level is an epistemologically independent task. Again the only way to avoid this conclusion is to deny that all claims of the form $p_n R_n q$ must be justified. But there is no reason to think that a sentence of the form of $p_n R_n q$ in a metalanguage is any less dubious than one of that form in an object language. Thus using a metalanguage will not avoid this argu-

ment. It is, incidentally, an argument similar to the one
used in the first objection raised previously against Carnap's
method—the objection based on the point that Carnap's
method for finding the extensions and intensions of the
designators of a language can succeed only if we already
know the extensions and intensions of the designators of a
different language, the language used as metalanguage (see
pp. 90–91).

I think that rather than debating further whether justifying sentences of the form of pRq involves us in a vicious
regress, we should give up the attempt to justify some claim
about the relation between language and reality, as, indeed,
the discussion of certain entailment characteristics of sentences gave us some reason to believe we could do. But
since we have had no more success with either formal or
available nonformal characteristics, have we reached the
point where we must conclude that we cannot answer 1?
Not yet, I think, for there is a further kind of objection to
this general approach, one which at the same time implies
that an alternative approach will succeed. The objections
previously discussed were all based on the assumption that
the question, "What is the relation between a language and
reality?" is a legitimate one. They were aimed either at some
particular attempt to answer this question, such as Wittgenstein's answer, or at showing that no satisfactory answer
could be found. The present objection, however, claims
that this assumption is wrong, because the question is not
legitimate; it is misguided because it sets us looking for a
relation R when there is none. Furthermore, this objection
goes, not only is this whole approach to question 1 wrong,
but once we see why it is wrong, we will see what is needed
to answer the question.

This line of attack is pursued by Ayer in *The Foundations
of Empirical Knowledge*. His attack is actually waged
against two questions often asked by philosophers who employ the approach of Carnap and the others: "How is it
possible for symbols to have meaning?" and "What is it

that they mean?" [23] He discusses the second question first and concludes that the reason the problem raised by this question

> appears to defy solution is that there is really no prob-
> lem to solve. We cannot find 'the other term of the
> relation of meaning' because the assumption that mean-
> ing is a relation which somehow unites a symbol with
> some other unspecified object is itself erroneous. What
> one is asking for when one seeks to know the mean-
> ing of a symbol is an explanation of the way in which
> the symbol is used. What form such explanations may
> take in particular cases I have already shown. But I
> cannot deal in the same way with the general case, for
> the simple reason that there is no general usage to
> explain. There is no one thing that all symbols mean.[24]

Having disposed of this problem by showing that to ask for the meaning of a symbol is to ask for the way it is used and maintaining that there is no general usage, Ayer can easily show that the first question is equally misguided. This question "is a product of the same confusion as the other. Again, it is assumed that meaning is a relation, analogous to loving or killing; but this time the puzzle is not to find the other term of the relation, but to discover the nature of the relation itself." [25]

For Ayer, then, both these questions are illegitimate because they assume that there is a relation between language and reality when no such thing exists. This does not mean that Ayer believes we can completely characterize a language without mention of reality, that is, merely by "the formal rules by which one symbol is connected with another." [26] Rather his view is:

23. See A. J. Ayer, *The Foundations of Empirical Knowledge* (New York, St. Martin's Press, 1955), p. 93.
24. Ibid., pp. 97–98.
25. Ibid., p. 104.
26. Ibid., p. 107.

> If a 'language' is to be capable of being used as a language, that is to say, for the purpose of communication, it must be characterized by non-formal rules, which connect some of its symbols, not with other symbols, but with observable states of affairs. What is not necessary, however, is that a symbol, the use of which is determined by such non-formal rules, should have any further connexion with what it symbolizes beyond that which is constituted by the existence of the rule. The answer to the question, How is it possible for 'red' to mean red is simply that this happens to be the symbol that we have chosen to refer to this colour.[27]

According to Ayer, any language must have some nonformal rules (what others have called ostensive rules, designation rules, or reference rules), but there is no other connection with reality. We are wrong, then, in looking for some relation R which connects all symbols or even all symbols of a certain kind with reality, because the only connection each particular symbol has is some nonformal designation rule for the use of that symbol. An example of such a rule is, I assume, the rule that in English the symbol 'red' refers to the color red. We need not go further and seek some relation between 'red' and this color or reality for the rule itself connects the two. Thus to find out what 'red' refers to we need not first find its relation, or the relation of its language, to reality; we need only see what it is used to refer to. If Ayer's answer is correct, then question 3 is misguided, for it sets us looking for one relation between language and reality. Instead we should try to answer question 2, "How can we find what 'p' refers to?" in another way. Ayer suggests that we should examine how 'p' is used; by so doing we will find the designation rule for that expression, and this is all we need to answer question 1 in any given case. Let us see, then, if this kind of answer to

27. Ibid.

question 2 is what we need to answer question 1 sufficiently for our purposes.

Ayer's designation rules, such as: 'red' (in English) refers to the color red, seem to be of the form $'p'Rq$. It may be objected this is not the case, for it makes out such sentences to be relational, whereas Ayer says they are not. But it must be admitted that for Ayer 'refer' is a term used to connect certain symbols to reality. Whether or not such rules are considered to be relational sentences is unimportant. What counts is that we not try to answer question 1 by attempting to find the nature of one relation which *all* symbols of a certain kind have. We must handle each symbol individually by examining its use. Saying that the designation rules for symbols can be put in the form $'p'Rq$ is not inconsistent with Ayer's view about how to establish a particular rule. We can put the point of Ayer's objection in this way: even if designation rules are relational sentences, we must not think that we need to examine some common relation in order to establish them. We can conclude, then, that for Ayer we are to answer question 1 for each particular expression by stating a designation rule of the form $'p'Rq$ for that expression.

Are designation rules as described by Ayer what we need to answer question 1? I think that they are not for the following two reasons:

> (i) Ayer's method of answering 2 cannot give us what we need to justify an answer to 1.
>
> (ii) The answer Ayer gives to 1, i.e. a designation rule, is not the kind of answer that we can use.

With regard to (i), Ayer claims that the answer to 2 is that we should examine how the expression $'p'$ is used. But question 2 presupposes a certain answer to another question, i.e. "Does $'p'$ refer to anything?" We have found that we must be able to answer such a question because whether or not certain expressions refer is relevant to how we decide among certain solutions to the traditional mind–body problem. It is also relevant to other problems and is the central point at issue in any debate about a theory of definite descriptions. It is, incidentally, a question parallel to the question we found Carnap must ask, "Is '*p*' a designator?" But on the basis of the conclusions we have reached in Part I, it would seem that we cannot answer the latter question for Carnap merely by examining how the expression is used, at least not in "nonparadigm" cases; and it seems it is just such cases in which we are interested. Thus unless we can either answer the latter question or find some way to avoid it, Ayer's view must be supplemented in some way. But I do not see how to do this without falling into the trouble we found facing Carnap.

The following example will illustrate how Ayer's way of answering question 2 is deficient. In deciding among the views of men such as Chisholm, Smart, and Ryle we must decide, first, whether certain mental-expressions have referents or whether, as Ryle claims, they function only as inference tickets. Second, if they do have referents, are the referents something nonphysical or not? For example, we can find by examining the way in which the word 'pain' is used that it is correct to use it to refer to certain sensations. Nevertheless although Ryle could agree to this, he would insist that 'sensation' refers neither to a thing nor an event and thus does not refer to something that can be either identical with or causally related to brain processes. On the other hand, Smart could also agree to the results of our examination but go on to insist that, contrary to Ryle, 'pain' refers to a certain kind of brain process because sensations are identical with brain processes. Chisholm could agree with Ryle and Smart about the way in which 'pain' is used, but he would opt for a dualistic conclusion concerning sensations and brain processes. Thus in the case of 'pain' and other words like it, discovering the way it is used does not provide the help necessary to decide the central issues of the mind–body problem. At this point someone might claim that the only sentences about linguistic reference are

those the truth of which can be discovered by examining
the way words are used, and thus the mind–body problem
if it requires something more is a pseudo problem. Such a
claim, however, is at least premature, especially so in the
light of the problems we have found confronting those who
have tried to show that it is a pseudo problem. The claim
may be correct, but because it is far from obviously correct
it must be established; the making of such a claim should
thus await the result of our discussion. We can, then, conclude that the first reason for rejecting designation rules
is sound.

But even if Ayer could avoid this first objection there is
another objection which claims that Ayer's kind of answer
to I does not provide us with what we need. To see the
force of this objection let us reconsider our purpose in asking question I: "What does 'p' refer to?" It is to find out
what it is that 'p' refers to, that is, the function of an adequate answer is to connect symbols, as Ayer says, "not with
other symbols but with observable states of affairs." We
can understand what Ayer means here by considering what
I shall call "ostensive answers." To explain what I mean,
let us take 'p' to be the expression, 'the presidential nominee
of the Republican Party in 1964.' One kind of answer to
question I, an ostensive answer, would consist of indicating
ostensively, by pointing for example, while saying something
like, "He is." Such an answer does what a nonformal rule
would do and what Ayer claims a designation rule does:
it connects symbols "not with other symbols but with observable states of affairs," that is it connects symbols to
reality. Any answer that does not do this is in some way
inadequate.

Let me illustrate the inadequacy of formal rules by considering the mind–body problem once again. Assume that
'S_1' is a specific sensation-expression and that 'B_1' is a specific brain-process expression such that S_1 occurs at time t_1
if and only if B_1 occurs at t_1. If we were to ask someone
holding a view such as Smart's what 'S_1' refers to, and if he

were to use a formal rule, he would have to answer by using something equivalent to the formal rule that 'S_1' refers to what 'B_1' refers to. But Smart wants to say more than this because he wants to make a particular claim about what it is that both 'S_1' and 'B_1' refer to. Thus he would want to answer question I by using a rule that would connect 'S_1' not with another symbol but with reality. His answer would, then, neither be equivalent to nor interpretable as a formal reference rule. It may be that what is needed are what Wittgenstein called rules of projection, but if this is so then Wittgenstein's objection against his own picture theory of meaning might also apply here. It may be that what is required for answers to question I—no matter how we approach it—are rules that get us outside language but which are at the same time expressible using language. However we are not ready to consider that now.

Our problem now is to see whether the kind of answer to question I that Ayer proposes connects 'p' with some particular state of affairs, whether such designation rules are—as Ayer claims—nonformal reference rules or whether they are merely formal reference rules that is, rules which express relationships among linguistic expressions. Some, but by no means all, of such rules are analytic. What I shall try to show is that designation rules of the form of:

I. 'p' (in L) refers to q

and sentences of the form of:

II. 'p' (in L) refers to what 'q' in this language, i.e. the language I am now using, refers to[28]

are logically equivalent and therefore that designation rules merely relate 'p' to another linguistic expression, 'q.' And

28. This way of stating II was first suggested to me by a paper by Wilfrid Sellars, "Notes on Intentionality" on which I was preparing comments for a symposium at a meeting of the American Philosophical Association, Eastern Division, Dec. 29, 1964. See *The Journal of Philosophy, 61* (1964), 655–68, for Sellars' paper and the abstract of my comments.

because designation rules are logically equivalent to statements of the form of II, they are not only formal rules but logically equivalent to the kind of formal rules that we have just seen are not adequate to formulate Smart's reductionistic position. Let me lay out the argument in the following way:

1. I and II are logically equivalent.
2. If I and II are logically equivalent, then I and II relate 'p' to the same thing.
3. II relates 'p' to a linguistic expression.

Therefore

4. I relates 'p' to a linguistic expression, i.e. I is a formal rule.

There seems to be no reason to doubt 2 and 3, but 1 is a problematic premise, because it can be attacked in two ways: by denying that I entails II and by denying that II entails I. There is, I think, just one objection to the claim that I entails II: if it were true that there were only one linguistic expression 'p' then I might be true, but II would be false because II, unlike I, entails that there are two expressions. Therefore I does not entail II.

The crucial objection to the claim that II entails I, which has been called the translation argument, involves the following:[29] If a sentence of the form of II such as A: " 'Russia' (in English) refers to what 'the largest country' in this language refers to," entails a sentence of the form of I, namely B: " 'Russia' (in English) refers to the largest country," then if A and B are translated into A' and B' in another language such as French, then A' should entail B'. But if it is logically possible that A' is true and B' is false, then because A if and only if A' and B if and only if B', it follows

29. This argument is derived from Alonzo Church, "On Carnap's Analysis of Statements of Assertion and Belief," *Analysis, 10* (1950), 97–99. This argument and other relevant points have been discussed by Wilfrid Sellars, "Grammar and Existence: A Preface to Ontology," *Mind, 69* (1960), 499–533.

that A does not entail B. Actually what is essential to this argument can be shown if we translate only B into B′ and see whether A entails B′. Following the rule of translation that says quoted passages remain untranslated, B′ is: " 'Russia' (*en anglais*) *se réfère au plus grand pays*." Does A entail B′? According to the translation argument, it does not because it is logically possible both that 'Russia' (in English) refers to what 'the largest country' in this language refers to, and that C′: " 'Russia' (*en anglais*) *se réfère au plus petit pays*," is true. But because A and C′ are consistent, but B′ and C′ are not, A does not entail B′, and therefore A does not entail B.

How are these two objections to be countered? Instead of meeting them head on, let me get at them indirectly by stating an argument in support of I. It uses:

III. '*q*' in this language refers to *q*
and goes as follows:

5. I and III entail II.
6. II and III entail I.
7. III is logically necessary.
Therefore
1. I and II are logically equivalent.

There are, I think, no problems facing 5 and 6, but the truth of 7 is surely open to debate. Thus 7 is crucial, doubly so because not only is it essential for establishing I, but also if 7 is true, then I entails III and consequently I entails that there are two linguistic expressions, contrary to what is claimed in the objection that I does not entail II.

I can find just three objections to the claim that III is logically necessary. The first two objections involve the central point of the translation argument, but I shall consider them first without making a translation. The first objection claims that a sentence of the form of III such as D: " 'Russia' in this language refers to Russia," is not a necessary truth, because it is surely logically possible that 'Russia' in this language refers to something different so that, for example, C: " 'Russia' in this language refers to the smallest country," is true. Thus because it is possible that C is true, C is only contingently false, so that it is possible that D is false. Consequently D is not logically necessary. However, because the possibility of being false cannot be deduced from the premise that it is possible that 'Russia' refers to something other than it does, another premise is needed to make the argument valid. What seems to be needed is the premise that if 'Russia' were to refer to something other than it does, this would entail the denial of D, i.e. that 'Russia' does not refer to Russia. The proper reply to this argument is to grant that it is possible that 'Russia' refers to something different, but to deny this entailment premise. Although it is surely true that if 'Russia' in this language were to refer to something other than it does, then it might, for example, refer to the smallest country, this would not affect the truth of D, for D, unlike B and C, mentions the same word that it uses, namely 'Russia.' Consequently if, for example, C were true and if that would require that 'Russia' have a different referent, then, although there might well be a change in the relationship between the word mentioned and the words used in B, there could be no such change in D because in it the word mentioned is the word used. Thus it seems to be logically possible that 'Russia' has a different referent and that D is true, contrary to the entailment premise. Indeed I think we can even make a stronger claim, namely, that it is logically impossible that 'Russia' in our language does not refer to Russia. Let me say why I think this is so. If D is false, then the denial of D is true. But anyone who asserts the denial of D would be claiming that the word he is mentioning does not refer to what he is using it to refer to in making the claim. That is, if such an assertion were true then the word 'Russia' would be used in the assertion to refer to something that it is incorrect to use the word to refer to. But if an assertion involves such a misuse of a word, then it follows that it is

either false or meaningless. Consequently if the denial of D
were true, then it would be either false or meaningless. But
because the denial of D is false or meaningless only if the
denial of D is not true, it follows that it is necessary that
the denial of D is not true. It is also necessary that if D is
false, then the denial of D is true. Consequently we can conclude that it is logically impossible that D is false.

It is at this point that the reason for making a translation
becomes apparent. If D is translated D': " 'Russia' (*en
anglais*) *se réfère à la Russie*," then it could be claimed that
if 'Russia' had a different referent but the referent of the
French expression '*la Russie*' remained the same, as is possible, then D' would be false. And because D' is a translation
of D, then D and D' are logically equivalent, and it is logically possible that D is false.

The first thing that can be said here is that it is not obvious that D' is a correct translation of D, and whether, if it
is, D and D' are logically equivalent. For one thing, D' is a
correct translation of D only if it is correct to follow the
rule of translation that no quoted passage is to be translated.
But although it may be that we should follow such a rule
when quoting what someone says, it is not clear that it
should be done in any other cases. It would seem that one
criterion often used for evaluating a translation is that the
translatans plays the same role in its language that the
translatandum plays in its language. If we were to adopt this
criterion then D' would not be a good translation of D, because D tells an English-speaking person what a word in
his language refers to, while D' tells a French-speaking person what a word in a *foreign* language refers to. However,
the main objection to this translation is that '*en anglais*' is
not a correct translation of 'in this language.' We were
forced to translate it as '*en anglais*' because we followed
the rule of not translating quoted passages. Indeed, we must
break the rule if we are to properly translate 'in this language,' and also if we are to arrive at a French sentence that
plays a role corresponding to the role of D, that is, D":

" '*la Russie*' *dans cette langue se réfère à la Russie.*" If D″ is the correct translation of D, then the translation argument fails. However, whether or not D″ is the correct translation of D we have seen reasons for rejecting D′ as the correct translation, and this is all that is needed to rebut the translation argument.

Furthermore, there is the very difficult question of what the criterion of cross-language logical equivalence should be. It would seem that the sentence that plays the role in French played by D in English would be the proper candidate, whether or not it follows certain rules laid down for a correct translation. Thus because what is important for the objection is not whether D′ is the correct translation of D, but whether it is logically equivalent to D, and because it is not clear that logical equivalence is a necessary condition of a correct translation, the problems surrounding translation seem only to confuse the basic question at issue, the question about logical equivalence. And here the question of sameness of role surely seems relevant.

I have produced an argument to show that it is logically impossible that D is false, and I have tried to show that translating D cannot be used to disprove this point. We can now raise the question of whether we can conclude from this that D is logically necessary. We cannot yet, because we have not considered what would be true if 'Russia' were not a word, and consequently not a referring expression. The second objection I wish to consider engages the problem at this point. It states that because it is possible that 'Russia' is not a word, it is possible that 'Russia' does not refer to Russia, so that D is not logically necessary. However, as with the first objection there seems to be an assumed premise, in this case the premise that if 'Russia' is not a word in this language, then this entails that 'Russia' in this language does not refer to Russia. Also, as with the first objection, it is this entailment claim I find mistaken. Let us consider the claim that 'glabob' in this language refers to glabob. Is this claim false because there is in this language no such word?

Would we say that it is false that glabobs eat meat because 'glabob' is not a word in this language? I think not. We would say instead that this claim is meaningless because it uses something that is not a word. Similarly, if 'glabob' is not a word in our language, then it follows that it is meaningless rather than false to say that 'glabob' in this language refers to glabob, and therefore meaningless to say that 'glabob' does not refer to glabob. Thus the entailment premise of the second objection is false.

The third objection, which is really a variation on the second, begins with the entailment claim that I made above, that is, if 'glabob' is not a word then it is *meaningless* to say that 'glabob' refers to glabob. This provides grounds for the claim that D entails that 'Russia' is a word. Because of this, and because it is contingent that 'Russia' is a word, it follows according to this objection that D is merely contingently true and thus not logically necessary. Although if 'Russia' were not a word, it would follow that D would not be true, it does not also follow that D would be merely contingently true. That would follow if D not being true entails that it is logically possible that D is false. But this entailment does not hold because something not being true entails that it is either false or meaningless, and if, as I have argued, it is logically impossible that D is false, then D being not true entails that D is meaningless, rather than false. Thus this objection fails as did the first two.

At this point someone might wish to point out that if D is a necessary truth as I have claimed, it seems to be quite different from many other necessary truths such as those of the form '*p* or not *p*,' because D, unlike those of the form '*p* or not *p*,' entails a contingent truth. It may be that D is a special kind of necessary truth, but it does not seem to be unique. Sentences such as: " 'bachelor' (in English) means the same as 'bachelor' (in English)" surely seem to be logically necessary, yet they entail that there is at least one word. We are faced with a similar problem concerning the obvious logical truth that all men are men which, according to the usual rules of quantification theory, logically implies the contingent truth that there is at least one thing. All I can say in reply to this point here is that such truths are contingently necessary. Indeed, if as has been claimed, analytic statements are true in virtue of the meanings of words, then analytic statements entail that there is at least one word and all analytic statements would also be contingently necessary. Admittedly this reply is not satisfactory, but it will, I hope, become better justified in the next chapter where I shall explain how it can be that D and other such necessary truths can also be, on another level, contingent.

I have, I think, rebutted all the objections to the claim that it is logically necessary that 'Russia' in this language refers to Russia. However, I have produced no argument to support the claim. Although I am not sure that one is necessary at this point, a quite reasonable argument can be constructed using the following three premises: *D* is true (which surely is acceptable); It is logically impossible that D is false (which I have tried to establish previously); If it is true that 'Russia' in this language refers to Russia and if it is logically impossible that 'Russia' in this language does not refer to Russia, then it is logically necessary that 'Russia' in this language refers to Russia. Although I am not sure this additional claim is true, I have been unable to find objections to it so that I shall accept it as true. Nevertheless whether that claim is true or not, unless there are objections to premise 7 that I have missed, or some I have considered can be revived, it seems reasonable to accept 7, that III is logically necessary. Thus we can conclude that 1 and finally 4 are justified, which is what I have been trying to establish.

Before we move on we must consider one more important point. It now looks as if all reference rules of the form of I are formal rules, and thus we have no rules to connect linguistic expressions to reality, i.e. no nonformal rules. Furthermore, this seems to open the way for an ad hominem objection against me. In Chapter 3 I claimed that Carnap could not translate sentences such as " 'p' refers to q" as " 'p' is equipollent to 'q' " because he could not handle at least one of his own reference sentences by such a translation. I further noted that what was needed was a nonsymmetric relationship, and that equipollence is a symmetric relationship. Given this, someone might well claim that " 'p' refers to what 'q' refers to" amounts to " 'p' has the same content as 'q' " and thus to " 'p' is equipollent to 'q.' " In such a way my objection to Carnap's translation could be turned against my own translation. I must admit that as I have stated my claim, this objection has force. However, my purpose in making the claim was to prove that designation rules are formal rules and consequently are not sufficient to express what Carnap and others such as Feigl, Smart, and Ryle wish to say. Carnap, for example, wishes to say that certain sentences of the form of III are false. He seems to claim, for example, that 'five' in the sentence, 'Five is not a thing but a number' does not refer to the number five, because this is a pseudo-object sentence and thus refers to the word 'five.' [30] Thus if Carnap is to avoid contradiction, he requires the use of some nonformal reference rule. Such rules cannot be equivalent to rules of the form of II, nor, I have claimed, are they designation rules. Thus, unlike Carnap, who claims that his translation holds for all reference sentences, I can avoid this objection by explicitly restricting my claim to only what I have called designation rules, and not to any other kind of reference rules that there might be. The objection seemed to apply to my claim because in talking of designation rules I seemed to be talking about all reference rules. Thus I seemed to be providing grounds for concluding that all reference rules are formal rules. On the other hand, I had in Chapter 3 and elsewhere given reasons for concluding that not all reference rules can be formal rules. This was done to set up a paradox to be resolved by recognizing the possibility of two kinds of reference rules: designation rules, which are formal rules; and

30. Rudolf Carnap, *The Logical Syntax of Language,* p. 285.

nonformal rules, which we shall be unable either to characterize sufficiently or to relate to what concerns us until certain results are obtained in the next chapter.

However, the above distinction, by allowing the possibility of the existence of nonformal rules of the form of I, also makes possible another objection against my position. If all rules of the form of I are formal rules, then designation rules, being of the form of I, are formal rules. But if, as I claim, some rules of the form of I are nonformal rules, then perhaps designation rules are nonformal rules. Let me in rebuttal indicate my reasons for thinking that whether or not there are any nonformal rules of the form of I, if any rules of the form of I are formal rules, then designation rules are formal rules. We have found that at least some sentences of the form of I are logically equivalent to sentences of the form of II. How can we decide which sentences these are? It would seem that if any sentences of the form of I are confirmed in the same way as sentences of the form of II, then those sentences would be the ones logically equivalent to sentences of the form of II and thus would be formal rules. We would confirm sentences of the form of II by examining the ways in which the relevant expressions are used. This is also the case with designation rules. The one feature of the rules Ayer discusses, the rules we have called designation rules, that has been most often emphasized in this discussion is that they are rules that can be discovered by examining the ways in which the relevant expressions are used. Thus we would confirm that a sentence of the form of I is a designation rule in the same way we would confirm a sentence of the form of II, that is, by examining the ways in which the relevant expressions are used. Because of this we can conclude that designation rules are those logically equivalent to sentences of the form of II and thus are formal rules.

It would seem, then, that designation rules can no more provide what we need to approach the mind–body problem via question I than does the kind of approach exemplified by Carnap's theory of meaning. Both approaches require supplementation, perhaps in the same way. Furthermore this is a predicament not just for the mind–body problem, but also for many other ontological problems. These others, such as the problem of universals and the problem of the nature of the external world, can be put as problems about the referents of certain key expressions, such as 'class' and 'physical object.' For each of these, all the points made against using Carnap's theory of meaning or Ayer's designation rules to get at the referents relevant to the mind–body problem apply mutatis mutandis. For example, the problem of expressing Smart's materialistic position using merely formal rules of reference is a problem not only for his mind-to-body reductionistic theory, but is a problem facing any kind of ontological reductionistic theory, be it the reduction of classes to individuals, or physical objects to sense-data, or any other. In all such problems what seems to be required is something other than formal rules, something that goes outside language—perhaps in just the way that Wittgenstein claims is impossible.

It seems, then, that Ayer's approach to question 1 will help us no more than Carnap's. But the above discussion suggests another possibility: the way to approach 1 is to give an ostensive answer. This seems to do for us what Wittgenstein claims any satisfactory answer must do: it gets us outside language to reality. Is this the kind of answer we can use? No, for at least this reason. Pointing or in some way indicating ostensively is not enough for ontological problems. It is true, for example, that we can indicate ostensively what "things" the word 'table' refers to. But this does not refute a Berkeleian, for example, because it is not relevant to anything he wants to claim. He wants to indicate that these "things" we are referring to by pointing are just particular bundles of sense-data, as is the finger that points. We cannot decide this issue by pointing; neither can we, it seems, by Carnap's or Ayer's approach.

Our conclusion, then, is that we have found no way to

approach question 1, that is, we can find no answer to question 2 by the three methods we have examined, for all are in some way inadequate. If we try Carnap's approach we can perhaps express in general terms the kind of answer we would give to 1, but we can not find what we need to establish the answer—the relation between language and reality. If we pick Ayer's approach we can produce an answer to 1, but not one that will do for our purposes because Ayer's designation rules are sufficient neither for formulating the kind of answers to question 1 for which we are looking nor for deciding among the various mind–body positions. If we choose ostensive answers as the sort of answers for which we are looking, then although we can connect symbols to reality, we can not say what we need to say— what it is that a given symbol is connected with. Thus we cannot find in any of these three ways what we need in order to choose among the views discussed in Chapter 3 about the relation of the linguistic mind–body problem to the traditional problem. Furthermore, if these are the only three approaches, it would also seem that we cannot find what we need in order to solve the traditional problem linguistically. But before we consider whether there is some other approach, we must first explore some of the consequences of the conclusions about question 1 and linguistic reference that we have reached in this chapter.

5. Internal and External Questions

In Chapter 4 we reached a conclusion which at first glance seems to contradict certain obvious facts. It seems to be true that people know what they are talking about and what the expressions of the language they use to converse refer to. That is, they know when it is correct and when it is incorrect to refer to certain things using certain expressions. And even when they do not know they can easily find out. They do not have to get involved in complicated theories of meaning to discover what a given expression refers to. That is, people do not seem to have trouble finding an answer to a question like question 1: "What does the expression '*p*' refer to?" This fact is the basis for Ayer's view about linguistic reference. The way people usually answer a question like question 1 is, as Ayer says, by means of a designation rule of the form " '*p*' refers to *q*." Sometimes they also use ostensive answers. In either case they provide satisfactory answers. These facts which no one should deny are the ones I seem to deny in Chapter 4.

I concluded, as have others, that it seems necessary to get involved in complicated theories of meaning and the relation between language and reality if we are even to begin to find an answer to question 1. I subsequently found that neither Ayer's designation rules, ostensive answers, nor both together can provide us with an answer to question 2, and unless the arguments in Chapter 4 have gone astray somewhere, these conclusions appear to be true. But they must be false if they contradict the obvious truths mentioned above. We have reached a pair of contradictory conclusions: first, that when we use language we have no trouble discovering what an expression refers to, and second, that we are unable to discover what such expressions refer to, or at best, have a very difficult time doing so. The paradox formed by this pair of conclusions must be resolved before we can continue. Because resolving the paradox will result in a considerable advance toward the goal we set out to reach, this is not a side issue. By resolving the paradox we shall be able to uncover the nature of those ontological problems such as the mind–body problem which led us to ask question 1 in the first place. One purpose of this chapter, then, is to resolve the paradox by showing that the contradiction is only apparent as indeed certain passages in Chapter 4 might lead us to believe. Another purpose is to draw out the consequences of the points made to show that the contradiction is only apparent.

My approach toward resolving the paradox involves four steps:

1. I wish to show that there are senses of 'refer' for which it is true to say that an expression refers, but that we cannot infer from this that anything nonlinguistic exists in any sense of 'exist.' This is a vital step because if there were no such sense of 'refer' then, as will be shown, we would be ontologically committed by our language and apparently committed to some very queer things. As a consequence, ontological problems such as the mind–body problem would be merely linguistic problems, and it would seem that the kind of answer to question 1—"What does the linguistic expression, 'p' refer to?"—for which we have been searching could easily be found by merely examining the language to which 'p' belongs, perhaps in the way that Ayer suggests. But we have seen reasons for concluding that such ways will not work, and thus the paradox which prompted these considerations would remain. A consequence of this step is that, instead of claiming that a language commits its users to certain

ontological positions, we should claim that it merely sanctions or prohibits the use of certain expressions in certain situations. This, as we shall see later, is important for our purposes. To develop the point involved in this step I shall use Quine's similar discussion in "On What There Is." [1]

2. I wish to show that even for any sense of 'refer' for which we can infer from " 'p' refers to something" that p exists, although we are ontologically committed to whatever it is that 'p' refers to, we are not thereby committed to any particular ontological theory about what it is that 'p' refers to. The second step is also important because if we could in any case infer that we are ontologically committed to p on the grounds that it is entailed by 'p exists,' which is entailed by " 'p' refers to something," then when in such a case the non-philosopher asks question 1 using a sense of 'refer' that entails 'p exists,' his concern would be the same as the ontologist's when he asks the question. But if such were the case, then we could not resolve the paradox, because if both the nonphilosopher and the philosopher were concerned with the same question then there is, contrary to our conclusion, no reason why the job of finding the answer is easy for the one and most difficult, if not impossible, for the other. In this step I shall be attacking some things Quine has said.

3. I shall explain just in what sense a language sanctions the use of its expressions and how this is relevant to the fact that a language does not ontologically commit its users. This step is primarily important as a preliminary to step 4.

4. With the apparatus developed to make the explanation mentioned in step 3 and the conclusions reached in the first two steps, I shall make a distinction between two species of question 1 which I shall

1. See W. V. O. Quine, *From A Logical Point of View* (Cambridge, Mass., Harvard University Press, 1953), Chapter 1.

use, first, to resolve the paradox and, second, to characterize ontological problems such as the mind–body problem.

Step 1

In order to establish step 1, I must first distinguish among certain senses of 'refer' so that we can work with just the sense or senses relevant to ontological commitment and the problems we are trying to solve. To do so, let us consider the words 'Alaska,' 'Pegasus,' 'loud,' and 'immovable.' For each of these words the following sentences seem, at least before philosophical scrutiny, to be true: "The word 'Alaska' refers to the largest state of the United States"; "The word 'Pegasus' refers to the winged horse captured by Bellerophon"; "The word 'loud' refers to loud things"; "The word 'immovable' refers to immovable objects." Thus each of these words seems to be a substituend for x in " x refers to y." Yet there also seem to be differences relevant to reference among these words. 'Alaska' and 'Pegasus' seem to be substituends for x in "x exists." However, neither 'loud' nor 'immovable' is such a substituend because they are not nouns. Furthermore, when 'Alaska' is substituted for $x,$ the resulting sentence is true, but when 'Pegasus' is substituted, the sentence is false for at least one sense of 'exist.'

Thus certain referring expressions function differently from others. We can distinguish between what we can call denoting expressions such as 'Alaska' and 'Pegasus' and ones such as 'loud' and 'immovable' which we can call descriptive expressions. In addition, we can distinguish between denoting expressions that denote—'Alaska'—and denoting expressions that do not denote—'Pegasus.' There is also a distinction between descriptive expressions that apply to or are true of something and those that are not. Let me first define what it is to be a referring expression in the way suggested at the beginning of the last chapter and then distinguish among four kinds of referring expressions as follows:

1. 'p' is a referring$_1$ expression $=_{df.}$ 'p' refers to something $=_{df.}$ it is correct (in some sense) to use 'p' to refer to something.

2. 'p' is a referring$_2$ expression $=_{df.}$ 'p' is a denoting expression $=_{df.}$ 'p' is a referring$_1$ expression, and 'p' is a noun expression which is a value of 'x' in 'x refers$_1$ to at least one thing that exists.'

3. 'p' is a referring$_3$ expression $=_{df.}$ 'p' denotes something $=_{df.}$ 'p' is a referring$_2$ expression and "'p' refers$_1$ to at least one thing that exists" is true.

4. 'F' is a referring$_4$ expression $=_{df.}$ 'F' is a descriptive expression $=_{df.}$ 'F' is a referring$_1$ expression and 'F' is a value of 'ϕ' in 'ϕ refers$_1$ to a property of x' where substituends for 'x' are denoting expressions.

5. 'F' is a referring$_5$ expression $=_{df.}$ 'F' is a descriptive expression that applies to (truly describes) something $=_{df.}$ 'F' is a referring$_4$ expression and for some value of 'x,' "'F' refers$_1$ to a property of x" is true.

It would seem, then, that the four words we have been considering are all referring$_1$ expressions, but only 'Alaska' and 'Pegasus' are denoting expressions. All denoting expressions are substituends for 'x' in 'x exists,' and because only nouns are such substituends, 'loud' and 'immovable' are not denoting expressions. Furthermore of the two denoting words it would seem that only 'Alaska' denotes, for while it is true that what 'Alaska' refers$_1$ to exists, this is not true of 'Pegasus' (for at least one sense of 'exist'). In picking 'Alaska' and 'Pegasus' as examples, I chose singular denoting expressions, but I could have chosen general denoting expressions just as well. Thus both 'human' and 'unicorn' are denoting terms, but only 'human' denotes anything because it surely seems false that 'unicorn' refers$_1$ to something existing. It should be noted that I am using the term 'denote' so that the question of whether or not a referring$_3$ expression denotes one and only one entity is to be answered by a theory of reference rather than by a definition of 'denote.'

The expressions 'loud' and 'immovable,' as we have seen, are not denoting expressions, yet since they attribute some property to things, they can be used to talk about things. Because of this they seem to relate in some way to reality, so that it appears correct to say that they can be used to refer to things. Both of them, then, are what I have called descriptive terms. That is, both terms can be predicated of a denoting expression such as 'sirens' and are such that when so predicated they attribute some property to sirens. Furthermore, 'loud,' but not 'immovable,' seems to refer$_5$ because although 'loud' truly describes many sirens there seems to be nothing to which 'immovable' truly attributes a property. Incidentally it does not follow from the fact that 'loud' truly attributes a property to certain objects and thus can be correctly used to refer to a property that the property loudness exists, unless the sense in which 'loud' refers to a property implies that it is correct to say that properties so referred to exist. This "unless" is the point we must take up next. But before we move on, it should be noted that all I have done thus far is provide five categories into which expressions can be sorted. I have not claimed that there are no other referring categories, nor have I provided any definitive sorting criteria. For example, in order to find out whether an expression is a denoting expression, we must establish a criterion for an expression being a value of 'x' in 'x refers$_1$ to at least one thing that exists.' To find out whether an expression is a descriptive expression, we must make clear what the criterion for an expression attributing a property is. This, however, we cannot do here, but something of what is involved in establishing such criteria will be discussed in Chapters 6 and 7, where we will consider, among other things, whether or not the term 'good' refers to a property, i.e. whether or not 'good' is a descriptive term.

It seems obvious that the only sense of 'refer' relevant to ontological commitment is 'refer$_3$' because it would seem that we should be ontologically committed to something only if it is true that it exists, and only in the case in which an expression denotes do we have any right to infer that something exists. Because of this let us rephrase question 1 for our present purposes as: "What does the expression 'p' denote?" As we shall find out later, however, we shall also be interested in question 1 interpreted as, "What does the expression 'p' refer$_5$ to?" It would seem, then, that there are senses of 'refer' for which we cannot infer from the truth of sentences such as " 'p' refers to something" that something exists. However, this may not be true. Someone might argue in a Meinongian way that because a certain expression refers in at least one sense such as 'refer$_1$,' 'refer$_2$,' or 'refer$_4$' we can infer that what it refers to exists in at least some sense. We must prove that there are no grounds for such a view because if we cannot, then there will be a very good sense in which it will be true to say that a language ontologically commits its users. This would be true because as we have shown earlier, designation rules of the form " 'x' refers to x" are analytic. Thus for example, the sentences " 'Pegasus' refers$_1$ to Pegasus" and " 'loudness' refers$_1$ to loudness" both seem to be analytic. If we are entitled to infer from the truth of these statements that what 'Pegasus' refers to and what 'loudness' refers to exist, we will be ontologically committed to the existence of certain things merely on the basis of the truth of analytic statements. In this way we could prove that all sorts of strange things exist. What this view in its most extreme form amounts to is a claim that, for any expression, if it refers in some sense, then either it, or if it is not a noun its noun form, denotes something. What I must do here is to show that there is no reason to think that we are ontologically committed to anything by any sense of 'refer' except 'refer$_3$.' Then in step 2 I show that even for an expression that refers$_3$ we are not ontologically committed to any view of what is denoted by the expression.

Essential to the view that we can infer the conclusion that something exists from the fact that an expression refers$_1$ refers$_2$ or refers$_4$, is the view that all referring$_2$ expressions denote something. If there is no argument to justify the latter, weaker view, then there is no argument to justify the former, stronger claim because there is no reason to think that all referring$_1$ and referring$_4$ expressions denote if many denoting expressions do not denote. I know of only one argument that can be used to justify the weaker view. It goes as follows: Although for one sense of 'exist' the sentence "What 'Pegasus' refers to exists" is false, there must be some other sense of 'exist' for which the sentence is true. For, even if "What 'Pegasus' refers to exists" is false (for one sense of 'exist'), what 'Pegasus' refers to must exist (in some other sense of 'exist') because even when we deny that what 'Pegasus' refers to exists, we are talking about or referring to what 'Pegasus' refers to, and there must be something we are talking about or referring to. Thus in some way what 'Pegasus' refers to must exist. To show that this argument is not sound I shall, as Quine does, employ the method developed by Russell in "On Denoting." [2]

Using Russell's technique, we can translate "What 'Pegasus' refers to exists" as follows: "At least one thing that exists is referred to by 'Pegasus,' and there exists no more than one thing referred to by 'Pegasus.'" On this translation the sentence is false. Is there still any reason to infer that what 'Pegasus' refers to exists (in some sense)? I think not on the basis of the argument given above and I can find no other. On this translation the sentence is false because the first conjunct is false. But if that is false, then "Nothing that exists

2. See Russell's "On Denoting," reprinted in *Readings in Philosophical Analysis,* pp. 103–15.

is referred to by 'Pegasus' " is true. But we can not infer from the truth of this sentence that what 'Pegasus' refers to exists for the above reason, because this sentence does not use the expression "what 'Pegasus' refers to," and therefore there is no reason to suppose that in uttering the sentence we are talking about or referring to what 'Pegasus' refers to. Rather we would seem to be referring to each thing that exists and denying that 'Pegasus' refers to any of these things. We can handle general terms such as 'unicorn' in a like manner. Although " 'unicorn' refers$_1$ to unicorns" is certainly true, it does not follow from this that for some sense of 'exist' the sentence "At least one thing that exists is referred to by 'unicorn' " is true, even though it is false for some other sense of 'exist.' For if it is false, then "Nothing that exists is referred to by 'unicorn' " is true. Again, as with 'Pegasus,' this sentence does not imply that what 'unicorn' refers to exists because the sentence would seem to refer to each thing that exists rather than what 'unicorn' refers to.

Thus there appears to be no reason to suppose that an expression, say 'p,' denotes anything unless the sentence "What 'p' refers to exists" is true for all senses of 'exist,' or, better, for the usual sense of 'exist,' since the other "odd" senses seem to be needed if and only if the argument we have destroyed is sound. That 'Pegasus' is a denoting (referring$_2$) expression provides no reason to claim that what 'Pegasus' refers to exists. Consequently that an expression refers$_1$ or refers$_4$ provides no reason to infer that what it refers to exists. Thus we have reached the conclusion of the first step in the attempt to resolve the "referring paradox," that is, the conclusion that there are senses of 'refer' from which we cannot infer that anything nonlinguistic exists. From this we can also conclude that language does not ontologically commit us in any way contrary to what would be true if we could infer ontological conclusions from analytic statements of the form " 'p' refers$_1$ to p." I shall now proceed to step 2.

STEP 2

What I wish to show now is that even for that sense of referring, referring₃, for which we can infer from " '*p*' refers to something" that *p* exists, we are only committed to what '*p*' refers to, whatever it is, but not to any particular ontological view of what this is. That is, merely because an expression of a language denotes, we are not thereby ontologically committed to any particular view of what there is. In this step, I shall turn Quine's argument upon certain of Quine's conclusions concerning ontological commitment. Quine concludes, in "On What There Is," from a discussion much like the above, that there is only one standard or criterion "whereby to decide what ontology a given theory or form of discourse is committed to; a theory is committed to those and only those entities to which the bound variables of the theory must be capable of referring in order that the affirmations made in the theory be true." [3] At another place Quine says, "an entity is assumed by a theory if and only if it must be counted among the values of the variables in order that the statements affirmed in the theory be true." [4]

The second formulation, although much like the first, talks of entities as values of variables rather than entities referred to by bound variables. For our purpose we shall wish to speak primarily not of entities but of the expressions which refer to these entities. In any case in which a theory employs such expressions, a criterion equivalent to Quine's is:

> A theory or form of discourse, T, is ontologically committed to an entity, *E,* if and only if *E* is an entity which, if the affirmations of T are to be true, must be referred to by some linguistic expression, *L,* which (1) is a constant of T and (2) can replace and be replaced by variables of T according to the laws of quantification.

3. Quine, p. 13.
4. Quine, p. 103.

Such constants are called substituends for variables. Thus *L*, which in our example is a substituend for certain variables of T, refers to *E*, which is a value of those variables. The expression *L* is what has been called "name" by logicians. It is, incidentally, the kind of expression we can do without, according to Quine, because whatever we might want to say using *L* we can say by binding the proper variables of T.[5] It seems clear that if we accept Quine's criterion we are ontologically committed to entities referred to by expressions of a language, whether they be bound variables or substituends for variables. Thus, it would seem, Quine's criterion requires explicit use of a theory of reference—which is what we are interested in.

One thing to note is that Quine's criterion is a criterion for what might be called "subjective" ontological commitments. As with other sorts of commitments, such as duties, where there are subjective commitments, there are also "objective" ones. We would be "objectively" ontologically committed to an entity if and only if the entity is referred to by an expression, variable or substituend, that denotes. We can, however, approach the problem from either kind of commitment because our aim can be either to find out in what sense, if any, someone's believing that certain sentences are true ontologically commits him to certain entities, or to find out in what sense, if any, certain sentences being true ontologically commits us to certain entities. In either case, what is important is that Quine's criterion involves the notion of denoting, for if and only if an expression denotes (it can be inferred from our assertions that an expression denotes), are we objectively (subjectively) ontologically committed to some entity or other.

As we have interpreted Quine's criterion so far, there seems to be nothing amiss. Quine, however, sometimes seems to think that the criterion is more powerful than it is. In "On What There Is," Quine claims, for example, that

5. Quine, pp. 7, 157.

logicism, a theory in the philosophy of mathematics, is committed to the same view on universals as medieval realism because it "condones the use of bound variables to refer to abstract entities known and unknown, specifiable and unspecifiable, indiscriminately." [6] But here Quine is claiming more than is justified on the basis of his criterion for ontological commitment. By his criterion, logicism is ontologically committed to whatever certain abstract terms denote or refer$_3$ to, if indeed they denote at all. But he cannot get from this premise to the conclusion that logicism is committed to abstract entities unless he provides another premise about what abstract terms denote, if they do denote. Thus, for example, only if an abstract term such as 'the number two' can be shown to *denote* the number two, or some such entity, can Quine reach the conclusion that logicism is ontologically committed to the same view about abstract entities as medieval realism. But if 'the number two' denotes, it might denote certain particulars rather than abstract entities. Or, if, as a logicist might, we define numbers as classes of classes, we are not thereby ontologically committed to classes by Quine's criterion. For all his criterion specifies is that a logicist is ontologically committed to whatever the expression 'class of classes' denotes. But the logicist may deny that this expression denotes, or he may claim that it denotes particulars, rather than abstract entities. This claim is certainly consistent with logicism unless Quine can establish the additional premises he needs to get from the fact that 'p' denotes something, i.e. from the fact that we are ontologically committed to whatever 'p' denotes, to the conclusion he desires, that we are ontologically committed to p (or p's).

In a later work, *Word and Object,* Quine draws the same kind of conclusion:

> We find philosophers allowing themselves not only abstract terms but even pretty unmistakable quantifica-

6. Quine, p. 14.

> tions over abstract objects ("There are concepts with which . . . ," ". . . some of which propositions . . . ," ". . . there is something that he doubts or believes"), and still blandly disavowing within the paragraph, any claim that there are such objects.[7]

The philosophers who assert sentences containing the phrases mentioned in the above quotation surely, as Quine says, use abstract terms and, what is more, at least imply that they are substituends for variables. But from a premise concerning commitments to the use of certain terms as substituends for variables, to infer the conclusion that we are ontologically committed to certain entities as the *values* of those variables is surely not legitimate without an additional premise concerning the reference of the substituends.

In the above quotations, Quine seems to be asserting that because certain philosophers have said or implied statements such as 'There are x's' or 'x's exist,' those men are ontologically committed to x's. Quine, then, seems to hold the view that I wish to refute in step 2. In order to see this view more clearly and to provide a more fruitful critical evaluation of it, let us put it in the form of a criterion of ontological commitment that is similar to—yet, as we shall see, importantly different from—Quine's. We can initially put such a criterion as follows:

> 1. A theory, T, is ontologically committed to an entity, E, if and only if 'E exists,' or some statement that logically implies 'E exists,' is used to make one of the affirmations of T.

If this criterion is correct, then any theory is ontologically committed to E merely because one of its assertions is or logically implies 'E exists.' Such a criterion differs from Quine's in two important ways. First, it makes no reference to values of variables or entities denoted; second, it is by

7. Quine, *Word and Object* (New York, M.I.T. Press, and John Wiley, 1960), p. 241.

itself sufficient for justifying Quine's claim that those who assert sentences such as 'There are concepts with which . . .' are ontologically committed to concepts and thereby to abstract entities. Quine may think that some such criterion is equivalent to his, but we shall see that none are because, although Quine's criterion provides a sufficient condition of ontological commitment, criteria such as 1 do not.

Let us examine the criterion. To find the mistake in it we need only remember the method of avoiding an ontological commitment to Pegasus considered earlier. There I utilized Russell's theory of descriptions to show that an assertion containing a term which seemingly denotes Pegasus could be paraphrased in such a way that there is no reason to think that there was any such reference to Pegasus. We can generalize this point, as does Quine, by saying that in any case where we can paraphrase a statement such as 'E exists' so that there is no reason to think that there is any reference to E, we are not ontologically committed to E. There is, then, at least one way to avoid the charge that we are ontologically committed to an entity, E, even when we assert 'E exists' or some statement which logically implies 'E exists.' For example, people sometimes assert statements such as 'Nothing exists now where once stood a thriving city.' Given the above criterion, it would follow that these people are ontologically committed to an abstract entity called "nothing." However we can paraphrase the expression 'nothing exists now' as 'there does not exist one thing now' which is an expression in which 'nothing' does not occur. Thus there is no reason to think I am referring to an entity called "nothing" when I assert the sentence and, as a result, no reason to think I am ontologically committed to this strange entity.

Thus this criterion will not do. It would ontologically commit us to more entities than there is any reason to think we should be committed to. This is, then, a criterion that does not provide a sufficient condition of ontological commitment. It follows that the view about ontology which states that a theory is ontologically committed to an entity E

merely because one of its assertions is or logically implies a sentence such as 'E exists' is mistaken. However, Quine's claims, which are correct if this criterion is acceptable, are not destroyed because this criterion fails. He stresses the importance of paraphrasing. We must stress it also if we are to find some way to avoid the above problems. We are not ontologically committed to entities in all cases in which we assert or imply a sentence of the form 'x exists,' but perhaps only in those cases in which we *must* assert—cannot avoid asserting—a sentence which is of that form or which logically implies one of that form, in order to say what we wish to say.

Let us now examine a criterion which accounts for this point. It would be expressed as follows:

2. A theory, T, is ontologically committed to an entity, E, if and only if 'E exists,' or some statement which logically implies 'E exists,' *must* be used to make one of the assertions of T.[8]

If this criterion is correct, then the ontological commitments of a theory do not follow merely from the assertions of the theory, but from those assertions which contain referring expressions that cannot be paraphrased away. It is, however, like the previous criterion in that it justifies Quine's claim concerning 'concepts' and abstract entities.

Criterion 2 also faces problems. If we take 'must' to express 'cannot be avoided in any way,' then sentences such as 'Hesperus exists' cause a problem. Although a theory using this sentence would seem to have an ontological commitment, it would not on criterion 2, because 'Venus exists,' which does not imply 'Hesperus exists,' can be used instead.[9] We can avoid this objection by taking 'must,' as we have

8. See W. Alston, "Ontological Commitments," *Philosophical Studies,* 9 (1958), 8–17, for a criterion of this kind.

9. The implication in criterion 2 must be logical, i.e. formal deducibility. If it were material, anyone who had to use a sentence which proves false would be committed to every value of 'x' in 'x exists.' If it were analytic entailment, we could not use meaning analysis, e.g. of 'nothing exists now,' to avoid commitment.

above, to express 'cannot be avoided by paraphrase,' but then the reverse of the 'Nothing exists' problem arises. We could paraphrase 'Venus exists' in a Quinean way as 'There is something which venusizes' which does not logically (tautologically) imply it. Thus again we would have no commitment regarding Venus. This is wrong. Criterion 2 fails on both interpretations of 'must.' Unlike the previously examined criterion, this one would not ontologically commit us to as many entities as it seems we should be committed to because this criterion does not provide a necessary condition of ontological commitment.

Is there any way to correct this second criterion in order to avoid the problem? It seems that any correction that will work must at least add to the disjunction on the right side of the criterion a disjunct such as "or some expression which refers to the same entity as 'E.' " More than this addition is needed to avoid all the problems such a criterion faces, but it is, I believe, necessary to avoid this one. However, because we have shown only that the second criterion does not supply a necessary condition of ontological commitment, there is still the possibility that it supplies a sufficient condition. This is all we require of a criterion, certainly all that is needed to support Quine's claim about 'concept' and the view I am trying to refute, my asserting 'E exists' (when I cannot paraphrase 'E' away) implies that I am ontologically committed to E. Let us consider, then:

3. If 'E exists,' or some statement that logically implies 'E exists,' must be used to make one of the assertions of a theory T then T is ontologically committed to E.

Let us also consider:

4. What 'E' denotes is F rather than E.

If 4 is true, then, even if T were to use 'E exists,' and it could not be paraphrased away, T would not be ontologically committed to E, but, instead, committed to F. Thus, because it is false that 4 conjoined with the antecedent of 3 implies that T is ontologically committed to E, then 3 is false.

It may be objected here that 4 is self-contradictory and therefore, because it entails any statement, entails both that T is and that T is not ontologically committed to E, with the consequence that 4 cannot be used to prove 3 false. It is true that we have found that " 'E' refers to E" taken as a designation rule is analytic, so if " 'E' does not denote E" is interpreted as " 'E' denotes something, but it is false that 'E' refers$_1$ to E," where the second conjunct is a designation rule, then it is self-contradictory. But we also found that such rules are formal rules, and we are here interested in theories of reference which involve nonformal rules, the kind of rules we have seen philosophers such as Carnap and Feigl need when they discuss what 'five' and 'sensation' refer to. And because no claim about the relationship between a linguistic expression and reality is self-contradictory, 4 as we are construing it is not self-contradictory. It might instead be objected that 4 and the antecedent of 3 are inconsistent when conjoined, so that although together they entail that T is committed to F, they also entail that T is committed to E. However, I see no reason to think this, unless 4 is self-contradictory, which we have just rejected because 4 entails " 'E' denotes something," which entails 'E exists.'

We can, I think, conclude that 3 is false, and, therefore, that 2 provides neither a sufficient nor a necessary condition of ontological commitment. How might we change 3 so that it is correct? Remembering that 4 and the antecedent of 3 entail that T is ontologically committed to F, we can try:

> 5. If 'E exists,' or some statement that logically implies 'E exists,' is (must be) used to make an assertion of T and what 'E' denotes is E, then T is ontologically committed to E.

However, although 5 correctly states a sufficient condition of ontological commitment, this formulation concedes me the point I wish to establish, that some premise involving a theory of reference is needed to make an inference from what is (or must be) asserted to a conclusion about ontological commitment. The only way that I can find to avoid nonformal rules and thereby, perhaps, a theory of reference is by realizing that the nonformal rule 4 entails the formal rule " 'E' refers$_2$ to F," which we have seen previously is equivalent to " 'E' refers$_2$ to what 'F' refers$_2$ to." Thus we might add to the antecedent of 3:

6. There is no expression not synonymous with 'E' that refers$_2$ to what 'E' refers$_2$ to.

This results in the sense of 'cannot be avoided' we need:

7. If 'E exists,' or some statement that logically implies 'E exists,' is used to make an assertion of T, and there is no expression not synonymous with 'E' that refers$_2$ to what 'E' refers$_2$ to, then T is ontologically committed to E.

This new addition, 6, when generalized, becomes what I shall call, modifying one of Ryle's phrases, the 'Fido'–Fido theory of reference.[10] This is the theory that for any referring$_2$ expression, 'p,' it is true that 'p' refers$_2$ to what 'p' refers$_2$ to, but for any other expression, 'q,' if 'q' is not synonymous with 'p,' then it is false that 'q' refers$_2$ to what 'p' refers$_2$ to. Although 7 expresses a sufficient condition of ontological commitment, and 6, which I have added to the antecedent of 3 to form 7, is not the statement of a nonformal rule, there are two reasons why I still want to claim that 7 involves us in a theory of reference. First, 6 entails the denial of the nonformal rule 4; second, the antecedent of 7 entails that if 'E' denotes, what 'E' denotes is E. Furthermore, if the justification of the addition in 7 is, as I assume it would be, that the 'Fido'–Fido theory of reference is correct, then we can reject 7—without, incidentally, hav-

10. See Gilbert Ryle, "Meaning and Necessity," *Philosophy*, *24* (1949), 69–76.

ing to reject 5—for the English language at least, because for English as ordinarily used we have more than one non-synonymous expression that denotes the same entity: 'Hesperus,' 'Phosphorus,' and 'Venus' all denote the same entity.

However, regardless of what I have claimed about what was added to 3 to form 7, we can conclude that because some nonanalytic reference rule, whether formal or non-formal, must be added to the antecedent of 3 to provide a sufficient condition of ontological commitment, we cannot infer ontological commitments from statements that assert that something exists. This is the point I have been trying to make in step 2. Part of the reason for this seems to be that in the language we have been using, English, we are not committed to talking in any one way about what there is. The objections to the first three criteria we examined were based on this fact, although it was used differently in each case. The objection to 1 involved the fact that we can paraphrase expressions; the objections to 2 and 3 involved the fact that several nonsynonymous expressions can be used to refer to the same thing. In English, as in other languages, we are permitted to use several expressions to talk about what there is; the choice is up to us.

However, the above conclusion may not bother the person who accepts any of the first three criteria we have discussed. He might well say that the problems arise not because there is something wrong with the criteria but because there is something wrong with the English language as ordinarily used. If there were a language such that one and only one of its expressions denoted each entity, then the users of that language would be committed to use one particular expression to denote each thing they wish to talk about; the choice of expressions would not be up to them. Thus for this language no additional premise about linguistic reference would be needed to infer validly from assertions to ontological commitments. We could in such a language read off a theory's ontological commitments directly from its assertions. For such an "ideal" language, then, all of the first three criteria would work.[11] But should we infer from this that in this case nothing but such criteria are necessary for finding ontological commitments? Let us see.

Suppose that someone constructed or discovered a language, S, which he claimed was "ideal." Suppose further that this language contained both sensation-expressions and brain-process expressions. Should we conclude that, at least for S, Feigl's identity thesis is wrong and that we are ontologically committed to both brain-processes and sensations, or should we conclude that S is not "ideal"? Or suppose that S contained brain-process expressions but not sensationexpressions. Should we conclude that sensation-expressions are unnecessary for an "ideal" language, or should we conclude that S is not "ideal"? In neither case would we know what to conclude unless the "inventor" or "discoverer" established his claim about S. But how could he do this? First, he would have to show that what I have called the 'Fido'–Fido theory of reference applies to all the denoting expressions of S. If this 'Fido'–Fido theory of reference were true of S, then if an expression 'p' denotes something, it could denote only one thing, p, and thus we would be ontologically committed to p if we asserted 'p exists.' Secondly, he would have to show that those denoting expressions of other languages that denote but which are not in S, denote entities which are denoted by some denoting expressions which are in S.

It is then necessary, in order to justify a claim that a language is "ideal," to show that one particular theory of reference applies to the language, i.e. the 'Fido'–Fido theory of reference. From this we can conclude that for the purposes of ontology there is no essential difference between an "ideal" language such as S, and "nonideal" language such as ordinary English. In both cases some premise about the reference of expressions of the language is needed in order to draw conclusions about ontological commitments. The

11. See Russell in his introduction to the *Tractatus*, p. 9, for a discussion of such an "ideal" language.

only difference is that whereas in the latter case the premise concerning linguistic reference is needed to justify the inference from assertions to ontological commitments, in the former case it is needed to justify the claim that the language in which the assertions are made is "ideal." Thus somewhere or other such a premise is necessary for any inference from language to ontological commitments. No language, whether S or any other, has a privileged position with regard to ontological commitments because for S, as for all the others, we would have the task of finding the relation between language and reality. And although the relation for S may be different from that for another language, the task is no easier. We are, then, no more ontologically committed to any entities just by adopting S, than we are if we use English. In both cases what results in our being ontologically committed to certain entities is not the language we use, but the theory of reference we apply to the language. This is true because only if we apply a certain theory of reference to a language can we arrive at the conclusion that we are not merely permitted to use a certain denoting expression to assert something, but are actually committed to use it.

The consequences of the above conclusion for the matters with which we are presently concerned are twofold: because none of the first three criteria of ontological commitment we have examined are by themselves correct, all at least require some addition involving a theory of reference; Quine cannot justify his claims that logicism and those who assert 'There are concepts with which . . .' are ontologically committed to abstract entities unless he justifies the 'Fido'–Fido theory of reference, or at least some instance of the theory. This is because his inference is valid without an additional premise about linguistic reference only if a criterion like one of the first three is itself sufficient. But we have just seen that no such criterion is sufficient. Thus Quine's claim is no better substantiated than the claim of his "Meinongian" opponents. Both have, in fact, made the same basic mistake.

Quine's opponents, as we have seen, seem to think that we are ontologically committed to entities such as Pegasus and unicorns, and Quine thinks certain people are ontologically committed to entities such as concepts. What accounts for this difference is that while Quine's opponents claim that all denoting expressions denote in some sense, e.g. that all expressions which are substituends for variables denote, Quine believes that only those expressions denote which are substituends for variables we must bind in order to make true assertions. But, as we have seen, we cannot get from either of these two positions about which expressions denote to the views these men hold about ontological commitments without some additional premise concerning linguistic reference. Common to both views—the point at which they can be criticized—is that they are based on what neither has substantiated, the 'Fido'–Fido theory of reference, a theory no more obviously correct for one language than for any other. In fact, as we have seen, it is surely incorrect for ordinary English. Thus whether or not it is true of any particular language is surely debatable; and from what we have seen concerning theories of reference, any attempt to justify it would seem to be at best a difficult task. The conclusion we reached when working with the English language still seems to be good when generalized to include all languages, whether "ideal" or not. In order to be valid, any inference from a premise that asserts or implies that some specific thing exists to a conclusion about a specific ontological commitment requires an additional nontrivial premise about linguistic reference. From this, the conclusion I have been trying to justify in step 2 follows. Although from " 'p' denotes" we can infer that p exists, we cannot validly infer in addition whether or not any particular ontological theory about what 'p' denotes is true.

Before we move on to step 3, let me point out how far we have come toward resolution of our paradox. It follows from the conclusion of step 2 that my asserting 'p exists' does not by itself entail that I am ontologically committed

to *p,* and, conversely, that my denying that I am ontologically committed to *p* does not entail my denying that *p*
exists. This logical wedge between existence and ontology
may perhaps show us the beginning of a way to resolve the
paradox. Those who are interested in the mind–body problem and other ontological problems can be understood as
asking about ontological commitments. However without
that wedge, if the conclusion to step 2 were false, then there
would be two serious consequences for the matters that
concern us here. First, and more importantly, it would be
impossible to resolve the paradox because being able to infer
the answer to the philosopher's question from the answer
to the nonphilosopher's question is not consistent with the
claim that the latter answer is easy to discover while the
former is most difficult if not impossible. Secondly, certain
ontological positions would be self-contradictory. It would
be impossible to admit that there are sensations but to claim
that we are not ontologically committed to sensations because the ontological position of materialism is true. An
identity theorist such as Smart might wish to make such a
claim, but unless the conclusion of step 2 is true, such a
claim is self-contradictory.

We have completed the discussion of step 2 and have
found some reason to think that the paradox might be
resolved by showing that question 1 when asked by philosophers is different from what it is when asked by nonphilosophers. But just what is the nature of these two different
questions, and what is the difference between them? We
must move on to step 3.

STEP 3

I have talked about being permitted rather than committed to use certain expressions in English. The concept
of being permitted by a language is central; it embodies an
essential point I have used in the argument against Quine's
views on ontological commitment. As such, it is also a
phrase essential to resolving the paradox. Therefore in order

to proceed we must unpack this expression, which, as we shall see, will take some long and involved work. That this examination is essential to our purpose can be further emphasized by noting that we are primarily interested in finding what it is to be permitted or forbidden to use a certain expression to refer to something. When put this way we can see that we have returned to the question we left unanswered at the beginning of Chapter 4. At that point I claimed that what I meant by " 'p' refers to q" could be expressed by "It is correct to use 'p' to refer to q," but I left until later the discussion of the word 'correct.' Now we can begin this discussion. By coming to understand what it is for a language to permit or forbid certain uses of expressions we shall be able to make clearer what it means to say that certain uses are correct and others are incorrect in the sense of 'correct' and 'incorrect' relevant to ontology. Once we have completed this examination of language, we shall not only be able to explain away the paradox but be prepared, finally, to see what we must do if we are to be able to answer the question posed at the beginning of this part of the book, question 1, "What does the linguistic expression, 'p,' refer to?" and to see what sort of problem the mind–body problem is.

Let us begin with a well-known analogy. A language, L, is in many ways much like the game of chess. In chess we are permitted to make certain moves in any given situation; we are forbidden to make others; we are committed to none. What is permitted or forbidden in chess is told us by the rules governing the moves of each piece. If we want to know whether this move by this piece in a given situation is permitted, we consult the rules for the piece. Such rules tell us how many spaces and in what directions the piece can move, whether and how it can jump and take other pieces. For each piece, then, there is what we can call an area of permitted moves. This area is demarcated by the rules—it is rule-bound. The set of rules for each piece marks off the boundaries of the kinds of moves it is permitted to make. Thus there is what we can call a pattern or network of moves any given chess piece is sanctioned to make by the rules which govern it. This pattern of moves is what I shall call the chess framework of the piece, and the rules which generate it are the rules of the framework. We can also talk about the framework of chess. The framework of chess consists of the framework of permitted moves of all the pieces. Thus it consists of all the frameworks of its pieces. It is generated by the set of rules governing all the chess pieces.

To say, then, that in chess a certain move is permitted is to say that it is a move within the framework of chess; it is a correct chess move, one which fits the pattern generated by the rules governing the piece in question. Thus we are committed by chess to do something only in this sense: if we are to move a certain piece, the move we choose must fit the pattern of moves; it must be within the framework of that piece. But we are not committed to any particular move unless the situation is such that there is only one move possible for that piece which fits the framework. However, what commits us here is not the chess framework but the existing state of chess affairs, what there is in this particular game of chess.

In a like manner we can say about a certain language, L, that using certain expressions in certain situations (making certain language moves) is in some cases permitted and in others forbidden. For each expression of L, then, there is an area of permitted or correct use marked off by the set of rules of L governing that expression. Thus there is a pattern or network of ways in which it is correct to use each expression, and this pattern is sanctioned by the rules. As with chess we can call such a pattern the linguistic framework of the expression, and the rules which generate the framework the rules of the framework. The linguistic framework of L, accordingly, consists of the frameworks of all the expressions which make up L; the linguistic framework of L is generated by the set of rules governing the expressions of L.

I must now indicate what the kinds of rules of the linguistic framework of a given expression, '*p*,' are. Since these are rules which govern the use of '*p*,' they would seem to be the kind of rules we could discover by an investigation of the ways in which '*p*' is used. In chess, again, the rules of the chess framework of a given piece are the rules which govern the moves of that piece. We could discover them by watching chess games and observing which moves of the piece are allowed and which are not allowed, and by asking about or trying out certain moves which we think might be permitted on the basis of what we have observed. The answer or response we would get would help us discover what we want. After such observation, questioning, and experimenting we could conceivably list the set of rules of the chess framework of that piece; and by doing this for all the chess pieces we could discover the framework of chess itself.

We could do a similar thing for '*p*,' and thus for the language it is a part of. By observing, questioning, and experimenting we could find the permitted ways to use '*p*' and thus discover the rules governing its use.[12] The rules we could discover by investigating the use of an expression are basically of two different kinds. One kind expresses the logical, and, for some people, the quasi-logical relationships the expression has—relationships such as what it entails, what entails it, what it implies or presupposes in various contexts of its use, what are its equivalents or near equivalents, in what contexts it is odd to use it, and in what contexts it is odd to question its use. The other kind of rules are what I have called reference, or designation, rules because they express certain referential relationships of an expression. As we have seen in the previous discussion of Ayer's

---

12. See Rudolf Carnap, *Meaning and Necessity*, pp. 233–47.

position, these rules could be expressed as formal rules such as: " '*p*' refers to what '*q*' refers to."

However, we should note here a difference between chess and a natural language. We can discover the rules of a natural language only by an investigation of the language. For chess, however, the rules are laid down. In this respect chess is closer to a constructed semantical system than a natural language. For both chess and a semantical system, the rules are originally constructed, not discovered, but this is not true of a natural language. It is in some sense given to us rather than constructed by us or anyone else. However I do not believe this difference affects the point of our analogy. There is nothing in principle wrong with approaching chess as a "natural" game, rather than a constructed game. Indeed there are some games played according to rules for which there are no rules laid down. Such games just grow as language does; they are not constructed. We can find out how to play them only by watching others and by trying various moves until we learn what is permitted and what is forbidden. This is, for example, the way—and in many cases the only way—someone can learn to play certain children's games. Yet children do learn to play such games.

But this difference points to another which to some may seem relevant to the purposes of our analogy. Chess and semantical systems are constructed so that there is no area of doubt about the permissibility of certain moves or uses. Natural games and languages, however, lack this precision because they are not constructed but evolve somewhat randomly. It is possible, then, and indeed for some it appears evident, that the rules we could discover about such games and languages would leave areas of correct use undetermined. I do not think that this difference is relevant to our purposes. We are using the analogy of the chess game not because it is chess, but because it is a game. We are comparing language with a game, and chess is a helpful example. We could just as well, although not so easily, have used basketball, or hide and seek, or some other game in which new rules are continually made to fill gaps in the framework of the game as situations, not previously covered by the rules, arise. Thus this difference between language and chess provides no reason why we should stop using the language–chess analogy. Nor do I think there are any further differences relevant to our purposes for using the analogy.

Since we have found no reason yet to discard the chess analogy, let us press it further. We can distinguish between two kinds of questions concerning chess pieces. Following Carnap's terminology in his article "Empiricism, Semantics, and Ontology," we can say that there are internal and external questions about such a piece which we shall call k.[13] An internal question about k is one whose answer comes under the jurisdiction of, or is covered by, the rules of the chess framework governing k. Thus an answer to an internal question is one which is sanctioned or prohibited (that is, wrong, according to the rules) by the rules of chess. An external question about k, however, is one whose answer is not under the jurisdiction of the rules of chess governing k. We can go further and distinguish between two kinds of internal and two kinds of external questions about k. The two kinds of internal questions about k are:

I,1. Questions whose answers not only are under the jurisdiction of the rules of the framework which govern k, but also can be found merely by consulting those rules.

I,2. Questions whose answers, although under the jurisdiction of the rules of the framework governing k, cannot be found merely by consulting those rules but require some kind of additional investigation as indicated by the rules.

The two kinds of external questions about k are:

13. Ibid., see pp. 205–21 concerning this distinction. My distinction, although derived from Carnap's, is somewhat different.

E,1. Questions whose answers lie outside the jurisdiction of the rules governing k, but are such that certain answers to them would entail a change in or addition to the rules governing k.[14]

E,2. Questions whose answers lie outside the jurisdiction of the rules governing k, but are such that none of the answers to them would entail a change in or addition to the rules governing k.

To see that there are these four kinds of questions about chess pieces, let us consider an example of each. The questions, "What is a chess king?" and "What does the expression 'chess king' refer to?" are examples of a type I,1 question when they can be answered merely by consulting the rules of the chess framework governing chess kings. For such questions an appropriate answer might be that it is (refers to) an object which can move in such and such ways on a chess board, can be castled, can be put in check, etc. We find this out merely by consulting the appropriate chess rules, assuming here, as throughout this discussion, that we are consulting rules expressed in a language we understand.

An example of a type I,2 question would be, "Is the black king in check?" The answer to this would come under the jurisdiction of certain rules of the chess framework because such rules would tell us what must be the case for a king to be in check. But consulting the rules is not enough in this case because we must in addition investigate the particular chess situation to see whether it fits the pattern generated by the rules governing the checking of kings.

A question we can use for an example of type E,1 question is, "Should we allow kings to move three spaces?" In asking this question we are asking whether we should change a particular feature of the chess framework, that is, change certain rules of the framework. Obviously this is an external

14. This is the one type of external question that Carnap considers. See pp. 205–21, esp. pp. 213–15.

question because the rules governing chess kings have no
jurisdiction here. And since we are considering a possible
rule change, this is a type E,1 question. Our answer would
have to be decided pragmatically by considering what best
suits what we take to be the purpose of the game of chess.
If we were to think that such a change would, for example,
result in a more intricate and challenging game, we might
possibly accept it. It would be a change in the framework
of the game and would thus make the game in some sense
a different game from the one with the old framework,
although in both cases we would be playing with the same
purpose in mind. Furthermore, it is plain, I think, that
such a change would affect answers to internal questions but
need not affect answers to any other external question.

A question used as an example of a type I,1 question can
also be interpreted so that it is an example of a type E,2
question. Thus if the kind of answer we are looking for to
the question, "What does the expression 'chess king' refer
to?" is one which describes the general characteristics of
certain chess pieces such as their general size, shape, and
material, then it would be a type E,2 question. Its answer
does not come under the jurisdiction of the rules of the chess
framework governing chess kings. No answer is either sanctioned or prohibited by these rules, although any answer
would come under the jurisdiction of the rules of some
other framework. Furthermore, an answer to this question
does not entail a change in the rules of chess. Thus the
question is a type E,2 question.

If the analogy between chess and language is to continue
to hold, it would seem that there would likewise be internal
questions of two types and, contrary to Carnap on whose
view there are only type E,1 external questions about language, external questions of two types concerning the
"pieces" which we use to play a language-game. As with
chess we can say that an internal question about such a
"piece," i.e. an element of language, would be one the
answer to which is under the jurisdiction of the rules of the

linguistic framework governing it. An external question would be one whose answer is not under the jurisdiction of those rules. Let us find examples of each of the four kinds of questions.

Using the English language, E, an example of a type I,1 question, would be: "What does the expression 'chess king' refer to?" We have previously found that when a proper kind of answer involves a description of the general physical characteristics of certain chess pieces then this question is external to the chess framework. However, it is a question internal to E because there are rules of E governing the answers. In the case of "What does the expression 'chess king' refer to?" there are designation rules of E governing which names and descriptions refer to whatever 'chess king' refers to. Furthermore, just such rules would function as answers to this question. That is, the question would be answered by a sentence of the form, "The expression 'chess king' refers to what 'p' refers to." Thus this is a type I,1 question for E because we can find the answer merely by consulting the appropriate designation rules of E.

An example of a type I,2 question for E would be, "Are there any chess kings?" or "Does the expression 'chess king' denote anything?" In order to answer this question we would have to follow rules like the ones used to answer the type I,1 question for E. And because chess kings are physical objects we would also have to use the rules governing 'physical object.' This is, then, an internal question. But such rules cannot by themselves provide us with an answer, for we must do more than merely consult the rules. We must also make an empirical investigation to try to find an object which meets the requirements expressed in the rules. Thus the question is an example of a type I,2 question concerning E.

For an example of a type E,1 question which according to Carnap includes all metaphysical questions, we can use, "Should we use the expression 'castled pawn' in E?" Here we are concerned with deciding whether to accept or change

certain rules of the linguistic framework of E. Thus if someone proposes to introduce a new expression into E or to
change the use of an old one, there is always the question
of whether there is any reason why we should use the new
or changed expression. The proper kind of answer to such a
question would be a practical one, based on a consideration
of the purposes for using E, and especially that part of E
directly relevant to the new or changed expression. If we
found out that introducing the new or changing the old
expression was better suited to the relevant purposes for
using E, if, for example, such a change made E more fruitful and efficient, and simpler to use in achieving those purposes, then we would have grounds for making the change.
Obviously such a question is an external one for E not
only because the rules of the framework of E have no
jurisdiction over any answer we give concerning the expression in question, but also because it is concerned with a possible change in the rules. Thus this is a type E,1 question.
Furthermore it is plain that, as with chess, such a change
in the framework of E will affect answers to those internal
questions governed by the changed or added rules, but need
not affect answers to any other external questions.

So far the language-chess analogy seems to hold in the
area in which we are interested. As we have laid out the
four types of questions there seem to be no a priori reasons
for denying that there is a type E,2 question for a language
just as there is for a game such as chess. It seems then, that
it is at least initially plausible that there are some type E,2
questions for a language. Now I wish to show that the kind
of problems with which we are concerned, and thus the
kind of questions we have been examining, can plausibly
be construed as being type E,2 questions.

We have seen questions of the form of question 1 as
relevant to ontological problems such as the mind–body
problem and the problem of the nature of the external
world. We can begin our investigation of such a question by
recalling the question used as an example of a type E,2

question for chess and a type I,1 question for English, i.e. "What does 'chess king' refer to?" We have seen that this question can be answered by stating a relevant designation rule of English. But consider how Berkeley might have answered such a question. Through Philonous he claimed that a cherry "is nothing but a congeries of sensible impressions, or ideas perceived by various senses."[15] For our purposes we could have a modern Berkeley say that 'chess king' refers to a bundle of sense-data. Could this ontological claim be an answer to an internal question of either type? It does not seem to be an answer to a type I,1 question because we cannot find such an answer merely by consulting the rules of the framework of 'chess king' which we learn both by observing the use of and by using that expression. It does not seem to be an answer to a type I,2 question either, because the designation rules relevant to 'chess king' seem to provide no information about how to evaluate the Berkeleian kind of answer. The kind of investigation relevant to type I,2 questions about 'chess king,' is an empirical investigation to find out whether anything meets the requirements of the rules, but this seems to be completely irrelevant. Thus it seems that the rules of the linguistic framework of 'chess king' will not help answer the ontological question. They do not apply; they have no jurisdiction at all. Consequently the question is neither a type I,1 nor a type I,2 question. It is an external question.

Here someone might object that although there is good reason to think that the ontological question is not a type I,2 question because no empirical investigation is relevant, the reason for deciding that Berkeley's answer was not an answer to a type I,1 question will not do. Indeed, Berkeley's answer should be considered a wrong answer to a type I,1 question because it violates the linguistic framework of 'chess king,' which refers to enduring, mind-independent entities while 'sense-data' refers to mind-dependent entities.

15. Berkeley, *Three Dialogues between Hylas and Philonous,* C. M. Turbayne, ed. (New York, The Liberal Arts Press, 1954), p. 97.

I do not know whether or not such claims about the reference of 'chess king' and 'sense-data' are derivable from rules of the linguistic frameworks of the two expressions (although I think that they are not), but even if such claims are so derivable, there is still reason to think that Berkeley was answering an external question. His dictum that we should "think with the learned and speak with the vulgar" might, in our terms, be transformed into the claim that in everyday conversation we should function within the frameworks of the languages we use, but that when functioning as philosophers in search of what there is we must go outside these frameworks. Furthermore, if Berkeley's claim is *obviously* false when interpreted as an answer to a type I, I question, then we should see whether there is some other way to interpret it which would make his position more plausible. This requires that we interpret it as an answer to an external question.

We have, then, some reason to consider the ontological question to be an external question. So far we are in agreement with Carnap. However, from this he infers that it is a type E,I question because he recognizes no other kind of external question. We shall, later, consider the reasons Carnap seems to have for recognizing only one kind of external question, but, leaving those aside for the moment, there seems to be no good reason to think that the above question is one about whether to change or adopt or keep a certain expression in a language. It seems to be a question which accepts that there is in English an expression, 'chess king,' whose use is governed by certain rules; it seems to be asking about the reference of *this* expression of *this* language, but it is asking this in a certain way. A nonphilosopher asking a question about what an expression refers to can be answered within the framework, by means of other expressions which according to the logical or designation rules of the framework either mean or refer to the same thing. Such answers inform him of other ways in which he is permitted by the appropriate rules to talk about what there is, and thus do not involve him with external questions. As we have seen, however, the philosophical question about 'chess king' cannot be satisfactorily answered from within the framework. It is an external question, and because answers to it such as Berkeley's accept the rules governing the expression, i.e. in no way imply a change in or addition to those rules, the ontological question does not seem to be a type E,1 question.[16] We have, then, an example of an ontological question that seems to be a type E,2 question.

We have now seen three different questions that can be expressed as "What does 'chess king' refer to?" and which can be interpreted as "What is it correct to use 'chess king' to refer to?" One was an I,1 question, the second was an I,2 question, and the third was an E,2 question. Their differences can be stated as differences among three different kinds of linguistic correctness. Let me state these differences; by so doing we shall at last answer that question asked at the beginning of the previous chapter about the kind of linguistic correctness relevant to ontological problems. We are interested in three different senses of "It is correct to use 'p' to refer to q." The first sense which is equivalent to the designation rule, " 'p' refers$_1$ to q," can be stated as:

> Using 'p' to refer to q is sanctioned by the rules of the linguistic framework of 'p.'

The second sense which is equivalent to " 'p' denotes q" can be stated as:

> Using 'p' to refer to q is sanctioned by the rules of the linguistic framework of 'p,' and 'p exists' is true.

16. This characterization of Berkeley also seems to differ from Strawson, whose view is something like Carnap's because he calls Berkeley a "revisionary metaphysician," that is, someone who attempts to reconstruct the structure of our conceptual framework. See *Individuals*, p. 9.

However the third sense, the sense relevant to ontological questions, is not so easy to characterize. But let us turn again to the chess analogy for help: in the case of the chess framework we could say that the answer to the type $E,2$ question about 'chess king' is not under the jurisdiction of the rules of the chess framework but is under the jurisdiction of certain rules outside the chess framework, namely the rules of the framework of English. Thus it is sanctioned by certain rules outside the chess framework. What corresponds to rules outside of the linguistic framework? If we remember that the rules of the linguistic framework are all formal rules, then it seems that what we are looking for are nonformal rules. Thus we can state the third sense of "It is correct to use 'p' to refer to q'' as:

> 'p exists' is true, and using 'p' to refer to q is sanctioned by (and perhaps only by) the nonformal rules of language relevant to 'p.'

It seems, then, that if there are rules that sanction ontological reference claims, they are nonformal rules, rules that connect linguistic expressions with reality. Thus they seem to function as Wittgenstein's rules of projection. But, it might be claimed, rules of projection are mysterious things, so mysterious that perhaps we should conclude that there are none. Let me sidestep this problem here by interpreting these three senses of " 'p' refers to q'' in another way. I shall emphasize two factors in order to bring out the distinction: that the internal senses are formal rules, and that we are interested in ontology and ontological commitment. Because of the second factor we are interested in referring$_3$ or denoting, because we can say that 'p' denotes something if and only if 'p' ontologically commits its users to something. Incidentally this does not conflict with the previous conclusion that no language by itself ontologically commits its users because 'p' denotes something and thus ontologically commits us only if what 'p' refers$_1$ to exists, and whether this is so depends not on language but on what

there is. Because of the first factor the internal senses of
" 'p' refers to q" are logically equivalent to " 'p' refers to
what 'q' refers to." Let me now state the three senses as
follows:

1. 'p' refers$_1$ to what 'q' refers$_1$ to.
2. 'p' refers$_1$ to what 'q' refers$_1$ to, and what 'p' refers$_1$
   to exists, i.e. 'p' ontologically commits us to what
   'q' ontologically commits us.
3. What 'p' ontologically commits us to is q.

Statements 1 and 2 are internal statements, for 1 is a
designation rule and 2 is sanctioned by 1 and by what there
is. Statement 3 we shall interpret as an external statement,
and thus it is not under the jurisdiction of any of the rules
of the linguistic framework of 'p.' Thus we can say that
what 'p' ontologically commits us to is not p, but rather q.
If we were to assert this using an internal statement we
would contradict ourselves because we would have to say
that what 'p' ontologically commits us to is not what 'p'
ontologically commits us to. This point is relevant to the
problem we saw facing Smart and other ontological reductionists. Someone such as Smart would agree that 'sensation' denotes, and that 'sensation' refers$_1$ to what 'sensation' refers$_1$ to, from which we could deduce that 'sensation' denotes what 'sensation' denotes. But Smart would
also want to claim that 'sensation,' although it denotes, does
not ontologically commit us to sensations but rather to brain
processes. If this claim were an internal statement, it would
entail that 'sensation' does not ontologically commit us to
what 'sensation' ontologically commits us to, and Smart
would be faced with the kind of contradiction which he
and other ontological reductionists can avoid by construing
their claims as we did Berkeley's, i.e. as external.

We have found above an example of each of the four
types of questions about elements of language. We have
concluded that, as for chess, there seem to be for a given
language two types of internal questions and two types of

external questions. With these distinctions in mind we are now ready to resolve the paradox set forth at the beginning of the chapter. The paradox arose because it seemed that we could conclude from the discussion in Chapter 4 that we cannot answer question 1 by using designation rules and ostensive answers, whereas it seems to be perfectly obvious that we can answer question 1 in this way. We are, then, ready to move on to step 4.

Before we do so, let me clear up two problems left unresolved in Chapter 4, where I stated that there were good reasons for claiming that rules such as " '*p*' refers to *q*" were formal designation rules, and also that there were good reasons for claiming that they were not formal rules. We are now able to see how this can be so. Designation rules are formal rules because they are internal statements, while the rules required by men such as Carnap, Feigl, and Ryle are neither designation rules nor formal rules, because they are external statements, and thus are not under the jurisdiction of the rules of the linguistic framework of '*p*.' It is because all such reference rules have generally been thought to be both designation rules and nonformal rules that the claims of Carnap and other ontological reductionists have seemed to verge upon self-contradiction. But because certain reference rules are external statements we can say both that there are good reasons to call internal reference rules—designation rules—formal rules, and that there are good reasons to call external reference rules nonformal rules.

I also said in Chapter 4 that I would later explain the sense in which necessary truths such as D: " 'Russia' in this language refers to Russia," are contingent. We can now see that given the framework of the English language, D is necessarily true, but that it is a contingent fact that English has the framework it has; indeed, it is even contingent that there is any linguistic framework at all. But when we ask whether a sentence is analytic, we are asking an internal question and thus can conclude that if it is analytic, it is necessarily true. But because which internal expressions are analytic sentences depends upon contingent facts about the relevant linguistic framework, we can also make the external claim that all analytic truths are contingent. With these two problems solved, we can return to the task at hand, step 4.

STEP 4

We can resolve the paradox facing us by concentrating on three claims we have already established:

(i) Question 1 as an internal question about what an expression denotes can be answered either by ostensive answers or by formal reference sentences.

(ii) Question 1 as an external question about what an expression denotes can be answered neither by ostensive answers nor by formal reference sentences.

(iii) Question 1, when asked for the purpose for which we have asked it, i.e. to help us solve the traditional mind–body problem, is an external question.

Let us consider claim (i). If question 1 is an internal question about what 'p' denotes, then, as we have seen, the answer to it comes under the jurisdiction of the rules of the linguistic framework of 'p.' Such an answer can be expressed as " 'p' denotes what 'q' denotes," which is a formal reference sentence. The other kind of answer to question 1 as internal is an ostensive answer such as " 'p' denotes *that*," said while indicating something. Although such an answer takes us outside the linguistic framework, it does so only in the sense that it involves more than language. But an answer to an external question is outside the framework in a different way—it lies beyond the jurisdiction of the rules of the framework. This is not true for an ostensive answer because just what kind of thing we are permitted to indicate ostensively is under the jurisdiction of the rules governing '*p*.' That is, if and only if we obey the rules of the framework of '*p*' do we employ the various permitted uses of '*p*' correctly, i.e. do we correctly call something '*p,*' whether or not we ostensively indicate it. If we do not know what is required in order to obey the rules, we would not know even what kind of thing to indicate. Therefore, ostensive answers are answers to question 1 when it is an internal question.

Having established claim (i), let us examine claim (ii). We might begin to establish it by saying that since formal reference sentences and ostensive answers are answers to 1 as an internal question, they come under the jurisdiction of the framework rules governing '*p*' and as such are not relevant to answers to an external question. But we can go beyond this by considering what kind of answer is required for 1 as an external question. We have interpreted 1 as an external question as, "What does '*p*' ontologically commit us to?" A satisfactory answer to this question is one which states what this is. Ostensive answers cannot do this because even if they imply that we are ontologically committed to whatever is indicated, they do not tell us what this is, as an answer to an external question must do. Thus ostensive answers cannot answer external questions. Similarly, no answers to question 1 as external are formal reference sentences because the most that a formal reference sentence can tell us is that certain expressions do or do not ontologically commit us to the same thing. But this does not tell us what we are ontologically committed to, as a satisfactory external answer must do. For example, we have seen that if Smart's answer about what 'sensation' denotes is a formal reference sentence, then it is not sufficient to decide the issue between a materialist, idealist, and neutral monist. Thus formal reference sentences are not sufficient to answer question 1 as external.

Claim (iii) is easily established by turning again to Smart as an example of someone interested in question 1 when it is asked for the purpose of solving the traditional mind–body problem. We have seen that for Smart's purpose, question 1 is external. Therefore it is external for our purposes.

We can now resolve the paradox easily. Formal reference sentences and ostensive answers can be used to answer question 1 when it is an internal question about what an expression denotes but not when it is an external question. But since question 1 is external when asked for the purposes for which we have asked it, i.e. as relevant to the traditional mind–body problem, formal reference sentences and ostensive answers cannot be used to answer 1 when asked for purposes such as ours. We have, then, resolved the paradox by distinguishing two species of question 1 and by showing what considerations are relevant to each. Thus because when we ordinarily use language, when we function as nonphilosophers, we are operating within some linguistic framework, i.e. when "we speak with the vulgar," our questions are internal ones. In such cases there is no trouble for us to find out what expressions refer to, and thus to know what we are talking about. A nonphilosopher asking about what an expression refers to is answered within the framework by means of other expressions which refer to or mean the same thing, or by ostensive answers. Such answers enable him to understand what he is talking about without becoming involved in external philosophical problems. In other words, such answers inform him of how he is permitted by his language to talk about what there is, but, in one sense, they do not tell him what there is. The philosopher "who thinks with the learned" is asking about what there is regardless of which language we use, and for this the kind of answers which satisfy the nonphilosopher will not do. Unlike the nonphilosopher, he is interested in a type E,2 external question.

In this chapter we have not only resolved a paradox left with us from Chapter 4, but we have also reinforced the arguments of Chapter 4 that designation rules and ostensive answers will not do for our purposes. But before we draw any final conclusions, let us turn to those reasons I attributed to Carnap for recognizing only type E,1 external questions because, obviously, if the reasons are sound then the claim that there are type E,2 questions although initially plausible would, in the last analysis, be incorrect.

Carnap's view, briefly, is that what appear to be type E,2 questions are either meaningless pseudo questions or really type E,1 questions in disguise. The reasoning behind his view is that if answering a question calls for a decision, then the question is practical, not theoretical, for a theoretical question calls not for a decision but for an assertion. He further seems to think that when ontologists ask a question like, "Are there numbers?" and ask it as an external question, many of them look for an assertion as an answer, not a decision, because they consider the question to be a theoretical one. But the answer to such a question is not a matter of assertion but a matter of decision, a decision about the effect of the use of the expression 'number' upon the fruitfulness, efficiency, and simplicity of a language. Thus the question is either meaningless or a practical one in disguise. In short, when meaningful, it is a question of type E,1. This is true for all external questions. They are either type E,1 questions, as they stand or in disguise, or else they are pseudo questions. Thus there is only one type of external question, type E,1. Indeed Carnap sometimes talks as if this is the kind of question in which ontologists are interested. Their mistake, according to Carnap, is in attempting to give as reasons for their answers not facts about the purposes of language but pseudo assertions such as "There are no numbers because none are given in immediate experience." But no matter what ontologists think they are doing, they are engaged in pseudo problems unless they are interested in type E,1 questions, and interested in them as practical questions about language to be answered by consideration of the purposes for which we use language.

The gist of this argument would go somewhat as follows:

1. Questions which do not take assertions as answers require decisions for answers.
2. No external questions take assertions as answers.

Therefore

3. All external questions require decisions for answers.
4. All questions which require decisions for answers are practical questions rather than theoretical questions.

Therefore

5. All external questions are practical questions.

Given the soundness of this argument, Carnap's next step to the conclusions that all external questions are practical questions concerning language is at least reasonable. The above argument is, however, dubious. I shall not consider the first premise here but only the second and fourth which are philosophically more interesting and less plausible than the first.

The only reason that I can find for holding the second premise, and I believe it would be Carnap's reason, is one based upon the claim that an assertion must be an empirically verifiable sentence. The argument here is that an assertion is a nonanalytic sentence which has a truth-value. But nonanalytic sentences with truth-values are those which meet the verifiability criterion of meaning. Thus, according to this argument, an answer to an external question cannot be an assertion because it is not empirically verifiable. The soundness of this argument, then, rests on the justification of the verifiability criterion. And, as has been amply shown by others, such a justification does not seem to be possible. We can emphasize the problem facing any attempt to justify it by pointing out that the criterion, if meaningful (which some may doubt), is neither analytic nor an empirically verifiable assertion. It would seem to be a metaphysical assertion. The correctness of this interpretation is bolstered by the fact that a justification of the criterion would require a strange kind of investigation, an "investigation" of the relationship between the language in question and reality, in order to find out whether only those sentences which are empirically verifiable correspond in some way with reality and thereby whether only those sentences have truth-values, i.e. are assertions. But if the verifiability criterion is an assertion, then since it is not an empirically verifiable assertion, it is a false assertion. That is, if the criterion is an assertion, it is a type E,2 assertion rather than an internal one, and, because it asserts that only internal sentences can be assertions, it is false.

In order to avoid the conclusion that the verifiability criterion is false, Carnap must show that it is not an assertion. And to show that a sentence which appears to be an assertion is not one because it is an answer to an external question, he would have to employ the criterion itself as a premise. But we cannot prove that a sentence is not false by using the sentence as a premise in the proof. Such an argument is circular. Thus Carnap has provided no grounds for rejecting type E,2 questions. We can conclude, then, that the verifiability criterion of meaning seems to be a false assertion (about the relationship between language and reality) because, first, if the criterion is an assertion then it is an assertion of type E,2 and consequently false; and, second, it does seem to be an assertion, and there seems to be no way to show it is not.

The fourth premise seems also to be based on the verifiability criterion of meaning. For Carnap, I take it, all theoretical questions are scientific-like questions; as such their answers are, in principle at least, verifiable. A decision, on the other hand, would seem to be for Carnap an answer to a question only when there is no empirical evidence on which to base an assertion. Therefore, since in principle at least all answers to theoretical questions are verifiable, then in principle again, no theoretical question would take a decision as an answer. Thus, if it can be shown that even in principle there could be no way to verify an answer to a question, then it would certainly seem that the question is, in Carnap's sense, nontheoretical. It follows from this, of course, that external questions are nontheoretical. But it does not follow from this that the important part of the premise is established, that is, that a question which can only take as an answer a decision must be a practical one.

Furthermore there seems to be no reason to believe that an ontologist would consider his questions as theoretical, in Carnap's sense of being questions whose answers are scientifically verifiable. But he might well claim that they are not practical questions either, although they do call for a decision because, even in principle, there is no scientific evidence available. For example someone might make a decision in favor of admitting abstract entities as part of the basic furniture of the universe because he believes that we can best "save appearances" in that way. And he would claim, I should think, that even though there could be no way to verify empirically his utterance that there are abstract entities, it is still an assertion about what there is, not a decision about what we should do, and certainly not a decision about what terms we should use in our language. Such an ontologist, then, would be claiming that his question, although nontheoretical, is also nonpractical in that it calls for an assertion. As with the second premise, there seems to be nothing wrong with this claim unless we hold that a sentence to be an assertion must be empirically verifiable, that is, unless we hold the verifiability criterion of meaning. But, as we have seen above, there seems to be no good reason to hold that.

Before we move on, it should be noted that we were in a sense unfair to Carnap in trying to use the method he developed in *Meaning and Necessity* to answer question 1 as an external question. On the basis of what he said in "Empiricism, Semantics, and Ontology," he was not interested in such a question in *Meaning and Necessity*. His method might nevertheless be applicable. Indeed, some of the things I have said in this chapter might seem to point the way toward overcoming the problem we found facing his approach.

The main problem Carnap cannot overcome is the problem of answering the question "Is 'p' a designator?" or, as we would put it, "Does 'p' refer to anything?" This is the question which we assume has been answered when we ask question 1, "What does 'p' refer to?" But since we are interested in 1 as an external question, we are interested in referring$_3$ (denoting) and thus designating$_3$. The first question to consider, then, is whether by using Carnap's approach we can find some way to answer the question, "Is 'p' a designator$_3$?" without getting involved in a Wittgensteinian type theory of meaning and the problems we have found for it. If we cannot, as it seemed in our previous discussion we could not, then we must conclude, as before, that Carnap's method will not help us.

However, since it seems that "Is 'p' a designator$_3$?" amounts to "Does 'p' denote anything?" it would seem that we may have found a way to supplement Carnap's method in order to answer that question and yet not get involved in the problems for a Wittgensteinian type theory of meaning. In the discussion of Quine and ontological commitment we have said that an expression 'p' denotes something if and only if for 'p': " 'p' refers to at least one thing that exists" is true. Furthermore, it would seem that we could find out whether or not 'p' denotes anything because it seems that, first, we could find out whether 'p' refers to something by the method Ayer advocates, by examining the ways in which 'p' is used in the language; and, second, we could find out the truth-value of the sentence by finding out the truth-value of, for example, 'p exists.'

Indeed, we have already implied that we could do this because we have used as an example of a type I,2 question one of the form "Does 'p' denote anything?" Perhaps, then, a possible way to answer question 1 that we have not examined is correct. We find out: first, whether 'p' is a denoting expression by examining how 'p' is used (as Ayer suggests), second, whether 'p' denotes something or not by finding the truth-value of a sentence such as 'p exists', and third, what 'p' denotes by employing Carnap's method. However I think that even with this division of labor we shall find that question 1 as an external question cannot be answered. Using the approach Ayer suggests to accomplish the first task is by itself insufficient, and Carnap's method seems to be of no help in accomplishing the third.

It is true that I used the question "Does the expression 'chess king' denote anything?" as an example of a type I,2 question. Furthermore, this question presupposes that 'chess king' is a denoting, i.e. referring$_2$ expression, which in turn presupposes that it is a referring$_1$ expression. It is also agreed that the approach Ayer suggests, an approach from within the framework of 'chess king,' is sufficient for discovering whether 'chess king' is a referring$_1$ expression, and that if any expression 'p' is a referring$_2$ expression, then finding out whether 'p' denotes anything is an internal task. However, these facts imply nothing about the task of establishing whether or not 'p' is a referring$_2$ expression. As I pointed out earlier in the chapter when laying out the five categories of linguistic reference into which certain linguistic expressions can be sorted, I did not provide a definitive sorting criterion. In many cases it would be questioning the obvious to require of someone that he justify his claim that a certain expression—'table,' for example, is a referring$_2$ expression. In such cases there is no need to establish the claim. In other cases, however, such a claim is by no means obvious and must be established. As was pointed out when both Ayer's and Carnap's approaches to question 1 were discussed, the question of whether certain expressions refer$_2$ (are designators) is not only of central importance to problems such as the mind–body problem, but also—unfortunately for such problems—a question that does not seem answerable by discoveries about how words are used. In these cases the question may not be an internal one. However, I shall not pursue this problem here because we shall examine it in detail in Chapter 7, where it unavoidably arises again.

But whether or not Ayer's approach is sufficient to the first task, Carnap's method does not seem to be of any help when applied to the third. In *Meaning and Necessity,* Carnap provides answers to question 1, which for him comes to, "What is the extension of 'p'?" To see how he does this and what is needed to justify his choice of extension, let us take as an example those designators which Carnap calls "predicators," that is, "Predicate expressions, in a wide sense, including class expressions." [17] Carnap claims that the extension of a predicator is the corresponding class. [18] From this he concludes that the extension of the predicate 'H' in his system, S_1, is the class corresponding to 'H,' which is the class Human, that is, the class which has as its elements humans. [19] If we are to use this method to answer 1 as an external question of type E,2, then the answer cannot be, "The extension of 'H' is the same as the extension of 'the class Human.' " It must rather be, "What the extension of 'H' is is the class Human," which as we have seen, comes to "What 'H' ontologically commits us to is the class Human." This, then, is the kind of answer that Carnap's method provides for question 1 as an external question. But it seems to be somehow beside the point. Its irrelevance can be brought out more clearly by considering the mind–body problem. Let us assume that in Carnap's semantical system there would be a predicator 'S,' such that the extension of 'S' is the class sensation. It is true that he would probably want to avoid such a predicator if he could, but we have seen just how difficult that would be. What is important here, however, is that claiming that the extension of 'S' is the class sensation seems to be irrelevant to the reason we are interested in question 1. Any consider-

17. Carnap, *Meaning and Necessity,* pp. 6–7.
18. Ibid., pp. 16 f.
19. Ibid.

ations someone might raise about the class sensation would be relevant to question I only insofar as we can use them to help decide whether or not sensations are identical with, for example, certain brain processes. Thus any concern with the class sensation would be with the problem of whether or not the class is identical with some other class. But, as Carnap says, two classes are identical if and only if their predicators have the same extension, that is, if and only if they apply to the same individuals.[20] The important question for our purposes, then, is whether or not sensation-predicators and certain brain-process predicators apply to the same individuals or to different individuals which always accompany each other. Unless this question is answered, question I cannot be answered. But the most that Carnap's method can tell us relevant to this question is that brain-process predicators have as their extension the class brain process just as sensation-predicators have as their extension the class sensation. This does no more than give us another way to state the problem. It cannot tell us whether the classes are identical. Thus Carnap's method does not seem to be of any help in accomplishing the task of answering question I. It is not only designed for a different task, but also seems inappropriate when applied to this ontological job.

It seems, therefore, that dividing the tasks between Ayer and Carnap brings us no nearer to an answer to question I as a type E,2 question than before. Is there no method we could use to solve this or any comparable problem? In the case of chess, it can be seen that the way to find an answer to a type E,2 question external to the chess framework is to conduct an investigation outside the jurisdiction of the rules of the chess framework. Relying on the language–chess analogy once again, we can conclude that the appropriate way to answer a type E,2 question external to any linguistic framework is to conduct an investigation which lies outside

20. Ibid., p. 18.

the jurisdiction of the rules of any linguistic framework. There is no problem about conducting an external investigation in the case of chess because there are frameworks external to the chess framework for which the investigation is internal. One such framework is a linguistic framework. As we have seen previously, a question external to the chess framework can be internal to a linguistic framework; that is, it will come under the jurisdiction of the rules of some linguistic framework, because chess is connected to reality—to chess pieces, for example—by certain linguistic expressions formulated according to the rules of some linguistic framework.

We can now see an important place at which the language–chess analogy breaks down.[21] There are frameworks whose rules can be discovered and which are external to the chess framework—such as linguistic frameworks. The rules of linguistic frameworks, as discussed earlier, are those discoverable by investigating the ways in which linguistic expressions are used. But there are no discoverable frameworks external to *all* linguistic frameworks. Thus an investigation external to all linguistic frameworks, unlike an investigation external to the chess framework or even external to the frameworks of all games, would be an investigation which does not come under the jurisdiction of the rules of any discoverable framework. But where there are no discoverable rules governing an investigation there are no available guidelines, no standards by which to judge the subject matter of the investigation, and thus no method of investigation. The conclusion we have reached, then, is that there are no external methods of investigation, i.e. no methods of investigation some part of whose subject matter lies outside the jurisdiction of the rules of all linguistic frameworks. Consequently we must also conclude that we cannot conduct an investigation which will provide correct answers to

21. I have discussed another place at which the language-chess analogy breaks down in "Malcolm's Mistaken Memory," *Analysis*, 25 (1965), 162–64.

external questions because such answers are discoverable only by external investigations. This is not to say, however, that there are no correct answers to external questions, but only that none are discoverable. If there were no rules external to the rules of all linguistic frameworks, then we could conclude that there are no correct answers to external questions. However, we have already discussed a kind of correctness which is independent of the rules of any linguistic framework. This is the correctness which results from the sanction of the nonformal, nonframework rules of language, the correctness we have seen relevant to answers to external questions. Thus, given the unavailability of nonformal rules, we can say both that there are correct answers to external questions and that there are no discoverable correct answers to external questions.

Our last conclusion can be shown in another way. Any method of investigation is either linguistic or nonlinguistic. That is, any method either has linguistic expressions as some part of its subject matter or has linguistic expressions as no part of its subject matter. But neither kind of method is external. All nonlinguistic methods are internal because all words involved in such methods are used rather than mentioned, so that the results of all such methods of investigation come under the jurisdiction of the rules governing the use of the words. Consequently these methods can be used only to investigate questions whose answers come under the jurisdiction of linguistic framework rules. That is, no nonlinguistic methods of investigation are external. An external linguistic method of investigation would be one that has as its subject matter those characteristics of linguistic expressions that are external to the frameworks of the expressions. However, such a subject matter could only be the nonformal, nonframework rules of language, that is, the rules connecting expressions to what there is, the rules that function like those Wittgenstein called rules of projection. Thus an external linguistic method of investigation would be the kind of method that we discussed when we examined Wittgensteinian theories of meaning. And since, as we found in Chapter 4, there seem to be insoluble problems for such theories, there are insoluble problems for any investigation seeking to discover what such theories express, i.e. nonformal rules of language. We can now also see that the trouble with Carnap's and Ayer's approaches to the external problem of linguistic reference was that they needed supplementation by an investigation requiring that we get outside language in a way we cannot.

At this point it would seem that we must conclude that we cannot conduct the kind of investigation needed to discover answers to question 1 as an external question. Thus we cannot solve external problems, such as the traditional mind–body problem, because they require answers to question 1 as external. Must we also conclude with Wittgenstein that philosophy, or at least that part of philosophy involving external questions, belongs to the realm of the mystical, the ineffable? There seems to be only one way left to avoid this conclusion. We must try to find some kind of relevant information by working within some linguistic framework. Which framework, if any, is required will be discussed in Chapter 6. It is important to note here, however, first, that there is no reason to think that internal investigations, i.e. the kinds of investigation used to answer internal questions about what there is, are at all relevant to external questions about what there is; second, that even if some internal investigations are relevant, none can provide a solution to any external problem, i.e. any problem expressed by an external question because, as we have seen, a solution can be provided only by an external investigation. The most we can hope for is that some kind of internal investigation will produce information which can be construed as evidence or clues, no matter how minimal, supporting one of the several alternatives we must consider in dealing with each of the external problems. Because external problems concern the reference of certain linguistic expressions, it seems that what we want to discover by means of an internal investigation are some internal facts about the relevant expressions which are clues to the external problems involving the expressions. In other words, we shall be hoping that language reflects what there is in such a way that by finding the "reflection" we will thereby find a clue to what there is.

On the basis of this last conclusion, our purpose in the next chapter will be to see if we can find some method of investigation to provide us with such internal clues to type E,2 external questions. There are three things we can say now about such a method. First, such a method will be purely a philosophical one because no other discipline is concerned with type E,2 questions external to language. Second, because the clues we shall be looking for are certain features of language, we must use a method of investigation suitable for examining language. We will, then, be using what we have called a linguistic method rather than a nonlinguistic method. The third point, by now obvious, is that we must choose a linguistic method to provide the clues we need which will allow us to remain within some particular linguistic framework. Although obvious, this point will be our main criterion when, in the next chapter, we examine three kinds of linguistic methods.

Before we move on, there is one last objection to consider. It might be claimed that the second point is based upon a faulty inference. I have inferred from the fact that we are hoping to obtain internal clues about external problems which involve certain linguistic expressions the conclusion that what we need is some kind of internal investigation of those expressions. Although such a linguistic approach is surely the most likely candidate, nothing has been said to rule out a nonlinguistic approach. Although it is true that no nonlinguistic investigation can produce a solution to an external problem, perhaps one could produce just those clues we need to guide our decisions about external problems. However, although I have given no reason for rejecting a nonlinguistic approach, I know of no helpful clues such an investigation could turn up. Let us once again consider the mind–body problem. The subject matter of an internal, nonlinguistic investigation relevant to the mind–body problem would be the empirically discoverable facts about minds and bodies. Such facts would come either from the relevant sciences such as psychology and physiology or, perhaps, from introspection. The facts these sciences provide are of no help. As was remarked in Chapter 2 when the double language theory was discussed, it seems that a one-to-one or at least a one-many psychoneurophysiological correspondence is a presupposition of the scientific investigation of minds and bodies, the scientific problem being to discover and specify the details of the correspondence. It was also remarked that this presupposition is equally compatible with all the alternative solutions to the mind–body problem. Consequently the sciences relevantly concerned with minds and bodies seem to be evidentially neutral regarding the mind–body problem.

The data of introspection are no more helpful. It might be argued, for example, that sensations and the like, when we intuit them, when we are directly aware of them by introspection, seem to be mental events or processes, and this "seeming" is evidence that they are mental events or processes. It must be admitted, I think, that there are data provided by introspection, and it can even be granted that this material is evidence in favor of the existence of mental events and processes. But the data are not evidence relevant to the mind–body problem because they cannot, for example, help us decide between the view that each sensation is identical with some brain process and the view that no sensations are identical with anything physical. Although we may intuit sensations in introspection, we do not also intuit that these sensations are either identical with or different from brain processes. Thus the data of introspection do not count as evidence either for or against the claim of an identity theorist that whenever we are aware of a sensation we are aware in a unique way of a brain process because sensations are identical with brain processes. Furthermore, the data could not help us decide among the various versions of the identity theory such as Feigl's "raw feel" version and Smart's materialistic version; nor among the various dualistic theories. Thus, like science, introspection seems to be evidentially neutral with regard to the mind–body problem.

Neither the internal investigations of science nor the intuitions of introspection provide the internal clues that we are seeking to help us handle the mind–body problem. Thus nonlinguistic internal approaches to the mind–body problem can be eliminated. The same conclusion will hold for the other external problems, such as the problems of the external world, the existence of God, free will, and universals. The results of science will not help decide the issue between the various competing views: Berkeleian Idealism and Realism, theism and atheism, free will compatibilism and incompatibilism, and nominalism and realism. Furthermore although some people have claimed that they can intuit the external world, God, free will, and universals, it is also true that many others are unaware of such intuitions and that there is no way to discover whether any such intuitions are veridical or illusory. Consequently, if any kind of internal method of investigation is to turn up clues relevant to external problems, it seems that it will have to be a linguistic method.

Before moving on to Chapter 6, let me briefly summarize the three conclusions of this chapter most relevant to the next:

> Certain philosophical problems such as the mind–body problem are problems external to any linguistic framework. They are type E,2 problems.

> Because we cannot solve external problems by an external investigation, we must attempt to find clues to the problems by means of internal investigations.

Because nonlinguistic internal methods of investigation seem to be unsuitable for finding internal clues to external problems, we must attempt to discover the clues by a linguistic method which is internal to some linguistic framework.

PART III

External Problems

6. External Problems and Philosophical Analysis

In Chapter 5 we concluded that the only way to approach external philosophical problems is to look for clues for their solution from within a given linguistic framework. Thus we shall be looking for certain features of a language which seem somehow to be due not just to the peculiarities of the language but rather to what there is (perhaps those features of language Wittgenstein called essential rather than accidental). In line with this, there seem to be two requirements any successful method must meet. First, it must not require us to go outside, but allow us to remain within, a given framework when our purpose is to answer external questions. Second, when so employed, it must provide us with some grounds, however slim, for justifying particular answers to external questions.

We found in Chapter 5 that a nonlinguistic method of investigation will not produce data evidentially relevant to external problems. Thus, any approach we try will involve a linguistic approach to question 1 which, if successful, will by itself provide answers to external questions. We must therefore examine linguistic methods to see if any meet the two requirements. At first glance it seems that any linguistic method would meet at least the first requirement. However, although this may be obvious when we employ such methods for certain purposes, it is not at all obvious, as we shall see, when we employ them for our purposes. We must, then, examine linguistic methods with regard to both requirements. Thus in this chapter I propose to examine what I

take to be the three general kinds of linguistic method. I
shall briefly characterize each kind, list the main purpose
for which it is used, and then try to find whether any of
these methods, when used for any of these purposes, meet
the first requirement. If any do meet the first requirement I
shall (in the next chapter) examine them more thoroughly
by returning once again to a brief examination of the mind–
body problem in order to see whether they meet the second
requirement.

Before we proceed, however, I should dispel a perplexity
that some may have about what I am doing. In Chapter 2
we examined certain solutions to what I called the linguistic
mind–body problem. The philosophical methods used to approach the problem were obviously linguistic ones. In Chapter 3 it was concluded that in order to be able to infer from
a solution of the linguistic problem a solution of the traditional problem, we would have to be able to find an answer to question 1: "What does 'p' denote?" But we found
in the following two chapters that the only way to answer
this external question is indirectly, from within a linguistic
framework, by some linguistic method. Here the perplexity
may arise: at one point I say that a linguistic approach to
the traditional problem must be supplemented by a consideration of question 1, but elsewhere I say that we may be
able to use a linguistic approach to answer question 1 and
thus solve the traditional problem. Thus, one might object,
if what I say at one point is true, then what I say at the
other must be false.

We can dispel this perplexity quickly. At the end of Chapter 3 I said that if we are going to use a solution of the
linguistic problem as a means to a solution of the traditional
problem we must also consider question 1. Thus linguistic
methods, when used for the purpose of solving the traditional problem by means of the linguistic problem, cannot succeed without answering question 1. But this does not
rule out the possibility of employing linguistic methods for
the purpose of helping to answer question 1. That is, if

using a method for one purpose will not work, it does not follow that using it for another will not work either. There is, then, no reason to give up our present inquiry on this account.

A relevant corollary is that there is no reason to solve the linguistic problem if we are interested in the traditional problem. This, in fact, could be inferred from the conclusion we reached in Chapter 3, i.e. in a certain sense a solution of the linguistic problem does not seem relevant to a solution of the traditional problem, because a linguistic approach via the linguistic problem must be supplemented by a linguistic approach to question 1. But we have also found that if we can answer question 1 we can thereby solve the traditional problem without considering the linguistic problem because we can put all the questions we need to ask into the form of question 1. For example, we can put the question Smart tries to answer as "What does the word 'sensation' denote?" which is a specific case of question 1. Thus because only linguistic methods are relevant to external questions and because the one and only question they must consider is question 1, our present examination of question 1 is not only necessary to see whether any approach to the traditional problem will succeed but actually is the only examination necessary for that purpose.

Let us now turn to a discussion of the three kinds of linguistic philosophical method, the three kinds of what we can call philosophical analysis, or, for our purposes, analysis. These three kinds of analysis can be employed for different purposes. When employed, for example, to solve the linguistic mind–body problem, it would seem that they do not require us to go outside language. We are interested, however, in finding whether they can remain within language when used for the purpose of answering type E,2 questions. I shall, primarily for identification purposes, call the three kinds of analysis that we shall consider: (1) meaning analysis, (2) reconstruction analysis, and (3) use analysis.

Meaning Analysis

Meaning analysis, briefly, is the linguistic method which defines a term (the analysandum) by providing an expression (the analysans) synonymous with it or with expressions containing it, such that the analysans so provided is one which will enable us to achieve the purpose for which the analysis has been made. As indicated there are two general forms such a definition can take. It can either be an explicit definition or a definition in use (a contextual definition). When we make an explicit definition of a term we provide an expression synonymous with it. Thus an explicit definition of the term 'human' would be 'rational animal.' For most philosophical purposes this kind of definition is considered to be of little value because whatever philosophical problems arise because of the analysandum will usually arise for any term synonymous with it. For this reason meaning analysis when done for philosophical purposes generally consists of attempts to provide definitions in use. In a definition in use, or a contextual definition, the analysans provides expressions synonymous with certain expressions containing the term in question, but it provides no expression synonymous with the term itself. Thus in a definition in use we "analyze away" the term which creates the problem we are trying to solve by making the analysis, and thereby we supposedly analyze away the problem. We have already seen an example of a definition in use. In the discussion of Quine and ontological commitment in Chapter 5 we discussed Russell's definition in use of definite descriptions. Such a definition analyzes away the definite description, thereby destroying one argument for the existence of such things as Pegasus, unicorns, and kings of France in the twentieth century. This, then, is an example of a contextual definition used for the purpose of refuting a philosophical argument.

Providing meaning analyses, especially definitions in use, has been and still is thought by many philosophers to be the only legitimate kind of philosophical endeavor, with the one exception of interpreting historically important philosophical views. The philosophers holding this view, the logical positivists, claim that the only kind of cognitive sentences (sentences with a truth-value) are those which are analytic and those which are synthetic a posteriori. Since the latter come under the domain of natural science, and since philosophy is not a natural science, philosophy can deal only with analytic sentences if, as is claimed for it, it is to be a cognitive enterprise. This is just what meaning analysis, and only meaning analysis, deals with: it consists of definitions, either explicit or contextual; and such definitions are analytic sentences. We can say, then, that for such philosophers, philosophy is restricted to only one kind of relation between expressions of a given linguistic framework, logical entailment.

At this point let us consider what seems to be the main purposes for which meaning analysis is used in order to see which, if any, are philosophical purposes and thus perhaps relevant to our task, i.e. to finding internal clues to external problems. I shall list six purposes and, where it seems helpful, give an example of how they have been used.

i. *To understand a certain expression* This kind of meaning analysis might be called a "real" definition as opposed to a nominal definition because we are concerned with a term which is used in a particular language and which we do not understand. Thus we want to find an expression which we understand and which is synonymous with it either in that language or in another. This kind of task is essentially lexicography and provides dictionary definitions. For such a purpose an explicit definition usually will do. To achieve such a purpose we need not go outside language. Generally this purpose for doing meaning analysis is not a philosophical one.

ii. *To give the meaning of a certain expression* This kind of definition can be called a nominal or stipulative definition. It does not apply to an expression in use; rather it is

used to define a new and usually technical term introduced
into the framework. This occurs in science and also in philosophy. The expression 'linguistic framework' is a technical
expression in philosophy. Definitions of this kind, like real
definitions, may either be explicit or contextual. However
they do in some sense require us to go outside a linguistic
framework in order to justify adopting them because they
cause a change in the framework: consulting the rules of the
framework will not help us decide if we are justified in making the definition. The existing rules have no jurisdiction
over them. But because such definitions do affect the framework, whether or not to adopt them is a type E,1 question.
This then is not the kind of external question in which we
are interested for we are interested in type E,2 questions.
However, we must consider whether or not we can approach
type E,2 questions by means of answers to type E,1 questions. This will be done when we examine reconstruction
analysis, which is itself a type E,1 task. Any objections to
doing reconstruction analysis for the purpose of solving external philosophical problems will also be objections to
meaning analysis when done for purpose ii.

   iii. *To reduce the number of undefined expressions*   This
is clearly a purpose for which we must use a definition in
use, for here we are trying to show that certain terms can
be eliminated because they are definable by means of others.
Thus we must be able to eliminate not only the terms in
question but also their synonyms because unless the term
and all its synonyms have been eliminated by definition,
the number of undefined terms has in no way been reduced.
But this can be done only if we define the term in some
way such that neither it nor a synonym of it appears in the
analysans. Thus we must use a definition in use. An example of using meaning analysis for this purpose is the
defining of all logical connectives in the propositional calculus in terms of Sheffer's stroke. Here what is achieved is
primarily logical simplicity and elegance. Another example
of this use of meaning analysis is Chisholm's contextual

definitions of the epistemic terms, 'unreasonable,' 'evident,' 'acceptable,' 'indifferent,' and 'dubitable' in terms of the expression 'more worthy of belief.' For example, " 'It would be unreasonable for S to accept h' means that non-h is more worthy of S's belief than h." [1] When done for this purpose, meaning analysis is obviously an internal task. Although we have given philosophical examples, this kind of internal task is not uniquely philosophical. It is essentially a subsidiary procedure which can be used in any discipline, mathematics, for example, to polish, tie together, or simplify a theory or argument. Ideally, as with the above examples, we should left with only one undefined expression. It may be that we can prove something about one or more of the defined expressions only by proving something about the expression by which they are defined. But if we are trying to construct such a proof, we are not using analysis merely to reduce undefined expressions but for a different purpose, in most cases for one of those purposes which are yet to be discussed.

iv. *To refute an argument* We have already seen an example of meaning analysis done for this purpose. Russell analyzes sentences containing definite descriptions into sentences which do not contain them. His purpose is to show that we need not use descriptions which seem to denote entities such as unicorns, and thus we need not accept the argument for their existence because it is based on the premise that we need to use such descriptions. This use of meaning analysis is also an internal task, and, furthermore, certainly a philosophical one. In fact any attempt which uses meaning analysis to show a philosophical argument is wrong because the argument uses an expression to mean something that it does not mean, or because it unjustifiably infers something from the use of the expression, would be an internal philosophical task, even if the argument itself is used to support a conclusion about an external problem. We can

1. Roderick Chisholm, *Perceiving,* p. 5.

say that using meaning analysis for this purpose where the argument in question is used to support an external conclusion is using analysis to show that what some philosophers may think to be internal clues to external problems are not such clues, because those philosophers have not seen how certain terms in their argument can be analyzed. Consequently using meaning analysis for this purpose, a purpose, incidentally, for which only a definition in use could be helpful, is important for philosophy. However, because its value is purely a negative one, it cannot alone be sufficient for our needs.

v. *To justify a theory*   This is one of the main philosophical purposes for using meaning analysis. We have seen several examples of the use of meaning analysis for this purpose in Chapter 2. Carnap tries to analyze psychological-expressions into physical-expressions, and belief-expressions into extensional expressions. Certain phenomenalists try to analyze material-object sentences into sense-data sentences. In these three examples the philosophers try to justify respectively linguistic monism, the theory of extensionality, and linguistic phenomenalism. In each case the task can be construed as an internal one, because all of the theories to be justified are theories about relationships among certain expressions of a given linguistic framework. Thus these three philosophical tasks are internal ones. Furthermore this purpose is one for which only definitions in use can be employed because, as in the three examples, the theories all claim that expressions of one kind are analyzable into expressions of a different kind. However, as we have seen, some philosophers have thought that the theories they were justifying were not merely theories about linguistic expressions; they have thought they were justifying theories about what there is; they have thought that they were "analyzing away" not just expressions but entities. Doing analysis for such a purpose is doing what is called reductive analysis. Because this deserves separate consideration I shall discuss it as purpose (vi).

vi. *To reduce entities*   Doing meaning analysis for this purpose, doing reductive analysis, involves contextually defining certain expressions which contain terms that seem to refer to one kind of entity, in terms of other expressions that do not contain these terms, but contain only terms referring to other kinds of things. Once the analysis is made, it is concluded either that the analysandum really refers to the entities referred to by the analysans, or is not really a referring-term. Although this has not always been understood, meaning analysis is only one part of the task of reductive analysis. The other part is justifying the inference from the analysis to the referent or lack of referent of the analysandum. Reductive analysis, then, involves approaching an external problem via a linguistic problem, an approach that we have seen cannot succeed without supplementation by consideration of question 1. Thus while reductive analysis is certainly a philosophical procedure relevant to our purposes, it is also an approach that is neither sufficient nor necessary for solving external problems. Indeed, whether or not it meets our first requirement depends upon whether we can find internal clues to external problems.

We have above briefly examined six general purposes for which philosophers and others have used meaning analysis. Only three purposes, (iv), (v), and (vi), seem to be peculiarly philosophical and relevant to our needs because only these seem to be in any way relevant to external problems. However, meaning analysis when done for these purposes, at least as it has been used so far by philosophers, is not adequate. Meaning analysis when done for purpose (iv), while relevant to external problems, is useful only in destroying defective arguments, not in justifying sound ones. When done for purposes (v) or (vi) it is neither necessary nor sufficient for solving external problems either because it concerns only linguistic problems or because it must be supplemented in such a way that it becomes superfluous.

Before we conclude that meaning analysis is of no help

to us, however, it should be recalled that we are not looking for a method sufficient for solving external problems at
present, but rather looking for some way to find internal
clues to external problems. Nothing so far has shown that
meaning analysis cannot provide such clues. There are, I
think, certain conditions under which it would be hard to
deny that a successful meaning analysis provided internal
clues. Let us assume that we have completed a meaning
analysis. We have, for example, analyzed material-object
sentences (M-sentences) into sense-data sentences (S-sentences) which are, presumably, counterfactual in form.
Thus some S-sentences, conversely, can be analyzed into
M-sentences and, furthermore, because synonymous expressions, if they refer, have the same referent, each M-sentence
refers to what some S-sentence refers to. But let us further
assume that there are some S-sentences, presumably at
least certain categorical S-sentences, which cannot be analyzed into M-sentences. While it follows from the above
that all M-sentences refer to what some S-sentences refer
to, it does not follow that all S-sentences refer to what some
or all M-sentences refer to. Furthermore, it is not unreasonable to assume that those S-sentences not synonymous
with any M-sentences would refer to sense-data, rather than
to physical objects. Given the above assumptions, can we
conclude that, because there seem to be sense-data and because all M-sentences refer to what certain S-sentences refer to, there are no such things as material objects but
merely sense-data? That is, since we can avoid using M-sentences, but not S-sentences, and some S-sentences seem to
refer to sense-data, are we justified in eliminating material
objects from the basic furniture of the universe? If we are,
then there seems to be an internal way to use meaning
analysis which, given the asymmetry of the analysis, fur-
nishes an internal clue to the external problem of phenomenalism versus realism, a clue which would provide
some grounds for picking phenomenalism as at least in part
a correct theory of what there is (whether there are *only*

sense-data, e.g. no abstract entities such as universals, is another question).

The question, then, is whether it is justified to claim that an asymmetrical analysis of M-sentences into S-sentences provides internal clues that are grounds for a phenomenalistic reduction. As it stands, it is not justified because there are two reasons for rejecting such a reduction that have not yet been considered. The first is based on the fact that we have assumed, in accordance with the analyses that have been attempted, that the S-sentences synonymous with M-sentences would be counterfactual conditionals. As such they would seem to refer not to actual sense-data but rather (shades of Mill) to the permanent possibility of sense-data. But counting permanent possibilities as part of the furniture of the universe seems strange indeed, surely stranger than material objects. Thus, given the situation as we have imagined it, there seems to be some reason for rejecting such a reduction. This objection can be raised against any use of this version of reductive analysis where the analysans is a counterfactual conditional.

Second, such a reduction is unjustified because it is not enough to show that M-sentences are asymmetrically analyzable into S-sentences; S-sentences might be analyzable into a third kind of sentence. For example, it may be that all S-sentences are synonymous with appear-sentences and with sensing-sentences. That is, it might be that a sentence such as 'The apple presents me with a red sense-datum' means 'The apple appears red to me' or 'I sense redly with regard to the apple,' and a sentence such as 'I see a red sense-datum, means 'I am appeared to redly' or 'I am sensing redly.' [2] If such sentences are, as claimed, synonymous with S-sentences, then they refer to whatever S-sentences refer to. But what is referred to is now not so obviously sense-data because, as with M-sentences, S-sentences can now be analyzed away. Thus it does not seem unreasonable for someone to claim that the S-sentences synonymous with

2. See Chisholm, especially Chapter 8.

M-sentences refer to material objects, while the S-sentences which are not synonymous refer to particular ways people are sensibly stimulated—either by material objects external to their bodies (as made explicit in the first set of examples) or merely by processes within their own bodies. In other words, although this kind of reductive argument might be convincing when used to reduce material objects to sense-data, it is not convincing when used to reduce material objects to ways in which people are sensibly affected. But if S-sentences are synonymous with sensing-sentences one conclusion is as good as the other.

It seems, then, that we can use the results of these two analyses either to show material objects are not sense-data —because S-sentences are synonymous with sensing-sentences—or to show that sensing-sentences refer to sense-data—because if not we get undesirable results when we consider what M-sentences refer to. Neither conclusion seems to be more plausible than the other. To decide between the two would involve going outside language to find what it is that such sentences refer to.

In order to eliminate these two reasons for rejecting the reduction, let us now assume that categorical M-sentences are asymmetrically analyzable into categorical S-sentences, and that no S-sentence is synonymous with any third kind of sentence. Are we now justified in concluding a phenomenalistic reduction on the basis of successful meaning analyses? Not yet, because there is still another possible reason for rejecting the reduction. It is not impossible that M-sentences are synonymous with certain S-sentences and that 'sense-datum' is not a referring$_2$-term. G. A. Paul has argued that it is wrong to hypostasize sense-data because S-sentences are merely ways of talking about how material objects look to us.[3] If Paul's argument is sound, then it is obviously a mistake to try to reduce material objects to

3. See G. A. Paul, "Is there a Problem about Sense-Data?" in Flew, ed., *Logic and Language, First Series* (Oxford, Basil Blackwell, 1955), pp. 101–16.

sense-data because there are no such things. The significance of this example is that there may be internal clues to external problems which can be gathered in other ways and which override any results of meaning analysis. Whether Paul's kind of approach provides such clues will be discussed in the next chapter.

Let us change our set of conditions once more. Let us assume that categorical M-sentences are asymmetrically analyzable into S-sentences, that S-sentences are not synonymous with any third kind of sentence, and that there is nothing else that could be an internal clue either for or against the reduction. Under such conditions, can we claim that a successful meaning analysis provides us with an internal clue to the external problem of phenomenalism versus realism? I think we must agree that under such conditions we *can* conclude that phenomenalism is the correct theory. On the other hand, I do not think that there is anything wrong with denying phenomenalism under these conditions, unless there is some independent reason for claiming that the relationship between M-sentences and S-sentences is an internal clue to the external relationship between material objects and sense-data. But if there is such a reason, it is certainly not readily available, as we saw when we examined Chisholm's analogous claim about the non-synonymy of mind-sentences and body-sentences. My point, then, is that under the above-stated conditions, neither affirming nor denying the reduction of material objects to sense-data is unreasonable.

It may be objected at this point that we have found the perfect situation for the use of Occam's razor because we have eliminated any grounds for rejecting a reduction. However, it is not clear that Occam's razor should be applied to external problems in this way. According to this principle, we are not to multiply entities beyond necessity, that is, if it is not necessary to assume the existence of some entity, then we should not assume it. But as stated, Occam's principle is elliptical because in stating that some entity is beyond necessity we mean that it is not necessary for some purpose or other. Thus we must spell out the principle more fully, and when we do that we shall find that there are two possible interpretations neither of which is obviously a help to a reductionist. The first is to interpret the razor as applying to those entities which are not necessary for the purposes of listing everything that there is. Occam's principle is certainly acceptable on this interpretation, but, unfortunately, provides no way of deciding which entities are unnecessary. Thus we cannot decide in favor of a reduction using the first interpretation. On the second interpretation the razor is to be applied to those entities not necessary for scientific explanations. This is probably the usual interpretation. However, although it is true that science should assume no more theoretical entities than are necessary for its theoretical explanations, it is not at all obvious that if an entity of any kind is scientifically superfluous then we should conclude that it does not exist. Thus although science should assume no more theoretical entities than are necessary for solving its particular internal problems, nothing follows from this about the applicability of the principle to external problems, unless what is good for science is good for philosophy which is by no means obvious. Nevertheless, even if we cannot justify an ontological reduction by Occam's razor, we can still conclude, as above, that if there is nothing else we can count as internal clues to external problems there is no reason against taking a successful meaning analysis as providing such a clue.

We cannot, however, let the matter rest here. We have been implicitly assuming not only that a successful meaning analysis can be carried out, but also that we can establish that it has been carried out. There are objections to both of these assumptions, objections which, if sustained, provide grounds for rejecting meaning analysis as a method for approaching external problems. Both objections are concerned with the fact that for a meaning analysis to be successful the analysans must be synonymous with the analysandum.

The first objection is based on the claim that there is no criterion for synonymy of expressions and, therefore, none for meaning analysis.[4] A meaning analysis is of the form '*p* if and only if *q*.' However the sense of 'if and only if' used must be appropriate for synonymy. That is, '*p* if and only if *q*' cannot be a contingent sentence but must be logically true. Thus, if we are to be able to determine when a meaning analysis is successful, we must be able to determine when a sentence of the form '*p* if and only if *q*' is logically true. But how can we do this? Following Carnap, we can say that a sentence is logically true if and only if its truth can be established on the basis of the rules of the framework alone.[5] Thus if we can establish that '*p* if and only if *q*' is true merely by consulting the rules of the framework, we thereby can determine that '*p*' can be analyzed in terms of '*q*.'

The rules of a linguistic framework can be discovered by observing, questioning, and experimenting in appropriate ways. Of all the rules we discover in this way, which are the ones we need? Certainly not quasi-logical or reference rules; neither can we use a rule which states that '*p* if and only if *q*' is analytic, for if we have to determine whether a sentence is logically true we will be no better off in determining whether it is analytic. In other words, we cannot use the logical rules of the framework as a criterion for meaning analysis because such rules are just what we produce when we make a successful analysis. The only other kind of rule that would seem to be at all relevant would be one about the interchangeability of '*p*' and '*q*.' Such a rule would state that '*p*' and '*q*' can be interchanged *salve veritate* in certain contexts. However which contexts are specified as relevant to synonymy is important. If all contexts are specified, then the notion of synonymy becomes too restricted to be used with regard to meaning analysis. In some contexts, such as

4. See W. V. O. Quine, "Two Dogmas of Empiricism," *From a Logical Point of View,* pp. 20–46.

5. See Rudolf Carnap, *Meaning and Necessity,* p. 10.

those of indirect discourse and belief sentences, 'bachelor' and 'unmarried male' are not interchangeable *salve veritate*. Nelson Goodman points out another such context. In sentences such as "The description 'a bachelor that is not an unmarried male' is a bachelor-description" we cannot substitute 'unmarried male' for 'bachelor' *salve veritate* because the sentence is true for 'bachelor' and false for 'unmarried male.' From this he concludes that no two words are synonymous.[6] However, because 'bachelor' and 'unmarried male' seem to be paradigms of synonymous expressions the correct conclusion seems to be that Goodman's criterion is too restrictive. But how are we to single out the relevant contexts? If we limit the contexts to extensional ones, then 'human' and 'featherless biped' would be synonymous and they obviously are not. The only way there seems to be to limit the contexts adequately is to say that if it is necessary that *p* if and only if *q*, then '*p*' and '*q*' are synonymous. But when we specify the sense of 'necessary' here, it seems to come to 'logically necessary' or, in other words, 'logically true.' But this cannot be our criterion for deciding whether '*p* if and only if *q*' is logically true. Once again we have gone in a circle.

Is there no way, then, which we can use to find out whether a sentence of the form '*p* if and only if *q*' is logically true, that is, whether '*p*' and '*q*' are synonymous, and thus whether '*p*' can be analyzed in terms of '*q*'? The only method left is one often used for checking analyses: the use of counter-examples. When we use this method to test a certain analysis, we try to find some example in which '*p*' could be true when '*q*' is not, or the converse. In this way we show that the equivalence does not hold. What is important here is the expression 'could be true.' For our purposes it must signify logical possibility. Thus when we use the method of counter-examples we are interested in finding

6. See Nelson Goodman, "On Likeness of Meaning," in L. Linsky, ed., *Semantics and the Philosophy of Language* (Urbana, University of Illinois Press, 1952), pp. 67–74.

some example in which it is logically possible that *p* and not
q; some example in which it is not logically necessary that
if *p* then *q*. Thus we are interested not in a sufficient condition of synonymy, but in sufficient conditions of non-
synonymy, or necessary conditions of synonymy. What
might they be? One obvious necessary condition of synonymy is that '*p*' and '*q*' are extensionally equivalent: But
this is of little practical help because few proposed analyses
fail to meet this condition. Interchangeability *salve veritate*
in extensional contexts is another necessary condition, but
it too is of little practical help. Interchangeability *salve
veritate* in all contexts is surely a sufficient condition of
synonymy, but, because, as we have seen, no pair of expressions meet it, it is much too restrictive as a necessary
condition. Any other candidates of which I am aware are
either too restrictive or of no practical help or involve logical modalities which put us back in the circle we have been
trying to escape.

It seems, then, that if we are to use the method of counter-examples we must use a rule of thumb. The kind of rule
we would need might state that an analysis is successful if
no examples generally agreed upon as being relevant to the
analysis are counter-examples. Thus a successful analysis
would be one where, although there may be dispute about
the relevance of certain examples which, if relevant, would
be counter-examples, none of them which are agreed upon
as relevant are counter-examples. However there is a question of why we should adopt this rule instead of any other
makeshift rule. Or why we should adopt any makeshift rule
at all? Furthermore where the area of agreement is small,
as does not seem unlikely in some cases, there seems to be
good reason to doubt the analysis. Faced with such a situation it may be better to give up trying to produce meaning
analyses and turn to reconstruction analysis.

Instead of considering this objection further let us turn
to another objection, one which if sound does indeed require us to give up meaning analysis for reconstruction

analysis. While the above objection claims that we cannot judge the success of an analysis because there is no criterion which we can use to judge success, the present objection claims that even if we have a criterion for a successful analysis we cannot produce one because of the nature of our language. A previously stated objection was that it does not seem possible to give a meaning analysis of M-sentences in terms of S-sentences. Although we talked above as if the analysis of M-sentences into S-sentences were possible, such an analysis has never succeeded, and there are good reasons for thinking it cannot succeed.[7] The present objection is a generalization of this. Like the preceding one, it claims that we cannot find out whether two expressions are synonymous. However, unlike the previous one, it claims that this is not necessarily true of all languages but is certainly true of ordinary language because the expressions of ordinary language are essentially vague and imprecise, or "open-textured."[8] In a similar vein it has been claimed that meaning analysis cannot be used upon the expressions of ordinary language because the objects to which each expression applies share at most what Wittgenstein calls a "family resemblance."[9] That is, these objects are at most more or less similar, there being no characteristics common to all. If this view is correct, then there is a counter-example to any proposed definition or meaning analysis which attempts to provide defining characteristics because there will always be something to which the analysandum applies but to which the analysans does not apply. Although this is a popular view of ordinary language, it is not clear that it rules out all contextual definitions, nor has it been proven, unless we can accept Goodman's arguments. However, that it is true

7. See A. J. Ayer, *The Problem of Knowledge* (Baltimore, Penguin Books, 1956), pp. 118–29; and Chisholm, pp. 189–97.

8. See Friedrich Waismann, "Verifiability," *Logic and Language, First Series,* pp. 117–44.

9. See Ludwig Wittgenstein, *Philosophical Investigations,* 65–67.

of many of the expressions of ordinary language, especially those relevant to philosophical problems, seems probable on the basis of the many attempts at the analysis of such expressions which have failed and the few which have been found acceptable.

If this second objection is sound, then we cannot, even in principle, give the meanings of such expressions precisely; we can merely indicate them roughly; we should talk of likeness rather than sameness of meaning, as Goodman says. But if we can only roughly indicate the meaning of an expression, we cannot give a term synonymous with it, because if we could, this would be to give its meaning precisely. To state roughly what an expression means is not to state an expression synonymous with it. Thus, since we cannot state a synonym of such expressions, we cannot give meaning analysis of them. For nonphilosophical purposes such as purpose (i), this defect is not important because such a rough indication is all that is needed. However if, as it seems, this is the best that can be done—either because of inherent vagueness or because of the lack of a criterion—then those who make analyses of the expressions of ordinary language are not doing meaning analysis but analysis of some other kind. Thus, although meaning analysis may be taken as one possible way to find internal clues to external problems, it seems that it is not in practice applicable to that language with which all analyses must begin, ordinary language.

It is because there seems to be this inherent vagueness or open texture in ordinary language that many philosophers feel justified in making the expressions of ordinary language more precise by giving them a precise definition. However, once they do this they are no longer doing meaning analysis because the relation between the analysandum and the analysans is not that of synonymy. This change in method is not thought to be illegitimate for it is a change which seems necessitated because of a defect of ordinary language, vagueness. Indeed it is often felt that by so clearing up the defects of ordinary language and only by clearing them up can many problems including philosophical problems be solved. Thus these philosophers can be said to consider meaning analysis as an ideal which cannot be reached because of the vagueness of ordinary language, so that it must be abandoned for what I have called reconstruction analysis; other philosophers who despair of meaning analysis turn instead to use analysis. It is time, then, to examine these two other kinds of analysis.

RECONSTRUCTION ANALYSIS

Reconstruction analysis is the linguistic method which in some way reconstructs certain features of the linguistic framework of a given expression, thereby changing its meaning in order to achieve some purpose or other. In this kind of analysis the relation between analysandum and analysans cannot be that of synonymy because the rules governing the use of one are not those governing the use of the other. In general we can say that the purpose of reconstruction analysis is to modify those rules governing the expression in question which are defective in some way, while preserving those rules which are not defective. Thus the ideal is to keep the meaning of the analysans as close as possible to the analysandum by reconstructing only that part of the framework of the analysandum which is defective.

In order to go more deeply into the examination of reconstruction analysis and to show more clearly the relation between meaning analysis and reconstruction analysis, let me consider Stephan Körner's discussion of what he calls "replacement analysis." Körner says that in replacement analysis we replace some expression which is in some way defective with another expression which is not defective in that way. There are two criteria any replacement analysis must meet. First, there must be a criterion of defectiveness, some criterion for deciding when an expression requires replacement analysis. According to Körner, "examples of criteria of defectiveness are vagueness, internal inconsistency, metaphysical commitments of an undesirable kind." [10] The second criterion is that we must work with a certain replacement-relation between the analysandum and the analysans in order to preserve those features, and just those features, of the framework that we want to preserve. Körner says that "examples of required replacement-relations are bilateral formal implication, bilateral intensional implications of various strictness, or a more or less clearly demarcated similarity." [11] He concludes that

> a brief and schematic description of problems belonging to what might be called replacement-analysis could be given in this way: given certain criteria of defectiveness and a replacement-relation—to replace a defective set of rules by another which is not defective and stands in the replacement-relation to the original set of rules.[12]

We can see that as Körner describes replacement analysis, it includes not only reconstruction analysis but also meaning analysis. But for meaning analysis the replacement-relation must be that of synonymy, while for reconstruction analysis the replacement-relation would seem to be almost anything but synonymy. Meaning analysis is, then, a limiting case of replacement analysis, the case where we can get rid of the defect by replacing one expression with another synonymous with it, e.g. Russell and his analysis of definite descriptions—if this can be called a meaning analysis rather than a reconstruction analysis. Thus given that ordinary language is vague, it is obvious that we cannot utilize the replacement-relation of synonymy, and therefore, in practice, meaning analysis reduces to reconstruction analysis.

Replacement analysis and, therefore, reconstruction analysis is, according to Körner, to be used where we find

10. Stephan Körner, "Some Remarks on Philosophical Analysis," *The Journal of Philosophy*, 59 (1957), 765.
11. Ibid.
12. Ibid.

that an expression we want to use for a certain purpose is in some way defective for that purpose, and we replace the defective expression with one that is not defective. If we make this replacement using meaning analysis, it would seem to be legitimate no matter what our purpose. However this does not seem so obvious if we use, as it seems we must, reconstruction analysis. Körner does not consider the purposes for which it is legitimate to use reconstruction analysis. It ought to be considered because, at first glance at least, it does not seem legitimate to "reshape" an expression just enough to solve a problem we could not solve before reshaping it. What we must do, then, is do what we did with meaning analysis. I shall examine those purposes for doing reconstruction analysis which seem relevant in order to find out which if any are purposes for which it is legitimate to use reconstruction analysis.

However, before we continue let me note here that reconstruction analysis is what I have previously called a type E,1 task because it is a task which, although it does not fall under the jurisdiction of the rules governing the expressions in question, does involve a possible change in some of the rules. When we discussed this in Chapter 5, I said that the criterion by which we judge whether or not to make such changes in a framework is how fruitful, simple, and efficient the changes would make the expression with regard to the purposes for which the expression is used, for example, the purpose of communicating factual knowledge. But at that point in the book we did not consider whether we can always justify changing the rules of an expression by claiming that there is a purpose for which the change makes the expression more fruitful, simple, and efficient. This is what we are interested in now.

There are two basically different kinds of reconstruction analysis. The first is the kind of replacement we make when we draw a distinction between two or more senses of an ambiguous expression. Some expressions can be used in two or more different ways; the rules governing their use do not explicitly distinguish between the several senses. In such a case we would make explicit the different senses of the expression, thereby replacing the defective set of rules governing the expression by two or more sets of rules not defective in this way. Here the criterion of defectiveness is ambiguity. An example of such a use of replacement analysis to reconstruct a particular set of rules is the distinction made and utilized in symbolic logic between the inclusive and exclusive senses of 'or.' I have also used this kind of reconstruction analysis when I distinguished several senses of 'refer.' These distinctions help to avoid certain confusions which might arise because of the ambiguity of 'or' and 'refer.' To avoid such confusions and to show where someone has gone astray because of such confusions seems to be the main, if not the only, purpose for doing this kind of analysis.

This "distinction analysis" is, then, one kind of reconstruction analysis. However because it reconstructs a linguistic framework only by making implicit differences explicit it materially affects neither external nor internal questions, but only the way some one might confusedly approach such questions. Distinction analysis is, then, a helpful and sometimes invaluable tool, but it is the kind of analysis which will help us answer question I only insofar as we may become confused by ambiguous expressions. It is helpful for any approach to any problem, but usually, as in our case, a method sufficient neither to solve nor to provide clues to the solution of the problem.

The second kind of reconstruction analysis is what has been called explication. Carnap explains that this kind of analysis, which is the

> task of making more exact a vague or not quite exact concept used in everyday life or in an earlier stage of scientific or logical development, or rather of replacing it by a newly constructed, more exact concept, belongs among the most important tasks of logical analysis and logical construction. We call this the task of

220   EXTERNAL PROBLEMS

explicating, or of giving an *explication* for, the earlier concept; this earlier concept, or sometimes the term used for it, is called the *explicandum;* and the new concept, or its term, is called an *explicatum* of the old one. . . . Generally speaking, it is not required that an explicatum have, as nearly as possible, the same meaning as the explicandum; it should, however, correspond to the explicandum in such a way that it can be used instead of the latter.[13]

According to Carnap, the requirements for a successful explication are four:[14]

  i. The explicatum must be similar enough to the explicandum so that it can be used in most cases in which the explicandum has been used.
 ii. The explicatum must be given an exact form.
iii. The explicatum must be fruitful for the purposes for which the explication is made. (This requirement is somewhat more general than the one Carnap proposes.)
 iv. The explicatum must be as simple as possible.

That explication is one kind of replacement analysis can be seen by examining the four requirements. The first is in a less precise way the requirement that there be a certain replacement-relation for each replacement analysis. The third is an obvious requirement and the fourth, which although not stated by Körner would certainly be acceptable to him, is the requirement that, all else being equal, the simplest explication should be chosen. The second requirement, however, shows that explication is not equivalent to, but merely one kind, of replacement analysis. It amounts to the criterion of defectiveness for explication, that is, vagueness. But vagueness is just one of many kinds of

13. Carnap, *Meaning and Necessity,* pp. 7–8.
14. See Carnap, *The Logical Foundations of Probability* (Chicago, University of Chicago Press, 1955), p. 7.

defects, explication would seem to be just one kind of replacement analysis. It is also a species of reconstruction analysis. Because the explicatum must be exact in order to correct the defect of vagueness, the explicatum can be at most somewhat similar to the explicandum; when we explicate, we change certain rules of the framework, that is, reconstruct them. Explication differs from distinction analysis in that distinction analysis merely makes explicit certain differences already implicit in the framework. That is, it changes certain rules of the framework of a language without changing the framework itself. Explication, however, not only changes certain rules but also the framework of the language as well.

Two examples of explication are the explication of 'fish' by zoologists as cited by Carnap, and the explication of 'probability' by Carnap himself. What the zoologists have done is to reconstruct the term 'fish' in such a way that such things as whales and seals are no longer called fish. The purpose of this explication was to make the term 'fish' more useful for the purposes of zoology; 'fish' had been somewhat defective in this respect. However, whether or not the defect was one of vagueness, as Carnap claims, may be questioned. Nevertheless the rules governing 'fish' were changed to correct a defect, and the change affected the framework of the language. Perhaps it is wrong to limit explication to just that kind of reconstruction analysis which has for its criterion of defectiveness vagueness. Perhaps we should include all those kinds of analysis which have as their criterion of defectiveness anything but ambiguity and as their replacement-relation anything but synonymy. All these have one thing in common, namely, they all not only change certain rules of the framework but change the framework as well. That this is perhaps what Carnap meant by explication may become more evident when we examine the second example.

As with other scientific terms, Carnap says, there is a classificatory sense of 'probability' of which the comparative and quantitative senses are explicata: "Classificatory concepts are the simplest and least effective kind of concept. Comparative concepts are more powerful, and quantitative concepts still more; that is to say, they enable us to give a more precise description of a concrete situation and, more important, to formulate more comprehensive general laws." [15] Carnap's aim in *The Logical Foundations of Probability* is to explicate the classificatory sense of 'probability' (the explicandum) in terms of a quantitative sense (the explicatum) in order to make that concept more fruitful for science. In this example it seems that unless we are to say that all nonquantitative terms are vague, the defect is not so much vagueness but that the concept does not lend itself to the mathematical formulation of scientific laws. Let us, then, use 'explication' as we did at the end of the last paragraph because it seems that taking vagueness as the criterion of defectiveness for explication does not best describe what actually takes place when people make explications. Moreover, by so doing we divide reconstruction analysis into two exclusive and exhaustive classes.

At this point let me review the ground we have covered. First, we have described replacement analysis and decided that there are three exclusive and exhaustive kinds of replacement analysis. First, there is meaning analysis, which replaces a defect without reconstructing any rules of the framework because its replacement relation is synonymy. Second, there is distinction analysis, which is one way to reconstruct rules of a framework but does not reconstruct the framework itself. Here the criterion of defectiveness is ambiguity. Third, there is explication, which reconstructs not only certain rules of the framework but the framework itself, and which may have a variety of criteria of defectiveness. That these three kinds of replacement analysis are exclusive and exhaustive can be shown as follows: one kind does not reconstruct rules while the other two do; one of the

15. Ibid., p. 12.

latter reconstructs rules but not the framework, the other also reconstructs the framework.

The second thing we have done is to eliminate both meaning analysis and distinction analysis as methods sufficient for our purposes. This leaves only one kind of replacement analysis—explication—to be examined. In both of the above examples the purpose of explicating was to make a term more useful for science. This certainly seems to be a legitimate use of explication. For one reason, it seems to amount to no more than defining a new technical term, which is purpose (ii) for doing meaning analysis. As in that case, we bring a new term into the language. Both are type E,1 tasks. The only difference between the two is that in the one case but not the other, we take as a basis some nontechnical term, a term whose original set of rules either may remain in effect (so that the term becomes ambiguous) or may gradually lose effect (as the scientific way of using the term becomes popular). Are there other purposes for which it is legitimate to use explication? It is certainly used for others. In fact it is used for all those purposes which were listed for meaning analysis. However since only purposes (iv), (v), and (vi) are relevant to philosophical problems, we shall consider only these three.

We can show that we cannot use explication for purpose iv, to refute arguments, by using a previous example, Russell's analysis of definite descriptions, which refuted an argument for the existence of things such as unicorns. The force of the refutation depends on showing that definite descriptions need not be used in the language because there are other expressions, meaning the same, but which are not definite descriptions. Thus the refutation is successful only if the analysans is synonymous with the analysandum. But if we must resort to explication to make an analysis, then this is evidence not that we can refute the argument but rather that refutation by analysis will not work. This may become more evident if we remember that the end result of explication is the same as the result of defining a new tech-

nical term. The question then would be: If we can show that
certain technical terms are translatable into certain other
expressions, have we thereby shown that, or provided
grounds for, the conclusion that certain nontechnical terms
similar in some degree to the technical terms are likewise
translatable? It would seem we have not shown this but
rather that the translation cannot be made because to make
it requires a technical term and thus a change in the framework. Another way of putting this point is that when we
are trying to make a translation and cannot, it is not that
the language is defective and needs revising; rather it is
that the translation and the refutation based on the translation cannot be made.

It is easy to see that explication for purposes (v) and (vi)
is also illegitimate. When we use explication for purpose (v)
we are using it in order to justify theories, in particular
theories which claim that expressions of one sort are translatable into sentences of another sort. We have examined
Carnap's attempt to translate psychological-sentences into
physical-sentences. Is explication a legitimate procedure for
such a purpose? Is it legitimate to change the rules governing psychological-sentences (or physical-sentences) in
order to make such a translation? It would seem not, for the
same reasons it was not legitimate to use explication for
purpose (iv). Thus we cannot use explication for purpose
(v). Furthermore, since it is illegitimate to use explication for
purpose (v), it is also illegitimate to use it for purpose (vi),
in order to reduce entities, because the first step in achieving
purpose (vi) is the making of a translation for which as we
have just seen explication is illegitimate.

It seems, then, that these three philosophical purposes for
which explication has been done are purposes for which it
should not be done. Should we now try to find other purposes for which explication is legitimate to see whether they
might help us? I think not because I believe that we can
show that there is something wrong in general with using
explication in order to answer external questions of type

E,2. A first, quick attempt to show this is the following: Because it seems that if we can approach type E,2 problems, we can do it only from within a given framework, and because explication is a type E,1 task, that is, an external task which modifies the framework, explication cannot be used to answer external questions of type E,2.

This is too quick, however, because the rebuttal is that, although it may be true that we cannot answer external questions by getting outside language (all languages), it does not follow that we must remain within any given framework. Why can we not pick one we want or reconstruct the one we are given? And once we have done this why can we not work from within the new or reconstructed framework? These questions must be answered if we are to show that explication cannot be used to answer external questions. In other words, what we must show is that we must remain not merely within some framework or other but within that framework with which we start, the explicandum framework, which, as we have seen, is the framework of ordinary language. Incidentally, if we show this it will not only rule out explication but also the construction of semantical systems as possible approaches to external problems because the only difference between the two is that explication is piecemeal replacement while construction of semantical systems is overall replacement.

We must work from within the framework of ordinary language to find clues for external problems because when we reconstruct a framework or construct a new one we must have some criterion of defectiveness. Thus, in order to be justified in changing or abandoning a framework we must be able to show that the framework is defective in some way. But how can we show that a framework is defective with regard to external problems? We cannot show it by showing that certain translations cannot be made, or that certain arguments cannot be rebutted, or that the framework fails to meet certain standards which some other, perhaps constructed, frameworks meet, because whether or not these are defects depends on whether the framework is defective. If the framework is not defective then the correct conclusion is that we should not make the translation, or rebut the argument, or use the standards of some other framework. In other words, we cannot claim that a framework is defective just because by using it we cannot do what we might want to do. For example, just because we may not be able to make certain meaning analyses that we want to make, we cannot conclude that the framework in question is vague and therefore defective. Perhaps the particular analyses should not be made. We can show that the framework is defective only if we have independent evidence that the analyses should be possible. Thus such criteria of defectiveness will not do. We need some other if we are to be justified in reconstructing or abandoning the explicandum framework, the framework of ordinary language.

The only criterion of defectiveness which seems to be at all relevant to explicating for the purpose of solving external problems is the defect of misleading us about what there is, or as Körner says, ontologically committing us in undesirable ways. That is, only if the framework of ordinary language leads us to ontological commitments which are in some way undesirable is it defective in any way relevant to external questions. But a linguistic framework cannot be defective in this way. As we saw in the last chapter, no linguistic framework ontologically commits us in any way. Once we are clear about this point there is no reason to think that it is the framework which misleads us about what there is. What can and often does mislead us, as we have seen, is not the framework of the language but some view or theory we might have about language, such as the 'Fido'–Fido theory of reference. It is only when we begin to talk about language as philosophers that we might become misled. It is not language which is defective but philosophers' views of language.

The conclusion, then, seems to be that ordinary language

is not defective in any way relevant to the solution of external problems. Thus because explication is justified for a certain purpose only when the language is defective for that purpose, explication is not justified for the purpose of solving external problems. We must, then, work within the framework of ordinary language when our purpose is to solve external problems. This conclusion not only rules out explication but also, once again, meaning analysis because ordinary language, as we have seen, does not seem to be suitable for meaning analysis. And since distinction analysis is not sufficient to the task we must conclude that we cannot use replacement analysis for the purpose of working with external problems. Only use analysis remains as a possibility.

USE ANALYSIS

One way to characterize this kind of analysis is as that method which consists in showing logical similarities and differences between sentences of known logical kinds and those of a different kind, whose logic is to be discovered. Once these similarities and differences are exhibited, general conclusions about the nature of the second set of sentences being examined are drawn. In light of these conclusions a new look is given to problems involving these sentences and quite often the problems are dissolved, or rather evaporate, because of the different way of looking at the logic of the sentences. For example, certain philosophers using this method claim that sentences such as 'A is right,' 'B raised his arm,' and 'C is vain,' which at first glance may seem to be descriptive (i.e. indicative sentences containing referring$_4$-expressions—expressions which attribute some property to A or B or C respectively), are not descriptive at all. The logic of these sentences is such, so it is claimed, that when we use them we are doing something different from describing—the sentences function respectively to commend something, ascribe responsibility to someone, or entitle us to infer something. In this way, as I shall briefly indicate, certain problems in ethics and the philosophy of mind have been handled.[16]

However, before I discuss these proposed solutions I would like to give some indication of how I am using certain key expressions which have already arisen in the discussion. The terms are: 'solve,' 'dissolve,' 'logical similarity,' and 'logical difference.' The first term, 'solve,' is used in such a way that to solve a problem is to answer correctly the question or questions in which the problem is formulated. The term, 'dissolve,' in contrast, is used in such a way that to dissolve a problem is to show that the question or questions in which the problem is formulated presuppose certain things which are not true. In other words, to dissolve a problem is to show that at least one necessary condition of the truth of any possible answer to the questions is false. Thus for the complex question, "Did you stop beating your

16. Some others whom it seems reasonable to interpret as using or implying this method are the following: J. L. Austin in "Other Minds," *Proceedings of the Aristotelian Society,* Suppl. Vol. 20 (1946), where he tries to show that because 'I know' is logically like 'I promise' in certain respects, it is a performatory utterance and thus not used to refer to some kind of mental event. R. M. Hare, in *The Language of Morals* (Oxford, Clarendon Press 1952), where in chapters 6 and 7 he compares and contrasts the logical features of 'good' and 'red' to show that 'good' is not the name of a property, either simple or complex. G. E. Moore, in "Is Existence a Predicate?," in Flew, ed., *Logic and Language, Second Series* (Oxford, Basil Blackwell, 1955), in which he considers interpreting the claim that 'exist' does not stand for an attribute as the claim that the way 'exist' is used in sentences differs from the way predicates such as 'growl' are used. G. A. Paul, in "Is there a Problem about Sense-Data," in which he compares the logic of 'sense-datum' with that of 'fovea' and with 'appears' to show that there is no reason to claim that "there are entities of a curious sort over and above physical objects" (p. 109) which are referred$_2$ to by 'sense-datum.' M. Weitz, in "Reasons in Criticism," *The Journal of Aesthetics and Art Criticism, 20* (1962), 436, where he claims that 'dramatically great' is not a name of a property because it is used in praise utterances, and the logical functioning of praise utterances differs from the functioning of predicates that describe properties.

wife?" there are only two kinds of proper answers, e.g. "I did" and "I didn't." A necessary condition of both kinds of answers is that the person being asked had been beating his wife. Thus if a problem for someone is to find out if a person stopped beating his wife, he would dissolve the problem, rather than solve it, by showing that the person had not been beating his wife. Whereas to solve a problem is to answer a question, to dissolve a problem is closer to correcting or curing the questioner. For this reason the method we are discussing has been called therapeutic. It functions primarily to cure philosophers rather than to solve philosophical problems.

The two other terms, 'logical similarity' and 'logical difference,' can best be understood by means of what might be called the logic of sentences. The logic of a sentence is the totality of those of its characteristics which we can discover by examining its use, such as what it entails, what entails it, what it implies or presupposes in various contexts, what are its equivalents or near equivalents, in what contexts it is odd to use it, in what contexts it is odd to question its use, and in what way—if at all—some kind of formal logic applies to it. These characteristics are what I mean by logical similarities and differences between two sentences.

However, not all such similarities and differences are important for our purposes. The ones in which we are interested are only those by means of which we can distinguish what we can call, borrowing a phrase from Waismann, "the language stratum" to which a sentence belongs,[17] for, supposedly, once we can assign a sentence to a particular language stratum we can infer things about it not otherwise discoverable. We are not interested, then, in the ways in which sentences are similar or differ with regard to those characteristics which a sentence has because it is unique:

17. See Waismann, "Language Strata," in Flew, ed., *Logic and Language, Second Series,* pp. 18–22. The concept of a language stratum is much like Ryle's category, discussed on pp. 38–41 and pp. 63–68.

those entailments of a sentence which are unique, its equivalents, and its distinct contexts of use. We are interested
rather in what I shall call "the stratifying" features, those
a sentence has in common with certain other sentences
which differentiate it as belonging to one particular language
stratum. If we can assign a sentence to a particular stratum
we shall be able to draw some conclusions concerning important extralogical facts about the sentence which, it has
been claimed, have philosophical importance: the sense in
which it is meaningful (e.g. descriptive, directive, performatory, or emotive); the way in which it can be verified (e.g.
by direct observation, by inductive inference from directly
observed facts, or by deduction from axioms); and what
theory of truth, if any, applies to the sentence (e.g. correspondence theory, coherence theory, or pragmatic theory).

Let us assume from here on that when we talk of the logic
of sentences we shall mean the stratifying features of sentences, and that when we talk of logical similarities and differences we shall mean stratifying similarities and differences. This brings out a major difference between use
analysis and meaning analysis. The latter is concerned only
with the relation of entailment, while the former is primarily
interested in quite different kinds of relations.

Before we move on, it might be helpful to look at some
examples of language strata. Some strata are easily discovered such as those differentiated by the distinct grammatical differences among the classes of questions, impera-
tives, exclamations, and indicative sentences. In these cases
the way, if any, in which the sentences are meaningful, verifiable, and true differs from stratum to stratum. Thus we
can say that sentences belonging to these different grammatical classes also belong to different language strata.
However, there may be other language strata not so obviously delineated by grammatical features. Thus within the
grammatical class of indicative sentences there seem to be
various subsets of sentences, such as the sets of material-
object sentences, sense-data sentences, laws of nature, math-

ematical propositions, ethical sentences, lines of poetry, etc. According to Waismann, each of these subsets has what might be called a distinct "logical style." [18] The sentences within each of these subsets have certain unique linguistic features in common. However, whether these distinct features, which can be discovered by use analysis, are or imply stratifying features, that is, whether these different subsets of indicative sentences are also language strata is a question we shall have to consider later because it is among these subsets that the method of use analysis has most often been used. By and large until recently sentences belonging to the grammatical class of indicative sentences have been relegated to either of two exclusive and exhaustive language strata. Indicative sentences were thought to be either descriptive (cognitive) or emotive. The method of use analysis, the method of exhibiting what I have called the stratifying differences and similarities of sentences, has been trying to replace, among other things, this dichotomy and the misleading conclusions drawn from it.

To illustrate this method, I shall briefly examine three attempts to employ use analysis to deal with the three sentences mentioned previously: 'A is right,' 'B raised his arm,' and 'C is vain.' The purpose of these attempts is to show that although all three sentences are grammatically indicative, as are descriptive sentences such as 'A is blue,' 'B's arm went up,' and 'C is blond,' they are not themselves descriptive. I shall at this point merely explain the three attempts. How successful they might be will be discussed later.

The first attempt to be considered is that by P. H. Nowell-Smith, who is concerned with the problem of what kind of properties ethical properties are. Nowell-Smith instead of trying to solve the problem, sets out to dissolve it by showing that terms such as 'right' and 'good' in their ethical use do not have certain logical features that terms referring to

18. Ibid.; see p. 19.

properties have.[19] As a consequence, 'right' and 'good' do not refer$_4$ to properties, and the problem about what kind of properties they refer$_4$ to is dissolved. He does this by showing that because there are important logical differences between indicative sentences such as 'x is right' and descriptive sentences such as 'x is blue,' the former sentences are not descriptive, and as a result their predicates do not refer$_4$ to properties. In so doing, he is primarily attacking Intuitionists such as G. E. Moore on whose view, claims Nowell-Smith, sentences such as 'x is good' are, like 'x is blue,' descriptive, the primary difference between the two being that 'good' refers$_4$ to a nonnatural rather than a natural property. Such Intuitionists, then, seem to presuppose that 'good' and 'right' refer$_4$ to some kind of property. Nowell-Smith, however, wishes to show that this is where they make their mistake. Using our terminology we can say that Nowell-Smith is claiming that they belong not to the stratum of descriptive sentences, but rather to a different language stratum, a stratum the members of which do not contain referring$_4$ expressions because only those expressions which are contained in sentences belonging to the stratum of descriptive sentences refer$_4$.

It will be noticed that in the above discussion we have been talking about referring$_4$ expressions (descriptive expressions), whereas in Chapter 5 we talked only about referring$_2$ expressions (denoting expressions) when we considered external questions. However there are not only external questions about what there is, about what entities we are ontologically committed to, but also about what kind of properties these entities have. Thus if a value for 'p' in question I is a referring$_4$ expression, then if we are asking an external question we would be asking what it referred$_4$ to; we would be asking what property of the entities this expression referred to. The answer would be something like, "What 'p' ontologically commits us to is the property q." It can be

19. See P. H. Nowell-Smith, *Ethics* (Baltimore, Penguin Books 1954), chapters 3 and 4.

seen, then, that there are two kinds of type E,2 external questions: one about entities, and one about properties.[20] For this reason let us stipulate that when we are talking about those kinds of referring which in general are relevant to external questions we are talking about referring$_6$, which means "either referring$_2$ or referring$_4$"; or about referring$_7$, which means "either referring$_3$ or referring$_5$." This will be helpful in future discussion.

Let us return now to Nowell-Smith's argument against the Intuitionists. I shall state in some detail his two main arguments so that we can later see more clearly the problems facing the approach he uses. In the first argument, Nowell-Smith claims that Moore is guilty of the same fallacy of which Moore had found the Naturalists guilty, that is, what Moore called the Naturalistic Fallacy. Actually, as Nowell-Smith interprets the fallacy it might more appropriately be called the Descriptivist Fallacy. This fallacy occurs, for example, when from a descriptive premise such as 'x maximizes pleasure' someone infers the normative conclusion 'I ought to do x.' This inference is fallacious because there is nothing logically odd about accepting the premise and asking, "Why should I do x?" Similarly, claims Nowell-Smith, if 'x is right' is descriptive, if it is used to refer to a property of x as it is for the Intuitionists, then between it and 'I ought to do x' there should also be a logical gap. It should not be odd to ask "Why should x be done?" while at the same time admitting that x is right. But Nowell-Smith says that the question is logically odd in such a context; from this he concludes that 'x is right,' unlike 'x maximizes happiness,' is not descriptive, and therefore 'right' does not refer to any kind of property.[21]

In the other argument I wish to consider, Nowell-Smith uses the 'is' and 'seems' distinction to try to show another

20. We briefly considered one way use analysis has been used regarding referring$_2$ expressions when we discussed Paul's approach to 'sense-datum.' See p. 228 n.

21. See Nowell-Smith, *Ethics,* pp. 36–43 for the first argument.

respect in which 'right' differs logically from descriptive
predicates such as empirical predicates. Empirical predicates are used to refer to certain properties a thing may
have or merely seem to have. Thus we can and do say "This
is blue," and "That seems blue." And there is nothing
logically odd about a man who realizes that he is color-
blind saying, "That seems grey to me, but I realize that it
is really blue." According to Nowell-Smith if ethical predicates are used to refer to properties, we should, as with
color predicates, be able to say, "That seems wrong to me,
but I realize that it is really right." But this is surely in
some way logically odd. Thus 'right' differs logically from
'blue,' and consequently 'right,' unlike 'blue,' does not refer$_4$
to a property.[22]

In the above two ways Nowell-Smith exhibits the logical
differences between 'x is right' and sentences such as 'x is
blue,' and he concludes that 'x is right' is not descriptive;
thus terms such as 'right' and 'good' cannot refer$_4$ to either
natural or nonnatural properties because they do not refer$_4$
at all. Nowell-Smith concludes that ethical discourse has a
logic all its own: it forms a unique language stratum. It is,
then, not descriptive; neither is it to be thrown in with all
other nondescriptive sentences because it also differs from
them. In this way Nowell-Smith breaks down the descriptive–emotive dichotomy by uncovering an additional language stratum—ethical discourse—in which we use language not to refer$_4$ to properties of things but rather, for
example, to commend. If Nowell-Smith has been successful,
then, he has found internal clues to an external problem
because his conclusion that ethical terms do not refer$_4$ to
properties is relevant to question 1 as an external question:
"What does 'p' refer to?" If he is correct, then it is illegitimate to ask 1 when we substitute ethical terms for 'p' because question 1 presupposes that the substituends for 'p'
refer$_6$. Nowell-Smith has not solved but dissolved an ex-

22. Ibid., see pp. 48–60 for the second argument.

ternal question some philosophers have been tempted to ask. In the light of this, it would appear that use analysis is the method for which we have been looking to provide the internal clues we need.

The second example of use analysis to be considered here is an attempt to handle another problem which appears to defy solution, the problem of human action. It can be formulated in the following question: "What is the difference between someone raising his arm and his arm going up?" If, as the question presupposes, there is a difference, it would seem that there must be some difference between the kinds of events or states which cause the arm to go up in each case. Traditionally there have been three different views about the unique cause which results in someone raising his arm rather than it merely going up. It has been thought that the cause of someone raising his arm is either some unique physical event—some unique brain process, or some unique mental event—an act of will or volition, or the person himself in some nondeterministic way. However, none of these three kinds of solutions seems to be satisfactory. The first leads us into the problems connected with free will and determinism, the second into the problems for dualistic interactionism, and the third leaves us with a mysterious causal force which has been called "the self" but which when we try to explain it usually leads us back to one of the first two kinds of solutions and their problems.

However, H. L. A. Hart, like Nowell-Smith, looks at this problem in a different way. It is wrong, he believes, to talk about what certain expressions are supposed to refer to until we have found whether the logical features of the sentences containing those expressions are the correct kind for such a job. For Hart, although sentences such as 'He raised his arm' and 'His arm went up' are indicative sentences, they have quite different uses. While the second is used descriptively, i.e. used solely to refer to something, in this case to some event, the first sentence is not. It is used to ascribe responsibility to someone for his arm going up,

rather than to refer to some event or process which differs
in some way from the kind of event or process referred to
by 'His arm went up.' [23] Hart reaches this conclusion by
comparing the decisions of judges with the sentences relevant to the problem of human agency; he finds many similarities between the two. He brings out the similarities by
exhibiting the logical peculiarities of judges' decisions and
then showing how sentences about human agency have
many of the same peculiarities. In light of these similarities,
Hart concludes that, just as a judge is not referring to a
property someone has—is not describing him—when he
gives his legal decisions, neither are we referring to something quite unique in a person when we use sentences such
as 'He raised his arm.'

For Hart, then, there is no problem connected with the
difference between someone raising his arm and his arm
going up because the question which formulates the problem presupposes that the two sentences 'He raised his arm'
and 'His arm went up' describe two different situations and
thus are in the same language stratum, the stratum of descriptive sentences. This is what Hart denies. Hart thus
dissolves rather than solves a problem, in much the same
manner as Nowell-Smith. And, therefore, in a like manner,
Hart seems to have found a method to obtain internal clues
to an external problem, the method we have called use
analysis.

The third attempt is concerned with the problem which
led us into this discussion, the traditional mind–body problem. As generally conceived, there are three kinds of possible solutions to the problem: body–no mind, mind–no
body, and both mind and body. None of these three kinds
of answers has been put forth satisfactorily. The first leaves
us with the problems of materialism, the second with the
problem of solipsism, and the third with solipsism plus some
problematic kind of causation whether the view be parallel-

23. See H. L. A. Hart, "The Ascription of Rights and Responsibility," in Flew, ed., *Logic and Language, First Series,* pp. 160 f.

ism or interactionism. Is there, then, no more satisfactory way to approach this problem? According to Gilbert Ryle, whose view we have already examined,[24] there is. Instead of considering the problem in terms of minds, bodies, machines, ghosts, and the like, Ryle suggests that we examine the words and sentences we use in our talk about such matters. Let us review Ryle's method and approach briefly. On one interpretation we can construe him as being interested in what we can discover about what I have called the stratifying features of the sentences containing such expressions. Thus, when we use mental terms we are not talking in the same language stratum as when we use physical terms with the only difference being that we are talking about two different worlds (the physical and the nonphysical world) or about two mutually exclusive kinds of substances. Rather we are talking in two different language strata about one world and one kind of thing—persons. Ryle's point is that all three traditional kinds of answers are wrong because they presuppose mistaken views about the stratifying logic of mind-sentences and body-sentences. These answers assume that questions about the relation of a person to his mind and the relation of his body to his mind are proper questions.[25] For Ryle they are not. Furthermore because the mind–body problem is essentially a problem about the relationship between mind and body, it presupposes that questions about this relationship are proper questions. However, if Ryle is correct, they are not proper questions and the mind-body problem is dissolved.

An example of the technique Ryle uses to establish his thesis is, as we have seen, the way he handles sentences such as 'A is vain.' For him this would be neither a sentence referring₄ to some mental states or episodes, such as feelings or pricks of vanity, nor one referring₄ to actual and possible behavior. We can see this by noticing what Ryle says about the sentence, 'He boasted from vanity.' According to Ryle

24. See pp. 38–41.
25.. See Gilbert Ryle, *The Concept of Mind,* p. 168.

this sentence explains why someone boasted by stating that in boasting he satisfied "the law-like proposition that whenever he finds a chance of securing the admiration and envy of others, he does whatever he thinks will produce this admiration and envy." [26] Such a sentence is what Ryle calls "a partly open hypothetical." It is, in this respect, law-like. A law is "an open hypothetical," an hypothetical the antecedent of which "can embody at least one expression like 'any' or 'whenever.' " [27] Consequently, according to Ryle, a law is merely an inference ticket; it is used solely as a license which permits us to make certain inferences. Thus laws are not descriptive sentences, and neither, concludes Ryle, are law-like sentences. Being law-like they, like laws, function as inference tickets rather than descriptive sentences.[28]

As I have interpreted his position, Ryle would say that sentences such as 'A is vain' are law-like and thus belong in the stratum of inference tickets rather than the stratum of descriptive sentences. Thus 'A is vain' does not predicate a property of A as do sentences such as 'A is blond' or 'A is six feet tall.' It merely licenses us to make a certain inference. In such a way Ryle attempted to handle all mind-expressions in *The Concept of Mind*. If no mind-expressions refer$_6$ to properties or entities either physical or mental, then it is wrong to ask about the relationships between mental entities and properties, and other entities and properties. Thus it is wrong to ask the questions which formulate the mind–body problem, and thus there is no mind–body problem. In such a way Ryle, like Nowell-Smith and Hart, provides what seem to be internal clues to external problems, clues that enable us to dissolve such problems.

From the preceding examples it would seem that use analysis may be the method we need to provide us with internal clues to external questions. At least this method

26. Ibid., p. 89.
27. Ibid., p. 120.
28. Ibid., see pp. 117–25.

meets the first requirement: it is a method which remains inside a given linguistic framework, the framework of ordinary language, when the purpose for using the method is to find such internal clues. It remains within the framework of ordinary language, which we have seen any successful method must do, because it merely examines the logical similarities and differences between sentences of that framework. In this respect it differs from explication. Because use analysis is also applicable to ordinary language, as it seems meaning analysis is not, and is constituted so that it is at least possible that it provides internal clues to external questions, as distinction analysis is not, we can conclude that use analysis and only use analysis is worth considering further. We are ready, therefore, to consider whether use analysis meets the second requirement. We can see that there is some question whether it does because in Chapter 3 we found problems for Ryle's approach to the mind–body problem, the external problem we have examined the most thoroughly. Therefore because, as we have just seen, Ryle's approach to the mind–body problem is an example of use analysis, the problems that we have found for his approach may be problems for use analysis in general. To see whether this is true, I shall return to a discussion of the mind–body problem and examine Ryle's and also Hart's approach in contrast to the approach of Smart and Chisholm. This will be the main concern of the next chapter.

7. *External Problems and Use Analysis*

In the last chapter we found that use analysis and only use analysis meets the first requirement for a successful approach to external problems. It remains within one linguistic framework, the framework of ordinary language, when it is used for the purpose of providing clues to an external question such as "What does 'p' refer$_7$ to?," i.e. question 1. Before we go on to see whether use analysis meets the second requirement, i.e. the requirement that it provide us with some internal grounds for justifying certain answers to external questions, let me first point out that in the last chapter, when examples of use analysis were examined, I stated the conclusions reached by those employing use analysis in the form: 'p' does not refer$_6$ (either refer$_2$ or refer$_4$) to anything, i.e. 'p' is not a referring$_6$ expression. Thus if I was correct in my characterization of use analysis, then the question which use analysis is designed to answer is not "What does 'p' refer$_7$ to?," which is question 1, but rather "Is 'p' a referring$_6$ expression?" Consequently we must accomplish two tasks if we are to achieve the purpose of this chapter. First, we must find out how use analysis is relevant to question 1 when use analysis seems to be used to provide answers to a different question: "Is 'p' a referring$_6$ expression?" Second, we must see whether we can justify answers to the latter question by relying solely on use analysis. I shall consider the former point first because if we cannot show the relevance of use analysis to question 1, there is no reason to consider the latter point.

We found a clue about how use analysis is relevant to question 1 in the last chapter. Use analysis is a method which seems designed to dissolve rather than solve problems expressible by question 1. Our present purpose, then, is to bring out clearly how it is that use analysis can dissolve these problems. What we want to find, in effect, is how it is that certain kinds of answers to "Does 'p' refer$_6$ to something?" which is the question use analysis is designed to answer, can dissolve question 1. Let us examine our schematic example of an answer to question 1, "What 'p' refers$_7$ to is q," in order to see what are the necessary conditions of any answer of that form. We know for substantive expressions that the following is true: 'p' is a referring$_7$ expression if and only if 'x refers$_1$ to at least one thing that exists' takes 'p' as a value, and is true when applied to 'p.' The first of these two jointly sufficient, necessary conditions of 'p' being a referring$_7$ expression is the definition of " 'p' is a referring$_2$ expression" (see p. 143). Thus 'p' is a referring$_7$ expression only if 'p' is a referring$_2$ expression and, therefore, only if 'p' is a referring$_6$ expression.

We also know that what 'p' refers$_7$ to is q only if 'p' is a referring$_7$ expression. Therefore we can conclude that what 'p' refers$_7$ to is q only if 'p' is a referring$_6$ expression. Consequently, because this is only a schematic answer to questions of the form of 1, we can say that a necessary condition of any answer to question 1 about an expression 'p' is that 'p' is a referring$_6$ expression. If 'p' in any specific case can be shown not to be a referring$_6$ expression, then it follows that there can be no correct answer to question 1 in that case. It is in this sense that problems expressible by question 1 can be dissolved. Such problems can be solved only if 'p' is a referring$_6$ expression. Thus such problems presuppose that 'p' is a referring$_6$ expression. If, however, we show that in a particular case the presupposition does not obtain, we thereby show that the question expressing the problem is incorrect and there is no problem, i.e. the problem is dissolved.

If we assume for the moment that use analysis can justifiably be used to find out whether expressions are referring$_6$ expressions, we can see how relevant use analysis is to external questions of type E,2, that is, how use analysis can provide clues to question 1 as an external question and thus clues to what there is. Let us return to the three examples of use analysis that we have already examined.

In these three examples the expressions being considered as possible substituends for 'p' are the three expressions 'right,' 'raising his arm,' and 'vain.' In the first example, question 1 would be, "What does 'right' refer$_7$ to?"—in other words, "What does 'right' describe?" Generally two answers have been given to this question. First, it refers$_7$ to a certain natural property of things; second, it refers$_7$ to a certain nonnatural property of things. But this question is legitimate and answers to it are possible only if 'right' is a referring$_6$ term. But if Nowell-Smith is correct, then 'right' is not a referring$_6$ term. Thus it is incorrect to ask question 1 about 'right,' and the problem about what kind of property 'right' refers to is dissolved. In this example use analysis is relevant to question 1 insofar as it can be used to answer questions about referring$_6$, because it provides us with internal grounds for the conclusion that it is incorrect to ask external questions of type E,2 about 'right' and presumably other ethical terms such as 'good.' This is also true in the other two examples. If Ryle and Hart are correct, then it is also wrong to wonder whether the expressions 'vain' and 'raising his arm' refer$_7$ to mental or physical properties of things.

However, this is not the only way in which use analysis may be able to provide us with internal clues to external questions. Let us assume that we have found that 'p' refers$_7$ to something. We then want to ask, "What does 'p' refer$_7$ to?" Can use analysis help us here? That it can may be shown in this way. The answer to question 1 is of the form "What 'p' refers$_7$ to is q." We know that this is true only if 'p' and 'q' refer$_7$ to the same things. And we also know that 'p' and 'q' refer$_7$ to the same things only if 'q' is a referring$_7$ expression. And 'q' is a referring$_7$ expression only if 'q' is a referring$_6$ expression. Thus what 'p' refers$_7$ to is q only if 'q' is a referring$_6$ expression. But, we are assuming, we can find out whether or not 'q' refers$_6$ by use analysis. If 'q' does not refer$_6$, then what 'p' refers$_7$ to is not q, and we have eliminated one possible answer to question 1. For example, we might ask "What does the substantive expression 'table' refer$_3$ to?" Let us assume that 'table' is a referring$_2$ expression, as it seems to be. One possible answer is that what 'table' refers$_3$ to are certain sense-data. But a necessary condition of this is that 'sense-data' is a referring$_2$ expression. This is where use analysis becomes relevant. We have already seen an example of employing use analysis for this purpose. After examining the use of sense-data sentences, G. A. Paul concludes that these sentences are just another way of talking about how things look to us. But since the way things look to us is not something that might exist, then 'sense-data' cannot be a substituend for 'x' in 'x exists.' Thus 'sense-data' cannot be a referring$_2$ expression, and, consequently, sense-data cannot be a possible answer to "What does 'table' refer$_3$ to?"

From this example we can see that insofar as we can answer questions about referring$_6$ by use analysis we can employ use analysis to eliminate certain answers to external questions in the form of question 1. We could, then, answer any specific case of question 1 in this manner if we could eliminate all possible answers but one. Thus, ideally at least, use analysis may be able to provide us with an internal way not only to dissolve but also to solve external problems. However, whether or not this ideal can be attained in a particular case, or indeed in any case at all, it is nevertheless true that if use analysis can eliminate certain possible answers it can be said to give us some grounds for judging answers to external questions.

Another way of putting this is to say that use analysis is a method which purports to give us clues about the language stratum to which any given expressions belong. Not all language strata are such that the expressions which belong to those strata are referring $_6$ expressions. Thus if by use analysis we can show that a certain expression belongs to a stratum the members of which do not refer $_6$ then we can infer that that expression does not refer $_7$ to something. This is what was done in the three examples discussed in the last chapter. The term 'right' was put in the stratum of commending rather than descriptive (referring $_6$) expressions; 'raising his arm' was put in the stratum of expressions that ascribe responsibility rather than the stratum of referring $_6$ expressions; 'vain' was put in the stratum of lawlike expressions rather than referring $_6$ expressions. In this way problems about what such expressions refer $_7$ to are dissolved because the necessary condition of any solution to such problems, that they are referring $_6$ expressions, does not obtain.

We have seen, then, that use analysis is relevant to, that is, provides internal clues to, external questions insofar as it is a method which can provide grounds for justifying answers to questions of the form, "Is 'p' a referring $_6$ expression?" We have, therefore, completed the first task facing us in this chapter. The second task is to find out whether use analysis provides such grounds. If we find out that use analysis is all that is needed to provide these grounds, then we will have found that use analysis meets the second requirement for a successful approach to external problems. In order to begin an examination of this point, let us turn again to the mind–body problem at a point where philosophers such as Chisholm and Smart disagree with those such as Ryle and Hart. All four men seem to agree on the correctness of linguistic dualism. However, in spite of this one area of agreement, their conclusions about the mind–body problem differ markedly. Both Chisholm and Smart believe this thesis is relevant to the traditional mind–body problem because it can be used to help supply a particular solution; it can be used to help supply a particular answer to question I when 'p' is replaced by mind-expressions and body-expressions. Ryle and Hart also agree that this thesis of linguistic dualism is relevant to the traditional problem but think that it is relevant for a different reason. It is not that this thesis can help supply us with an answer to question I but rather that by examining the use of the two different kinds of expressions we can find that certain expressions relevant to the problem are not substitutable for 'p' in question I and thus question I should not be asked about those expressions.

Chisholm claims that linguistic dualism is evidence for a traditional mind–body dualism of some sort. That is, he claims that a linguistic dualism is evidence upon the basis of which we can conclude that mind-expressions refer$_7$ to mental phenomena, and body-expressions refer$_7$ to physical phenomena. Smart, on the other hand, uses the linguistic dualism with Occam's razor to conclude that (at least certain) mind-expressions and (at least certain) body-expressions refer$_7$ to the same thing, brain processes. Thus although each arrives at a different answer to question I when asked about the mind–body problem, they agree that it is legitimate to ask question I about both of these two different kinds of expressions. Ryle and Hart disagree with both of these solutions. Taking, as we have, 'A is vain' as an example of the kind of expression Ryle discusses, we can ask according to both Chisholm and Smart, "What does 'vanity' refer$_7$ to?" Smart might say that it refers$_7$ to certain brain states and Chisholm might claim it refers$_7$ to certain mental states. But Ryle, as we have seen, claims that 'vanity' is not a referring$_6$ expression and therefore he would claim that both these answers are wrong because any answers to question I about 'vanity' are wrong.

There would be a similar disagreement about 'He is raising his arm' and 'His arm is going up.' Presumably Smart would claim that part of the difference is that while 'his arm going up' merely refers$_7$ to certain overt behavior, 'his raising his arm' would in addition refer$_7$ to some brain process. Chisholm seems to think that part of the difference is that the latter, unlike the former, refers$_7$ to some mental act.[1] Hart, however, while agreeing that there is a difference in addition to the differences in meaning between the two expressions, claims that the difference is not that 'his raising his arm' refers$_7$ to something different from or in addition to what 'his arm going up' refers$_7$ to, but rather that 'his raising his arm' is used to ascribe responsibility to someone for his arm going up, so that it does not refer to anything other than the arm going up. Thus for Hart the question "What other than his arm going up does 'his raising his arm' refer$_7$ to?" is illegitimate because it presupposes that 'his raising his arm' refers$_7$ to something in addition to his arm going up, and for Hart it does not.

The central difference between Chisholm and Smart on the one hand and Ryle and Hart on the other is that they disagree about the answers to questions of the form "Is 'p' a referring$_6$ expression?" Ryle and Hart are directly interested in this question while Smart merely assumes or presupposes an answer to it. Chisholm, although at one point he considers a factor relevant to this question, does so only very briefly.[2] The question to consider now is, as-

1. See R. M. Chisholm, "Review of *Intention*," *The Philosophical Review, 68* (1959), 110.

2. Ibid. At this point in the review Chisholm considers the sentences 'I raised my arm' and 'My arm went up' and says that if there is any reason for ascribing responsibility when using the first but not the second sentence "(and I can not believe that the philosopher is in a position to deny that there is), then, I should think, this reason must pertain to someone's act and thus presuppose that there is a difference between my raising my arm and my arm going up." Thus Chisholm's claim is that only if 'raising my arm' refers$_7$ to some act by me are we justified in ascribing responsibility to me for the occurrence of my arm going up. Thus if Hart is to justify his claim about sentences such as 'I raised my arm' he must show that the reason does not refer$_7$ to anything about me different from my arm going up. Hart would, I should think, claim that the difference is not in me but in the circumstances under which my arm goes up, because the reason, in general, for ascribing responsibility

suming that Ryle and Hart have correctly characterized the logical similarities and differences between the sentences they are all interested in and certain other sentences, should we thereby conclude that the answers Ryle and Hart give to the question "Is 'p' a referring$_6$ expression?" are justified, or would it still be reasonable to give the answer which both Chisholm and Smart accept? If we answer that the only reasonable course is to accept the conclusions of Ryle and Hart, then we will have found out that use analysis meets the second requirement.

A clue to how we should answer this question can be found by looking once again at the criticism of Ryle's thesis made in Chapter 3.[3] There we found that Ryle infers that mind-expressions belong to the category, or what we have called stratum, of law-like sentences rather than to the stratum of reports or descriptive sentences. And because sentences belonging to this stratum do not refer$_6$, Ryle can be said to conclude that mind-expressions do not refer$_6$ and thus do not refer$_7$ to something. Ryle, Hart, and Nowell-Smith all provide arguments to justify their conclusions. Two questions will be asked about each of these arguments. First, do the arguments justify the conclusions, have these men established all the premises needed to make their arguments valid? Second, if they have not done so, can we find some other way to justify their conclusions?

We are interested in whether the conclusions of Ryle, Hart, and Nowell-Smith that certain indicative sentences have a nondescriptive use are justified on the basis of what they have shown concerning certain logical similarities and differences. Although Hart and Ryle emphasize logical simi-

------

is to "check crime and encourage virtue" (Hart, "The Ascription of Responsibility and Rights," p. 166). In specific cases we ascribe responsibility when and the way we do because certain laws concerning crime and virtue (legal and moral laws) apply to the particular circumstances. We justify these laws by their utility in checking crime and encouraging virtue.

3. See pp. 65–69.

larities with nondescriptive sentences and Nowell-Smith emphasizes logical differences from descriptive sentences, their approaches are basically the same. They and others like them move to a conclusion about the use of certain sentences which phrase the problems they are considering, from premises about the logical similarities or differences between these sentences and certain other sentences whose use seems to be clear. They then use this conclusion either to solve or to dissolve the relevant problem. Let us examine the form of the argument as Nowell-Smith uses it because he has dealt with it most specifically:

1. Indicative sentences of the form 'x is blue' are descriptive sentences; they contain expressions that are referring$_4$ expressions.
2. Indicative sentences of the form 'x is right' differ logically from indicative sentences of the form 'x is blue' in respects A, B, C, ...

Therefore

3. Indicative sentences of the form 'x is right' are not descriptive sentences.
4. The predicates of nondescriptive sentences are not referring$_4$ expressions, i.e. do not refer$_4$ to a property.

Therefore

5. The ethical predicate 'right' does not refer$_4$ to a property (either natural or nonnatural).

This argument has three premises. Premise 1 certainly seems to be true. Color predicates seem to be perfect examples of descriptive predicates. If they do not refer$_4$ to properties, then no predicates do. Premise 2 is the kind of statement which Nowell-Smith and the others presumably establish by examining the logical features of sentences such as 'This is right.' We will for our purpose assume that it is true. Statement 4 on the other hand is a premise which we can show to be true by definition. An indicative sentence is descriptive if and only if it contains a predicate which is a descriptive expression, i.e. a referring$_4$ expression. Thus a nondescriptive indicative sentence does not have a referring$_4$ expression as its predicate. Thus premise 4 is true. If the argument is valid, then it seems that we have established its conclusion, that is, that 'right' is not a referring$_4$ expression.

However, the argument as it stands is not valid. What seems to be required is a premise that relates logical characteristics of sentences to their being descriptive. This is achieved if we replace premise 1 with:

> 1′ Sentences logically unlike indicative sentences of the form 'x is blue' in respects A, B, C, . . . are not descriptive.

Nowell-Smith and the others do not seem to consider this premise, perhaps because they think that it is obviously true. Indeed this is the case with Nowell-Smith. "To say that goodness is a property commits us to the very debatable assertion that the logic of 'good' is like that of 'blue,' 'loud,' and 'round.' " [4] The assertion Nowell-Smith mentions is not merely debatable but is false if what he has shown about the logic of ethical predicates is true. But the reason he thinks that anyone who says that goodness is a property is committed to this debatable assertion seems to be that he accepts without question the claim that if P is a property then 'P' functions in sentences logically like predicates such as 'blue,' 'loud,' and 'round.' This claim approximates premise 1′.

Is premise 1′ obviously true as Nowell-Smith and the others seem to think? It is, I think, only if 'descriptive' is used in premise 1′ in a sense different from that required to make 4 analytic, so that anyone who thinks that both 1′ and 4 are obviously true is guilty of equivocation. Let me show this. Premise 1′ is analytic if we use the term 'descriptive' in such a way that to say a sentence is descriptive is

4. P. H. Nowell-Smith, *Ethics,* p. 64.

to say that it is logically like empirical sentences of the
form 'x is blue' in respects A, B, C, . . . This is the way
logical empiricists and some of their descendants often seem
to use 'descriptive.' I shall call this the narrow sense of the
word. However there is another sense which I shall call
the broad sense. It is the sense we have used above to
make 4 analytic. Thus a sentence descriptive in the broad
sense is an indicative sentence whose predicate is a descriptive expression, a referring$_4$ expression.

Although if we use 'descriptive' in the narrow sense, $1'$
is true, 4 is no longer analytic and certainly not obviously
true because 4 would read: 'The predicates of sentences
which are not logically like empirical sentences in respects
A, B, C, . . . , are not referring$_4$ expressions.' In this
case, although the argument would be valid and 1 and $1'$
true, there surely would seem to be some doubt about 4.
Thus anyone who uses 'descriptive' in this narrow sense
would have to establish a premise such as 4, which no one
has done. On the other hand, if we use 'descriptive' in the
broad sense, then although 1 and 4 are true and the argument valid, $1'$ would need to be established—and these
men have not done so. In this case $1'$ would be: "Sentences
logically unlike indicative sentences of the form 'x is blue'
in respects A, B, C, . . . do not have predicates that are
referring$_4$ expressions." This sentence is not obviously true.

Thus Nowell-Smith and the others must justify either
premises like $1'$ or those like 4 in order to justify their conclusions, but they have not done this. Consequently they
have not justified dissolving certain philosophical problems.
Thus they have not refuted someone who might insist, for
example, that the sentence 'A is right' is descriptive, because
if the sentence is true, then A has the property referred to
by 'right.' Indeed a defender of ethical intuitionism might
agree with Nowell-Smith that 'right' and 'blue' differ logically in many important ways, but he would explain the
differences in another way entirely. Ethical predicates differ
logically from empirical predicates not because they do not

refer$_4$ to properties but because they refer$_4$ to properties of an entirely different kind.[5] They have certain logical characteristics which are what we can call the linguistic symptoms of nonnatural, nonempirical properties, symptoms which are, obviously, quite different from the symptoms of empirical properties. Surely this is prima facie as likely an explanation as Nowell-Smith's. In a similar manner someone who thought that in using 'He raised his arm' we are in part referring to some kind of mental event, could nevertheless agree that the sentence is like judges' decisions in certain ways. Furthermore, even given what Ryle says about the logic of 'vanity,' there is nothing inconsistent in maintaining that 'vanity' and other expressions like it refer$_4$ to mental (nonempirical?) states of certain persons, and are consequently descriptive in the broad or nonempirical sense.

We have found that Nowell-Smith, Hart, and Ryle have not established the conclusions that they reached via use analysis, because they have not justified one of their premises. Because which premise it is depends on how the term 'descriptive' is used, let us use 'descriptive' in the broad sense as we have been doing throughout the book. Thus the premise these men have not justified is premise 1', which for referring$_4$ expressions becomes: Sentences logically unlike indicative sentences of the form 'x is blue' in respects A, B, C, . . . , do not have predicates that are referring$_4$ expressions. Given this interpretation of 'descriptive,' premise 4 is, as we have seen, analytic, and premise 2 can be established by use analysis. But premise 1' is not analytic, and use analysis is not relevant to establishing it. Consequently because use analysis alone does not provide grounds for deciding which expressions refer$_6$, use analysis does not meet the second requirement. Since we have concluded that use analysis was the last possibility for supplying internal

5. See W. Frankena, "Obligation and Motivation in Recent Moral Philosophy," in A. I. Melden, ed., *Essays in Moral Philosophy* (Seattle, University of Washington Press, 1958), pp. 47–51, for a detailed discussion of this point.

grounds relevant to external problems, must we also conclude that there is no way to obtain such grounds? The only possible way to avoid this conclusion is by showing that premise 1′ *can* be established by some internal method. If we can do this, then we can supplement use analysis with this method and thereby produce an approach to external problems that meets the second requirement.

Premise 1′ can be established if and only if we can establish that only sentences that have certain logical features in common with empirical sentences can be said to be descriptive in the broad sense. Thus, more generally, if premise 1′ is correct, then any descriptive sentence must have certain logical features. This brings up two problems: first is the problem of establishing that an expression must have some logical features if it is to be a descriptive expression; second is the problem of establishing just which these features are. Neither of these tasks is easily accomplished. If, as many philosophers claim, many if not all general terms are family resemblance terms, then it may very well be that 'descriptive' is such a term also, so that the expressions it applies to have no defining characteristics and thus no essential features, whether logical or some other kind. There is, then, a reasonable doubt about whether expressions must have some logical features or other if they are to be descriptive. But even if we could establish that some logical features are essential, how are we to establish which ones they are?

Once we put the second problem this way we can see that we have come full circle back to the problem that arose in our examination of Carnap's theory of meaning in Chapter 4. We found that Carnap's method could not provide us with a way to distinguish which expressions are designators, and, consequently, which expressions refer$_6$. At that point we concluded that to justify claims that certain expressions are designators, we must justify a premise of the form: Sentences in language L are in relation R to reality if and only if the expressions have the additional characteristics *a, b, c, ...*[6] We also concluded that a theory such as Wittgenstein's picture theory of meaning seemed designed to establish such a premise. Indeed, we can put the two problems that we are presently considering, using Wittgenstein's terminology in the *Tractatus,* as the problems of showing, first, that some logical features of expressions are essential for their representing, and, secondly, just which of all the various features are essential rather than accidental, i.e. which features are not merely due to the peculiarities of the specific language. The problems stated in this way seem to be problems that, according to Wittgenstein, require us to go outside language. Thus they would seem to be external problems. If this is correct, then the problem of establishing premise 1′ is an external problem, and, consequently we can justify employing use analysis to provide internal clues to external problems only if we can solve one particular kind of external problem to which use analysis does not apply. However, because we have eliminated the other possible approaches to external problems, we must conclude that, if Wittgenstein is correct, use analysis fails to meet the second requirement.

But must we conclude that Wittgenstein is correct? Is there no way we can justify the claim that certain logical features are the linguistic symptoms of referring[6] expressions without going outside the relevant linguistic framework? Nowell-Smith's discussion of properties provides one possible way. He says that because 'property' is a technical term of the logician we must, in order to find out which adjectives refer to properties, examine the adjectives "that most typically fit what the logician has to say about properties; and these are the names of empirical, descriptive properties."[7] But aside from the fact that we cannot validly infer the required conclusion from the premises we can construct from Nowell-Smith's claim, this kind of attempt will fail

6. See pp. 93–95.
7. Nowell-Smith, p. 64.

because at least some nonempirical adjectives such as mathematical adjectives and surely logical adjectives typically fit what the logician says about properties. Indeed, if we are to rely on the logician who allows such diverse adjectives as 'blue,' 'tautologous,' and 'infinitesimal' to refer to properties, the most plausible conclusion to draw is that properties have at best a family resemblance, and therefore there are no features, logical or otherwise, essential to an adjective referring to a property.

We must conclude, I think, that Nowell-Smith's way of supplementing use analysis fails. Furthermore, I can think of no more promising approach to premise 1′ that remains within the relevant linguistic framework. I think, therefore, that we must end by agreeing with Wittgenstein that the problem of justifying premise 1′ is an external problem, and consequently that no attempt to supplement use analysis by an internal approach to 1′ will succeed. However we have been assuming that what we need is a deductive argument. Perhaps an inductive argument relying solely on use analysis will suffice. Consider the following:

> i. All predicates known to be referring$_4$ expressions have logical characteristics A, B, C, ...
>
> ii. Predicate 'p' lacks characteristics A, B, C, ...
>
> *Therefore it is probable that:*
>
> iii. Predicate 'p' is not a referring$_4$ expression.

Here, it would seem, only use analysis is needed to establish the truth-values of the two premises. Unfortunately there is one preliminary task for which use analysis is not relevant, i.e. the task of deciding which predicates are known to be referring$_4$ expressions. Empirically-minded philosophers will claim that only empirical predicates are known to be referring$_4$ expressions, while others, more metaphysically inclined, will want to include other predicates as well. Which claim should we accept? We cannot justify accepting either claim because we are involved in what is preliminary to the task of justifying claims about which expressions refer$_4$. Thus to accept one claim would be to beg the question against the opposing view. It seems that we must substitute for (i) something like (i'): All predicates agreed to be referring$_4$ expressions have logical characteristics A, B, C, ... The only possible candidates for such predicates are empirical predicates and the issue might be quickly settled. But this argument has unsatisfactory consequences also, because the area of agreement may be so small that many cases which seem unquestionable may be eliminated. Consider, for example, if someone claimed the thing-language was theoretical and only the phenomenal language was descriptive. If arguments of this form are inductively valid, then this phenomenalist claim would be inductively justified. Giving such an advantage to the most restricted view represented in any debate is question-begging in its own way.

Thus it seems that we must provide some grounds for claiming that certain logical characteristics are in an important way relevant to referring$_6$, i.e. are what I called linguistic symptoms of referring$_6$. But, unfortunately, showing this takes us right back to premise I', which we have been unable to find any internal way to justify. It surely seems, then, that use analysis must be supplemented by some internal method suitable for establishing premise I' if we are to obtain internal grounds relevant to external problems. But it also seems clear that no such method is available. Consequently, we have reached the conclusion that neither use analysis nor any other method can provide clues to an external question such as "What does 'p' refer$_7$ to?"— question I.

An ad hominem objection might be raised at this point. In Chapter 5 I claimed that the question "Does the expression 'chess king' denote anything?" is a type I,2 question, but in the present chapter I seem to claim that such a question involves us in external problems which there is no way to solve.[8] Thus it would seem that I have made contra-

8. See p. 169.

dictory claims. However, it should be remembered that in Chapter 5, although I claimed that to establish whether a referring$_2$ expression denotes something is a type I,2 task, I left for the present chapter the question about what kind of task it is to establish that an expression is a referring$_2$ expression. We have now concluded that the latter task is an external one. But although this has consequences for establishing whether an expression denotes something, there is nothing inconsistent in claiming that an internal task involves us in an external task when that means that solving the internal problem presupposes that the external problem has been solved. Thus the objection fails.

However, the way I have avoided the above objection might lead someone to raise a new one. If establishing that an expression refers$_7$ to something presupposes that it has been established that it is a referring$_6$ expression, and the latter cannot be established as I have argued, then the first cannot be established. But this contradicts the obvious truth acknowledged in Chapter 5 that we very often do establish that expressions denote. The reply to this point, as was mentioned in Chapter 5, is that in some cases there is no need to establish that an expression is a referring$_6$ expression, e.g. the expressions which are agreed to be referring$_6$ expressions, so that in such cases establishing that they denote does not presuppose any external task. It is generally agreed that at least substantive expressions that are material-object expressions, and predicable expressions that are empirical predicates, are referring$_6$ expressions, and that we can find out by empirical investigation whether for any particular use they refer$_7$ to something. But which other expressions refer$_6$ and thus which, if any, refer$_7$, must be established in some other way. The attempt to do this that we have just examined, use analysis, compares the logic of these acknowledged cases of referring$_6$ expressions with those in question and draws its conclusions on the basis of the logical similarities and differences between the two. This procedure we have found cannot be justified because we have no way of finding which, if any, of the logical features of these acknowledged cases are essential to their referring$_6$ to something. In Chapter 5 I picked as my example of a type I,2 question a physical-object expression, the kind of expression used by use analysis as a standard for non-standard cases. Showing that such expressions denote presupposes no external task. But in the present chapter, I have been talking only about expressions where there is some question about whether they refer$_6$, i.e. nonstandard cases. Showing whether these expressions denote presupposes an external task. Thus what is stated in the present chapter does not contradict what was stated in Chapter 5.

We have tried to find whether use analysis meets the second requirement of a method suitable for our purposes. In order to do this we first discovered its relevance to question I; then we showed that those who have employed use analysis have not established one premise needed in the argument to justify their conclusions. From this we concluded what additional justification is needed, and then found that the justification could not be supplied. Thus we answered the question with which we started the chapter, for we have found that use analysis fails to meet the second requirement. It will not provide us with internal evidence for answers to external questions of the form of question I. Therefore use analysis, like all other methods we have examined, cannot provide grounds for answers to external questions, those questions which are peculiarly philosophical.

Where does this leave us? In the next chapter, the concluding one, I shall try to tie together the various strands we have been following, show the kind of knot that results, and suggest what seems to be the only way out of the tangle—short of cutting the strands and giving up altogether.

Summary and Concluding Remarks

Let me summarize the conclusions reached thus far. We began with a brief examination of the mind–body problem, which was taken as representative of a certain group of philosophical problems, a group which, as we discovered later, consisted of what I called type E,2 external problems. In the first chapter this external mind–body problem, the traditional problem, was discussed, and three alternative solutions were explained. In the second chapter the three "parallel" solutions to the linguistic mind–body problem, the problem not about minds and bodies but about mind-expressions and body-expressions, were examined. Thus these first two chapters presented the raw material from which the central issue of the book was to emerge. The specific nature of that issue began to take shape in Chapter 3, in which four different views about the relationship between the traditional problem and the linguistic problem were examined. We were led to this examination because, for one reason, certain philosophers have thought that the relationship between the two problems, for example, that of identity or that of evidence to hypothesis, has important consequences for solving or dissolving the traditional problem. It was also important for what developed later because it was by means of this examination that we began to see the significance of that question that concerned us throughout the rest of the book which I called question 1: "What does 'p' refer to?" In Chapter 3 we found that we must be able to answer question 1 if we are to substantiate any one of the views about the relationship of the linguistic problem to the traditional one.

It was in order to find some way to answer question 1 that we began in Part II to examine theories of linguistic reference. Here we became directly concerned with what was developing into the central issue of the book; we began the search for some way to answer questions of the form of question 1. As the search progressed, however, it became more than just the task of finding the relationship between the linguistic mind–body problem, and the traditional mind–body problem. We began to see it as the task necessary for either solving or, as the case may be, dissolving any external problem. This search began in Chapter 4 with the examination of theories of linguistic reference. We started with Carnap's theory of meaning as representative of one kind of approach to the problem of reference, the problem expressed in question 1. This theory, and consequently those like it, were found not to be sufficient for the task. They needed some supplementation because we can employ the theories only if we have some way to find out to which expressions of a language the theories apply. That is, we needed some method to find out which expressions are referring expressions, or in Carnap's terminology, which expressions are designators. Wittgenstein's picture theory of meaning seemed to be the kind of supplementation required because it was a theory which provided us with a view of the relationship between a referring expression and what it refers to.

However, objections to the picture theory and to any theory which tries to find the relationship of language to what there is, including the objections of Wittgenstein himself, seemed to eliminate this kind of theory of reference, and thus Carnap's theory, from consideration. We then examined Ayer's view of linguistic reference, which is that we need not and indeed should not look for some one relation between language and what there is as Wittgenstein had done; we should look for what I called the designation rule for each expression. Such rules, claims Ayer, are the reference rules for expressions, and they can be found by examining the uses of the expressions. But this approach to question 1 was also found to be unsuitable. Designation rules could not be used to solve the problem then facing us, the problem of answering question 1 in order to show the relationship of the linguistic mind–body problem to the traditional problem.

At this point in the discussion it seemed that we had arrived at a paradoxical conclusion. People certainly know what they are talking about, know how to use expressions to refer to things, know what the expressions they use refer to. In cases when they do not know what someone is referring to, it seems that they can readily find out by using Ayer's method with some supplementation by ostensive indication. But in Chapter 4 we seemed to have arrived at the conclusion that we cannot find out what expressions refer to or at least that it is a very difficult philosophical task to do so, and that Ayer's method, even when supplemented by ostensive answers, will not work. Thus unless we could find some way to resolve this paradox it would seem that we had gone far astray in our attempt to find how to answer question 1 because any conclusion which implies that people do not know what the expressions of their language refer to or which implies that they must be philosophers to find this out certainly is misguided. This was another important step toward our final conclusion because the manner of resolving the paradox provided the basis for differentiating between that group of problems of which we have taken the traditional mind–body problem as representative, and any other kind of problem.

In Chapter 5, this paradox was resolved by differentiating between external and internal problems and then showing that while the traditional mind–body problem—and thus the problem of reference appropriate to it—is an external problem, the problems nonphilosophers might raise about linguistic reference are internal problems. At this point our scope had been enlarged. We were no longer merely interested in the relation of the linguistic mind–body problem to the traditional problem, nor were we even interested just in the traditional problem. Our task had become the attempt to answer the question, "How can we find a solution to an external problem, one example of which is the traditional mind–body problem?" We also found out that this question can be replaced by another, "How can we find answers to questions of the form of question 1 when it is considered as an external question?" In other words we found that if and only if we can answer questions the form of question 1 can we solve any external problem. We then continued our search with this broadened problem in mind. We first examined nonlinguistic approaches to external problems and eliminated them quickly because none can produce data which are evidentially relevant to external problems. We were left, then, with only linguistic methods which we examined in Part III.

In Chapter 6 we divided linguistic approaches into three kinds. We eliminated the first two kinds, meaning analysis and reconstruction analysis, both of which we found to be species of what Körner calls replacement analysis. The main reason for rejecting these methods is that it is legitimate to apply replacement analysis to an expression in order to achieve some purpose only if the expression in question is defective in some way relevant to that purpose. But, as was pointed out in Chapter 5, language is in no way defective relevant to external problems because language does not ontologically commit us in any way and thus does not mislead us about what there is. This left us only with the third kind of linguistic method, use analysis.

We examined use analysis in Chapter 6 and more thoroughly in Chapter 7 and found that use analysis is relevant to question 1 if and only if it can be used to answer the question, "Does 'p' refer$_6$ to something?" This is the same question we found Carnap's theory of meaning could not answer and which we tried to answer using Wittgenstein's picture theory. We found use analysis no better in this respect. From the conclusions found by use analysis, i.e. con-

clusions about certain logical similarities and differences between certain sentences, we found that we are not justified
in inferring anything about the reference of the expressions
in these sentences. Use analysis, as the other methods, was
not sufficient for our purposes.

The previous discussion, then, shows that we have examined the various approaches to external questions and
found them wanting in some respect or other. There seems
to be no method to provide us with answers to external
questions. However, this is not our final conclusion. One
more question remains to be answered: Must we infer
from this conclusion that we should give up any attempt
to deal with external philosophical problems because we
can discover no solution to any of them, i.e. because there
is no method that can provide grounds sufficient for handling external problems? If we must draw this inference,
then we must abandon many of the central problems of
philosophy. Some philosophers do not need to be urged
to give up such metaphysical problems, but for others, if
all the philosophical problems that can be characterized
as external are abandoned, not much philosophical is left.
Let us consider, then, if there is not some possible alternative. We know this much: if we are to find some alternative,
it will involve certain assumptions needed to supplement
the method we choose to approach external problems. This
is one additional conclusion we can draw from the previous
discussion. It is not a startling one for it comes to no more
than saying that there is no assumptionless philosophy.
With this additional conclusion in mind, let me suggest an
alternative to the complete abandonment of philosophy; let
me suggest the kind of assumptions which seem needed to
avoid the first, pessimistic alternative and then suggest a
sense in which these assumptions may be said to be justifiable. If I can indeed find a way to produce some kind of
justification of these assumptions, then there should be no
reason to abandon these problems, but rather some reason

to embark on a course like the one I am about to suggest.

Our conclusions suggest the kind of assumptions we need. In Chapter 7 we found that in order to be justified in employing use analysis to answer question 1, and thus external questions, two questions must be answered. First, "Are there certain logical features that an expression has if and only if it is a referring$_6$ expression?" The second question, which presupposes an affirmative answer to the first, is, "What are these logical features an expression has if and only if it is a referring$_6$ expression?" Because we could not find how to answer these two questions, we could not justify employing use analysis to solve or dissolve external problems. The assumptions we must make, I suggest, are just those which function as answers to these two questions. First we must assume that there are certain logical features an expression must have if and only if it is a referring$_6$ expression. Second, we must assume just what those logical features are. What we are to assume, in effect, is some particular version of a premise like premise 1′, that premise needed by men such as Ryle, Hart, and Nowell-Smith to justify moving from their conclusions about logical similarities and differences to conclusions about the reference of the expressions in question. Such a premise, incidentally, is also one version of the premise we were trying to establish in Chapter 4 in our attempt to find what is needed to supplement Carnap's theory of meaning, i.e. the premise that a sentence has referential meaning if and only if it has characteristics a, b, c, ... What I am claiming, then, is that we should assume first that some version of this premise is correct and second that certain logical features are the correct values of the variables a, b, c, ... I am, then, making explicit those logical features of language that men such as Nowell-Smith and Ryle have assumed to be the criteriological features of referring$_6$ expressions insofar as they employ use analysis to solve or dissolve external problems. One important reason for making these assumptions explicit will become evident when we come to examine in what sense these assumptions might be justifiable.

However before we move on to consider justification, let me give examples of various candidates for these criteriological features. Nowell-Smith, as we saw, tries to show that ethical predicates such as 'right' are not descriptive or referring$_4$ predicates by showing that they lack certain logical features. These features would be for Nowell-Smith the criteriological features of referring$_4$. For example, he claims that 'right' is not descriptive because, unlike descriptive predicates, it results in a logically odd sentence when substituted for 'x' in the sentence form 'This seems x to me, but I realize that it really is not x,' and also in the sentence form 'This is x but why should I do it?' Other candidates for criteriological features of referring$_4$ predicates can be gleaned from the many discussions of the predicate 'exist.' It has been claimed that 'exist' is not a descriptive predicate because it lacks certain characteristics, for example, because it is not a predicate in symbolic logic, because it produces a logically odd sentence when substituted for 'x' in 'Some tame tigers do not x,' and because when 'exist,' unlike descriptive predicates, is substituted for 'x' in 'Tigers x' the resulting sentence can be restated as 'There are tigers' in which the only predicate term is 'tigers.'

The assumptions I have suggested are those needed to supplement use analysis. At this point someone might wonder why, since no method is sufficient by itself in the sense that all methods require certain assumptions, I have picked just those assumptions which are needed for use analysis. Why could we not, for example, employ some form of replacement analysis and assume what we need to make it sufficient for our purposes? In other words, if no method is justifiable without certain assumptions why should we pick one method rather than another? Each of the competing alternatives is less satisfactory than use analysis in one way or another and consequently should be discarded in favor of use analysis. Each alternative faces at least one of the following difficulties that use analysis does not face. Each alternative either requires an assumption which seems to be false or at least highly dubious or one which is not open to any kind of justification, or is a method that, unlike use analysis, is not applicable to all external problems. Let me indicate my reasoning by a brief examination of the various alternatives. We can first distinguish between linguistic and nonlinguistic methods, and within the class of linguistic methods between those methods that consider only the formal relationships of linguistic expressions, i.e. the relationships among expressions, and those that consider the nonformal relationships of linguistic expressions, i.e. the relationships expressions have to things nonlinguistic.

We can eliminate all nonlinguistic methods first. In Chapter 5, when we were looking for some method of investigation that could provide data relevant to external questions, it was concluded that there are no external nonlinguistic methods of investigation and that the data of internal nonlinguistic methods are evidentially neutral with regard to external problems. That is, we found that the conclusions reached by nonlinguistic investigations, unlike the conclusions reached by use analysis, provided no evidence at all relevant to external problems. It is true that use analysis requires assumptions to justify the conclusions it reaches, but the assumptions needed are importantly different from those needed to make a nonlinguistic approach relevant. Although it may be true that no assumption is needed for nonlinguistic methods to justify the conclusions they reach, there are two reasons why the assumptions needed to make the conclusions relevant to external problems are less satisfactory than those required by use analysis. Consider again the mind–body problem. The results of the relevant sciences might be, for example, that certain sensations occur when and only when certain brain processes occur. The results of introspection might be, for example, that I am experiencing a certain specific sensation. But such results can be made relevant to the mind–body problem only by assuming either that each mental event is identical with some brain process if each mental event occurs when and only when one particular brain process occurs, or that whatever is intuited in introspection is not identical with anything physical, or some other equally ad hoc assumption. That is, the assumptions required to make these nonlinguistic results relevant are applicable to only one external problem. Consequently a nonlinguistic approach, unlike use analysis, would require a unique set of assumptions for each external problem. It would, therefore, require more assumptions than are needed to handle the problems, and, more importantly, it would make impossible the one kind of justification available for assumptions, that is, justification by reference to a large body of problems handled by a method of investigation when it is used in conjunction with the assumptions. Consequently the two reasons why nonlinguistic methods are less satisfactory than use analysis are: first, it would multiply assumptions beyond necessity; second, there would be no way to justify the assumptions made.

We must turn to linguistic methods if we are to find a viable alternative to use analysis. Let us first consider those methods concerned with the formal relationships of linguistic expressions. We have already examined two of these in some detail in Chapter 6, meaning analysis and explication. The only other possibility I can find is a method which examines the formal referential relationships among linguistic expressions, a method we can call reference analysis. Take meaning analysis first. Meaning analysis is used to discover which expressions are synonymous and which are not. From such results the only conclusion about reference that we can infer is that synonymous expressions have the same referents. We cannot infer what it is they refer to or whether certain nonsynonymous expressions have the same referents. Thus for meaning analysis we would have to assume what the synonymous expressions relevant to each external prob-lem refer to and whether the relevant nonsynonymous ex-pressions refer to the same things. But making such assump-tions amounts to assuming the solutions to specific external problems. Therefore, as with nonlinguistic methods, some of the assumptions required to supplement meaning analysis are not justifiable. Furthermore, meaning analysis also in-volves the additional assumption that it is applicable to the expressions of ordinary language and this, as we have seen, is a dubious assumption.

There is no doubt that reference analysis is relevant to external problems. Discovering the formal reference rela-tionships among certain expressions is a vital step in solving certain external problems. Unfortunately, however, as we have seen in Chapter 7 and elsewhere, not only is the ques-tion of whether two expressions such as 'brain process' and 'sensation' refer to the same things not answered by an in-ternal investigation of the two expressions, but the task sometimes presupposed by reference analysis, the task of finding whether an expression refers$_6$, is an external one. Thus, for reference analysis, not only must we assume that certain expressions refer$_6$ or that they do not, but also what it is they refer to, because reference analysis can discover at most whether certain referring$_6$ expressions refer to the same thing. Once again we must assume answers to specific versions of question 1, which amounts to merely assuming solutions to external problems.

The third kind of linguistic method of investigation that considers formal relationships is reconstruction analysis, or explication. As previously stated, explication is one kind of replacement analysis, and what is common to all kinds of replacement analysis is that one expression is put in some replacement relationship with another, so that the replace-ment of the one by the other corrects some defect of lan-guage. What is essential for explication, therefore, is that there is some defect of language that should be corrected. The most natural thing to do would be to assume that language is defective with regard to external questions, that, for example it misleads us about what there is. However, we have previously found that language is not defective in this way. What may be defective is some theory of reference we apply to the language but not the language itself. Consequently we cannot use explication with such an assumption because the assumption is false. However, another assumption, sometimes used with explication, may be helpful. Expressions are quite often legitimately explicated to correct defects in language when it is used in science. It might be, then, that certain scientifically motivated explications will be relevant to external problems. For example, it may be that psychological terms such as 'sensation' will be explicated for the purposes of science in such a way that it will be correct to locate each sensation in the place where the corresponding brain process is located. Such a change in the term 'sensation' would eliminate certain conceptual objections to the identity theory. The assumption we might use, then, is that scientifically motivated explications are philosophically relevant. However, although this assumption may be quite acceptable, it is not the only assumption needed because even if 'sensation' were explicated so that it would be synonymous with 'brain process' there are still the assumptions needed relating synonymy and reference. The major drawback of this approach to external problems, however, is that while expressions relevant to the mind–body problem may undergo science-motivated explication, it is unlikely that expressions relevant to the problem of the external world will be so affected, and it is clear that expressions relevant to other external problems will not be affected at all. Thus explication, bolstered with the assumption that philosophy should follow science, will not be relevant to most external problems and thus should be discarded in favor of use analysis, which applies to all external problems.

There are, I think, only two kinds of linguistic methods of investigation that consider the nonformal relationships of linguistic expressions, those that consider the relationship of referring and those that consider the relationships of expressions to the various nonlinguistic contexts of their use. Because use analysis considers expression and contexts, the only alternatives left are those involving theories of reference; and because no method of investigation can supply a theory of reference, what we must do is assume a certain theory of reference and use it to handle all questions of the form of question 1. This is the kind of approach to question 1 that we examined in Chapter 4 when we considered the views of Carnap, Ayer, and Wittgenstein. We would have to assume that only certain expressions refer$_6$ and thus only certain expressions refer$_7$. However, there are two ways we might do this. One approach would consist in assuming specific answers to questions of the form, "Is 'p' a referring$_6$ expression?" These are the questions use analysis with its assumptions is designed to answer. The other is to assume a general criterion that can be applied in specific cases. However, although both approaches are directed toward answering the same question, there is a basic difference. The only way to justify assumptions about which expressions refer$_6$ is to use some one criterion for all cases—the second approach—rather than handling each case individually—the first approach. This is because the only way we have found to justify assumptions is by judging how successful they can handle a body of problems. Thus if we make each assumption about referring$_6$ as each particular external problem arises, we cannot justify any assumption. This rules out the first alternative. What we need are some assumptions we can use to answer external questions, which we can justify in some nontrivial way. The second alternative seems to do this because it requires us to assume that only those expressions which meet a certain criterion refer$_6$. In this case, we assume a certain theory of reference by assuming this criterion. If we take this approach we do not thereby assume answers to external questions but must in each case see whether the expression in question meets the criterion. Here then we would attempt to supplement an approach to external problems, not by a theory such as the picture theory, but by assumed internal clues to the external problems. This alternative, then, looks promising.

There are two ways to implement this alternative. The first is to assume certain characteristics as criteriological. However, once we remember that the only characteristics available and appropriate would be certain logical features of expressions, then it becomes apparent that this approach reduces to the method of use analysis, for we would employ use analysis to find out which expressions meet the criterion. Thus this case is not really an alternative to use analysis.

The other approach involving a theory of reference is an approach that assumes that the 'Fido'–Fido theory of reference is the correct theory when applied to certain terms of certain languages. As we have seen, this theory of reference does not apply to the English language as ordinarily used, but it could be applied to an "ideal" language. However, because we cannot show that some language is ideal, we must assume a criterion for choosing some language as ideal or, in other words, a criterion for choosing those terms of some language to which the 'Fido'–Fido theory applies. The one available candidate, and the only one I can think of, is a criterion that specifies that the 'Fido'–Fido theory of reference is to be applied to a term if it is one of the undefined primitive constants of a semantical system which consists of these constants and the resources of symbolic logic, and which is adequate to construct all statements necessary for science. Such an approach is surely relevant to the mind–body problem. If both 'brain process' and 'sensation' are needed for science and both are needed as primitive terms in a systematic reconstruction of the language of science, then given the above assumption, we could conclude that the identity theory is false. However, many of the expressions most relevant to other external problems, such as 'God,' 'free will,' 'sense-datum,' 'good,' and 'beautiful,' are surely unnecessary for the vocabulary of science. How are we to deal with such terms? If we use the assumption as stated above, then we are assuming that being a scientifically necessary undefined primitive term is only a sufficient condition for applying the 'Fido'–Fido theory; there would be no way to apply this approach to most external problems. On the other hand, if we assume that being such a term is both a sufficient and a necessary condition of the applicability of the theory, then we are committed to what surely is a dubious assumption, namely, that expressions such as the above and all other expressions which are not necessary for science are not referring expressions. Consequently this approach to external problems is less satisfactory than use analysis because it is irrelevant to most external problems or because it involves a dubious assumption.

We have now examined the most plausible alternatives to use analysis. We have found that each involves an assumption which is apparently false, dubious, unjustifiable, or too limited in scope. We have also seen the assumptions required by use analysis, and there is no reason to think them false, dubious, or limited in scope. I have also claimed that they are open to a kind of justification, so that use analysis is more satisfactory an approach to external problems than any of its alternatives. However, I have not shown to what extent and in what manner we can justify these assumptions. Let me do so now. I have suggested that we should assume that certain, and only certain, logical features of ordinary language are possessed by those expressions which refer$_6$. Thus these logical features are to be the assumed criteriological or symptomatic characteristics of referring$_6$ expressions. How can we justify such a criterion? The answer is, as already implied, that it can be justified pragmatically by considering how fruitful the method utilizing the criterion is when applied to a certain class of problems, i.e. external problems. Thus to justify this criterion we must have this class of problems available. Let me now briefly indicate reasons for claiming that certain philosophical problems are external problems.

I have used the mind–body problem as a representative

of a certain class of philosophical problems, problems characterized as external problems in the sense that if they are
problems which are to be solved rather than dissolved, then
we are required to answer certain questions of the form of
question 1. We have also briefly considered three other
problems held to be external: the problem of the nature of
the external world; the problem of whether goodness is a
property, and if it is what kind of property it is; and the
problem of human agency. In all three cases, we found that
the question of whether certain expressions were referring$_6$
expressions, and if so what they referred$_6$ to was of central
importance. Three other problems have been cited but not
even briefly considered—the problem of whether existence
is a property, the problem of whether aesthetic predicates
such as 'dramatically great' refer$_4$ to properties, and the
problem of universals. That the first two are external problems can be understood by realizing that all the considerations relevant to dealing with the problem of whether goodness is a property apply mutatis mutandis to any other problems about properties. The third, the problem of universals,
is not so easily recognizable as an external problem. However, the facts that general terms, predicates, and thus
properties are related and that Quine's view about logicism
and medieval realism arose in the context of ontological
commitment give us some reason to think that this is an external problem.

Let me provide additional reasons for considering the
problem of universals to be an external problem by first giving a rough approximation of the three major medieval positions as traditionally stated, and then by restating them so
that they can be seen to be answers to one specific version
of question 1. The three views are ultrarealism, moderate
realism, and nominalism. Ultrarealism, attributed to William
of Champeaux, is the view that universals are substances
existing in and essential to a group of particulars; moderate
realism, attributed to St. Thomas Aquinas, is the view that

although only particulars are real entities, each particular has a certain essential characteristic in common with certain others, which characteristics are the universal elements in reality; and nominalism, attributed to Roscelin, is the view that universals are mere words, collective terms, which by convention we use to talk about certain groups of particulars. We might also consider conceptualism, the view that universals are concepts or ideas used to think about groups of particulars. Let me now restate each of these positions in terms relevant to question 1. Ultrarealism is the view that each general term refers$_2$ to one substance existing in and essential to a certain group of particulars; moderate realism is the view that each general term refers$_2$ to a group of particulars, each of which has a certain essential characteristic; nominalism is the view that each general term refers$_2$ to a group of particulars that are grouped merely by convention; conceptualism is the view that each general term refers$_2$ to a concept or idea used to think about a certain group of particulars.

When we consider the second formulation of these four positions (and similar formulations of positions not mentioned, such as Plato's *ante rem* view), we can see that all of them can function as answers to the question, "What do general terms such as 'human' refer$_2$ to?" This is a specific version of question 1. Does 'human' refer$_2$ to a unique substance, either existing in or separate from the particulars to which it applies; does it refer$_2$ to each particular to which it applies, either in virtue of a certain characteristic common to them all or merely by convention; does it refer$_2$ to a certain concept? How are we to decide among these alternatives? Perhaps there really is no problem and all these answers are fundamentally mistaken.[1] However, whether the problem of universals is to be solved by answering question 1 or dissolved by showing it is an illegitimate question, it

1. See D. F. Pears, "Universals," in Flew, ed., *Logic and Language, Second Series,* pp. 51–64.

certainly seems to be an external problem because it concerns question 1 as an external question.

Other problems that have not yet been mentioned are also classifiable as external problems. Two of the most important are the problem of the existence of God and the problem of free will and determinism. The first can be stated as the problem of whether the term 'God' refers$_3$ to something, and if it does, what it refers$_3$ to. The assertion that this is an external problem is supported by the fact that the external problem of whether existence is a property is crucial for one important proof of the existence of God, the ontological argument. Indeed, the ontological argument can be interpreted as an inference from the definition of the term 'God' to a conclusion that God exists. As with all arguments that move from premises about language to a conclusion about what there is, there is a missing premise. In this case it is the premise that 'existence' refers$_4$ to a property, the justification of which is, as we have seen, an external problem. As with most of the other external problems, there have been claims that the problem of the existence of God is not a legitimate problem because it presupposes that 'God' is a referring$_2$ term, which it is not. It has, for example, been claimed that religious utterances are not assertions and thus are neither true nor false, because they are compatible with any observable state of affairs and thus are not verifiable.[2] But, as we have seen, whether verifiability is a necessary condition of an utterance having a truth-value is itself an external problem.

The basic issue in the problem of free will and determinism is whether the two are compatible or not. Paradoxically there are convincing arguments for both views. Consider the following argument for the incompatibility of free will and

2. See A. J. Ayer, *Language, Truth and Logic* (New York, Dover, n.d.) pp. 114–20; and Antony Flew, "Theology and Falsification," in Antony Flew and Alasdair MacIntyre, eds., *New Essays in Philosophical Theology* (London, The Student Christian Movement Press, 1958), pp. 96–99.

determinism.[3] First, no one has free will to do something even as simple as raising his arm if some event that is a necessary condition of his arm going up and is not within his control does not occur. Secondly, if determinism is true, then if at any time my arm is not going up it follows that some previously occurring event is a causally sufficient condition of my arm not going up. Furthermore, if determinism is true, then for any event, there is a previously occurring event that is causally sufficient for its occurrence, so that some event before my birth is causally sufficient for my arm not going up now. But if some event is causally sufficient for my arm not going up now, then the nonoccurrence of this event is a causally necessary condition of my raising my arm now. It follows from the above that at some time before my birth, at a time at which I had no control over what occurred, a necessary condition of my now raising my arm did not occur. From which we can conclude that my arm, or anything else, not moving entails that I do not have free will to move it, and my arm, or anything else, moving entails that I do not have free will to refrain from moving it. Consequently, determinism being true entails that neither I nor anyone else has free will. Determinism and free will are incompatible.

Let us turn to another argument, one used to establish that free will and determinism are compatible.[4] Let us assume that although my arm is not going up now, I raised it just a moment ago with ease and have done so many times under conditions quite similar to those that now obtain, often in response to requests to raise it. These not unusual

3. This argument is derived from a debate between Richard Taylor and Keith Lehrer. See Keith Lehrer, "Doing the Impossible," and Richard Taylor, "Not Trying to do the Impossible," *Australasian Journal of Philosophy, 42* (1964), 86–100; and Keith Lehrer, "Doing the Impossible: a second try," *Australasian Journal of Philosophy, 42* (1964), 249–51. I am indebted to Professor Lehrer for helping me become clearer about the central point at issue between Professor Taylor and himself.

4. See Lehrer, 91–96.

facts surely seem to constitute evidence sufficient for establishing that it is probable that I can raise my arm now although it is not now going up. This is the first premise. Secondly, this evidence is surely compatible with determinism and, furthermore, in no way seems to be sufficient for establishing that it is improbable that my arm not going up is determined. We need one more premise, a theorem of the calculus of probability, i.e. if it is true that a hypothesis h is more probable than not on the basis of evidence e, but it is false that a hypothesis h' is more probable than not on the basis of e, then h does not entail h'. Given these three quite reasonable premises, we can conclude that it is false that my having free will to raise my arm at a time when it is not going up entails that it is not determined that my arm not go up at that time. Thus free will and determinism are compatible.

There is surely something paradoxical here. We have two quite plausible arguments that are used to support conclusions that are contradictory. There seem to be only two ways to resolve this paradox. One is to deny that the occurrence of an event before my birth which is not within my control but is causally sufficient for my arm not moving now entails that my arm going up now is not within my control. The other way is to reject the canon of evidence used to make it probable that I can raise my arm when it does not move. Both of these ways of resolving the paradox, it seems to me, involves us in an external problem, although, as we shall see, the two problems are quite dissimilar.

If we are to provide some reason for denying the entailment, the following, in rough outline, provides a beginning of what I think must be done. We must establish that it is a mistake to claim that sentences such as 'He did it,' 'It is within my control to do it,' 'I decided to do it,' 'He chose it of his own free will,' and the like belong to the same stratum as causal-sentences such as 'His arm going up was caused' and 'Everything that occurs has a cause.' A review of the claims of H. L. A. Hart about 'He raised his arm' will indicate how such a stratum difference can be used to make the point. If we take what Hart says about 'He raised his arm' to apply to all free-will sentences, then we can conclude that they belong to the stratum of expressions used to ascribe (or assume) responsibility for certain kinds of things that occur, rather than to the stratum of expressions used to describe, and scientifically explain and predict what occurs. Given this stratum difference we can, with Hart, hold that while 'His arm went up' describes a certain event, an event causally explainable, 'He raised his arm' ascribes responsibility to someone for that same causally explainable event. Thus someone raising his arm now would be compatible with there being an event that occurred before his birth which was not within his control and was causally sufficient for his arm moving. But because someone raising his arm entails that its going up is within his control, it follows that I can have the movement of my arm within my control even when some event sufficient for its movement is not within my control. Obviously this is not all that must be done; it must also be shown that I can have the movement of my arm within my control when some event sufficient for its not moving is not within my control. This might be worked out by showing that sentences such as 'He could have raised his arm but he didn't,' which entails that it was within his control to move his arm when it did not move, is used to ascribe responsibility to someone for his arm not going up. However, no matter how, or whether, this argument can be worked out, my point has been made. That Hart's attempt to place 'He raised his arm' in a certain stratum seems to be the kind of approach needed, is enough to allow us to conclude that the attempt to resolve the paradox at the root of the free will problem by denying a certain entailment involves us in the external problem of justifying a claim about the stratum to which certain expressions belong.

   If we take the other way out, if we deny a certain canon of evidence, then we become involved in one of the central epistemological problems, the problem of refuting the sceptic about knowledge. This problem, I wish to claim, is external in its own unique way. The epistemological sceptic, unlike the ontological sceptic who doubts the existence of certain things, doubts that we can attain knowledge of things such as the external world, other minds, the past, the future, and free will. This is contrary to what most of us believe, because we accept certain canons of evidence which allow us to infer that we have these kinds of knowledge. The sceptic, however, challenges us to justify the use of these canons. This surely seems to be a legitimate challenge because he can show us not only that there are cases where we go wrong using these canons, but also that there are other canons such that if our evidence satisfies them, we will not be led to mistaken conclusions.

How can such a sceptic be refuted? Let us briefly examine three specific attempts. First, consider A. J. Ayer who attacks many of the sceptic's claims on the problem of the knowledge of other minds. In this case, as always, the sceptic denies that there is any such knowledge because the only evidence available is hardly sufficient. I can establish that certain behavior of other bodies is like the behavior of my body that accompanies certain of my own mental events, but to conclude from this that there are mental events accompanying this behavior of other bodies is to make an inference that does not even meet the requirements of a sound inductive argument. Ayer's answer, in brief, is that because it is logically impossible to use any more restrictive canon successfully, the sceptic is demanding of us something that it is logically impossible to achieve. Ayer concludes from this that we can dispense with the sceptic's challenge.[5]

Norman Malcolm, who has also considered the problem of other minds, has argued against the sceptic about our knowledge of the past in a manner importantly similar to Ayer's approach. Malcolm claims that the sceptical hypothesis that the world began to exist just five minutes ago

5. See A. J. Ayer, *The Problem of Knowledge,* pp. 214–22.

with its population "remembering" a wholly unreal past so that their statements about the past are mainly false is a logically impossible claim. One of his arguments goes as follows. Because apparent memories being in agreement with each other and with the "records" of the past entail that the apparent memories are verified as true, and because apparent memories being verified as true entails that the past they describe existed, it follows that it is logically impossible that a population with their memories in agreement with each other and with the "records" of the past "remembers" a wholly unreal past. Here Malcolm, like Ayer, claims that the sceptic's claim involves a logical impossibility and thus can be dismissed.[6]

P. F. Strawson has used similar arguments to refute the sceptic who claims that induction is not justifiable. Because in an inductive inference the truth of the premises does not guarantee the truth of the conclusion, we seem to need some way to justify our use of one particular rule of inductive inference when there are an infinite number of other rules available. But, claims the sceptic, we cannot justify this rule by deduction from premises established independently of induction, nor, obviously, by induction, so that there is no way to justify the inductive rule we use. Strawson replies to the request to justify induction in two ways.[7] First, if this request is interpreted as a request to show that relying on inductive procedures is reasonable, then we can easily meet the request by pointing out that relying on inductive procedures is part of what it means to be rational. His second reply is much like Ayer's. He claims that although it makes sense to ask for the justification of any specific use of induction, it does not make sense to ask for a justification of induction in general, because in this case it is impossible to

6. See Norman Malcolm, "Memory and the Past," *The Monist,* 47 (1963), 255–62. I have criticized Malcolm's position in "Malcolm's Mistaken Memory," *Analysis,* 25 (1965), 162–64.

7. See P. F. Strawson, *Introduction to Logic* (London, Methuen, 1963), pp. 256–60.

produce a standard that can be used to evaluate induction.

In each of these cases the sceptic challenges the adequacy of a certain canon of evidence and provides some reason for his challenge. In each case he is answered by the claim that because his challenge involves something it is logically impossible to achieve, his position is not legitimate. Furthermore, although 1 think that none of these three men has established his claim, there surely is something important to be gleaned from each. It may well be that, as these men seem to imply, the canons of evidence we use are so closely linked to the linguistic frameworks of certain key epistemological terms that to challenge the canons from within these frameworks would involve violations of the rules of the frameworks and result in something logically impossible. Once again we seem faced with a paradox which can, however, be resolved by considering the sceptic's questions about these canons, including the one we use to justify certain free-will claims, as external questions. Thus the second way out of the paradox embodied in the free-will problem may, like the first way out, involve us in an external problem. This external problem, is, however, quite different from external metaphysical problems, because although producing an answer to question 1 solves an external metaphysical problem, it is by no means sufficient for solving an external problem about canons of evidence. Just what is sufficient, if anything, is a topic for another, quite different book.

I have above tried to sketch some of the major philosophical problems which seem to be external metaphysical problems. The way to solve or dissolve them, I have suggested, is to employ use analysis with certain assumed logical criteria for referring. The way to justify such a set of criteria is, I have suggested, to employ them to solve or dissolve the above-mentioned and any other external problems. Insofar as the set of assumed criteria we choose allows us to solve or dissolve each of these external problems, it can be said to be justified. My suggestion, then, is that we must select the set of criteria we are to use by trial and error, using finally that set which most fruitfully, efficiently, and simply solves or dissolves all external problems for it is that set we can be said to have justified pragmatically. By doing this we will not only pragmatically justify our assumptions about which features of ordinary language a referring$_6$ expression and only a referring$_6$ expression has, but we will also justify the conclusions we reach about each specific external problem. We have seen that we can justify in any particular case all the premises necessary to reach a conclusion about the specific external problem except a premise such as premise 1′. But it is just this premise which we pragmatically justify when we justify a certain set of assumptions. Thus, because we can justify in some way or other the premises needed, the conclusion we reach for any specific external problem can be said to be justified in some sense.

I have above outlined the program I suggest to avoid the pessimistic conclusion that we should abandon all attempts to consider external philosophical problems. I have suggested what seems to be the sort of assumptions we need and the sense in which they can be justified. Some people undoubtedly will disagree with this suggested program. Yet, if the conclusions we have reached are correct, there seem to be but two alternatives open to us. We must either give up a major part of philosophy because its conclusions do not meet a certain standard of justification or pursue that part of philosophy on the basis of certain explicit assumptions which may be justifiable in a way that does not meet that standard. Perhaps we shall find that no set of assumptions even meets this "weakened" standard of justification. But until it has been shown that this is the case, and there seems to be no a priori reason to think that it is, I can find no reason not to pursue these philosophical problems in a way such as the one I have suggested.

Index

Abstract entities and terms, 150 f., 160, 207. *See also* Universals

Alston, W., 153 n.

Analysis: distinction, 218 f., 222 f., 239; reductive, 205; reference, 266 f.

MEANING, xx, 200–10, 218, 222 f., 239, 261, 266; six purposes of, 201–05; objections to, 210–16

RECONSTRUCTION, 213 f., 216–27, 261, 267. *See also* Explication

REPLACEMENT, xx, 216, 261, 267; criterion of defectiveness for, 216, 220, 221, 225

USE, xx f., 216, 228–39, 261 f., 269, 271; and external problems, 240–57

Aquinas, St. Thomas, 272

Austin, J. L., 228 n.

Ayer, A. J., xvii, 47 n., 185 ff., 190, 214 n., 259 f., 269, 274 n.; on reference, 121 ff.; on other minds, 278 f.

Behaviorism: psychological, 5 f.; logical, 17 f., 117

Belief-sentences, xi, 25 ff., 32–34

Berkeley, G., 137, 171–73, 175, 193

Black, M., 109 n.

Brandt, R., 76

Brentano, F. C., 71 f.

Broad, C. D., 9

Carnap, R., 15, 84, 114, 116, 125, 134 f., 176, 190, 211, 269; theory of meaning, xv ff., 86 ff., 102 f., 113, 136 ff., 252, 261, 263; linguistic monism, 18–25, 39, 204; on relation of linguistic to traditional problem, 56 ff.; on external questions, 180 ff.; on explication, 220 ff.

Category: ontological, 11, 13, 16; linguistic, 16, 52; logical, 16, 38, 40 f., 45, 49, 52, 63, 67 f., 247; mistake, 64–66

Champeaux, William of, 272

Chisholm, R. M., xiv, 44, 125, 202, 203 n., 207 n.; linguistic dualism, 27–34, 244 ff.; on relation of linguistic to traditional problem, 71 ff.

Church, A., xv, 86, 128 n.

Cornman, J. W., 51 n., 78 n., 279 n.

Correctness, linguistic, 85, 162, 188 f.; three kinds, 173–75

Daitz, E., 104 f.

Definition: contextual, 200 ff., 214; explicit, 200

Descartes, R., 8 ff.

Designator, 88 f., 93 f., 117 f., 121, 184, 186

Ducasse, C. J., 9 f.

Entailment and logical implication: Carnap on, 88; and translation argument, 128 ff.; distinction between, 153 n.

Equipollence, 25, 58–60, 135

Ethical intuitionism, 232 f., 250 f.

Explication, xx, 219–24, 239, 266, 267; four requirements for, 220. See also Analysis. RECONSTRUCTION

Expressions: referring, 60–61, kinds of, 84, 142–44; denoting, 142 f.; that denote, 142–44; descriptive, 142–44, 233 f., 235, 244, 248 ff., 264, broad sense of, 250, 251 f., narrow sense of, 250

Extension and intension, 87, 89 f., 121

Extensionality, thesis of, 25 f., 204. See also Intensionality

External problems, xxi, 190 f., 253 ff., 261 f., 280 f.; internal clues to, 190 f., 193, 201 ff., 209, 234 f., 238 f., 240, 242–44, 253, 257; linguistic approaches to, 191–94, 197–239, 261, 266–71; nonlinguistic approaches to, 191–94, 261, 265 f.; and philosophical analysis, 197–239; and use analysis, 240–57; and science, 270 f.; list of, 271 ff. See also Questions: EXTERNAL

External world, problem of, 3, 137, 193, 243, 272

Family resemblance, 214, 252

Feigl, H., xii ff., 74, 77, 158, 176, 193; double language theory, 34 ff.

Feyerabend, P., 107 n.

Flew, A., 274 n.

Formal and material modes of speech, 23, 57 f. See also Pseudo-object sentences; Syntactical sentences

Framework, chess, 163 ff.

Framework, linguistic, xviii f., xxi, 163 ff.; and canons of evidence, 280. See also Ordinary language

Framework, rules of. See Rules, of a framework

Frankena, W., 251 n.

Free will and determinism, problem of, xi, 3, 193, 274–76

Frege, G., 28, 86

God, existence of, xi, 193, 274

Goodman, N., 212, 214 f.

Hare, R. M., 228 n.

Hart, H. L. A., 235 f., 239, 242, 244 ff., 251, 263, 276 f.

Hempel, C., 23; linguistic monism, 17 ff.

Hobbes, T., 4 ff., 13 f., 55

Human agency, problem of, 235 f.

Ideal language, 100 f., 104, 157–60, 270

Identity: cross-category, 76; theoretical, 75 f.

Induction, problem of, 279 f.

Infinite regress, 90, 119–21

Intensionality, 30 f. See also Extensionality, thesis of

Intentionality: linguistic thesis of, xiv, 27 f., 71–73; criteria of, 28 f.; nonlinguistic thesis of, 71

Introspection, 192 f., 265 f.

Knowledge of the past, problem of, 278 f.

Körner, S., xix, 216 f., 220, 226

Language and reality, 95, 102, 106 ff., 113, 117 f., 121 f., 137; accidental vs. essential features of, 101, 197, 253. *See also* Pictures, their link with reality

Language–chess analogy, xviii, 162, 165, 170, 187; breakdown of, 188 f. *See also* Framework, chess

Language, ideal. *See* Ideal language

Language, ordinary. *See* Ordinary language

Language, private. *See* Private language

Language stratum, 229–31, 237, 243 f., 247, 276 f. *See also* Category, logical

Language, structure of. *See* Sentences, structure of

Language, vagueness of. *See* Ordinary Language, vagueness of

Laws of projection. *See* Rules, of projection

Lehrer, K., 275 n.

Leibniz, G. W., 10

Lewis, C. I., xv, 86

Linsky, L., 85 n.

Logical form of representation, 98–100, 106. *See also* Language, and reality; Pictures, their link with reality

Logical implication and entailment. *See* Entailment and logical implication

Logical positivism (empiricism), 201, 250

Logical similarities and differences, xxi, 228–31, 247 f., 256

Logicism. *See* Universals, problem of

Malcolm, N., 188 n.; on knowledge of the past, 278 f.

Material object. *See* External world, problem of; Sense-data and material objects

Meaning, theory of, xvi, xix, 85 ff., 184, 252. *See also* Picture theory of meaning; Reference, theory of; Verifiability criterion of meaning

Meinongian position, xiv, xv, 110, 145, 159 f.

Metaphysical: questions, 169; problems, 262, 280

Mill, J. S., 207

Mind–body: PROBLEM, LINGUISTIC, xii, 15–52, 199; relationship to traditional problem, 53–80, 138, 258 f.; is identical with traditional problem, 54–63; shows there is no traditional problem, 63–70; is evidence for a solution to the traditional problem, 70–78; has no relationship to the traditional problem, 78 f.

PROBLEM, TRADITIONAL, xii, 3–14, 137, 162, 179, 192, 236 ff.

THEORIES, LINGUISTIC: monism, 17–25, 36, 39, 204; double language theory, 24, 34–52, 74; dualism, 25–34, 244 f.

THEORIES, TRADITIONAL: materialism, 4–8, 36, 51, 55, 69, 137, 178; epiphenomenalism, 6; parallelism, 6, 8, 10 f., 35, 36; dualism, 8–11, 35, 40 f., 69, 245; double aspect theory,

11–14; identity theory, 13, 77, 158, 192 f., 268; idealism, 52, 69, 178; neutral monism, 52, 178
Moore, G. E., 228 n., 232

Necessary truths: how they are contingent, 133 f., 176 f.
Nowell-Smith, P. H., 231 ff., 235, 236, 242, 247 ff., 254, 263 f.

Occam's razor, 36, 37 f., 51, 209 f.
Ontological commitment, 140 f., 145 ff., 159 f., 174 f., 186, 200, 226, 261; criteria of, 148, 151, 153, 155, 156; objective vs. subjective, 149
Ontological problems, 137, 140–42, 171, 172
Ordinary language, xx f., 157 ff., 270, 281; framework of, xxi, 225 f., 240; vagueness of, xx, 101, 214 f., 219–22
Ostensive answers, 126, 138, 139, 178, 179 f.
Other minds, problem of, 25, 278

Paradox, referring. See Referring paradox
Paraphrasing, 153–55; and entailment, 153 f., 153 n. See also Translation
Passmore, J., 109 n.
Paul, G. A., xxi, 208, 228 n., 233 n., 243
Pears, D. F., 273 n.
Permitted by language. See Sanction, linguistic
Phenomenalism: linguistic, 36, 117, 204; traditional, 3, 206–09, 255

Philosophy and science, 50, 51, 192 f., 201, 210, 265 f., 268, 270 f.
Physicalism, 18 f., 21, 24–26
Picture theory of meaning, xvi, 95–102, 253, 261; objections to, xvi f., 102–22, 127. See also Meaning, theory of
Pictures: abstract vs. representational, 96, 109, 111; their link with reality, 96–98, 106–12, and sentences, 99 f.; their link with what they picture, 96 f., and sentences, 100
Plato, 273
Predicates and properties: aesthetic, xi, 253 f., 272; ethical, xi, 145, 232–35, 242, 244, 248 ff., 264, 272; empirical, 234, 250 f., 253, 254 f., 256; nonnatural, 251; existence and, 264, 272, 274. See also Expressions, descriptive
Private language, 19 f., 46–49
Problems: to dissolve, 228 f., 234 f., 236, 241, 273 f.; to solve, 228 f., 234 f., 236, 241, 273 f.
Properties. See Predicates and properties
Pseudo-object sentences, 57–60, 62–67. See also Formal and material modes of speech; Syntactical sentences
Putnam, H., 75 f.

Quasi-syntactical sentences, 58. See also Pseudo-object sentences
Questions: EXTERNAL, xviii, xxi, 139–94, 166 ff.; two types of, 167; and ineffability, 190. See also External problems

INTERNAL, xviii, 139–94, 166 ff.; two types of, 166

NONPHILOSOPHERS', xviii, 141, 172, 179

PHILOSOPHERS', xviii, 141, 173, 179, 257. *See also* Metaphysical

Quine, W. V. O., xv, 86, 146, 184, 200, 211 n., 272; on ontological commitment, 148 ff., 159 f.

Reality and language. *See* Language and reality

Reductionistic theory, 128, 137, 175 f., 209 f.

Reference, linguistic, xiii ff., xv, 50, 83–138. *See also* Expressions, referring

Reference, theory of, 84 f., 144, 149, 155 f., 159, 259, 268, 269; 'Fido'–Fido theory, 156–60, 226, 270 f. *See also* Meaning, theory of

Referring, characteristics that are criteria for, xvi, 94 f., 102, 113 ff., 263 ff., 271, 280 f.; formal, 114, 115–17; nonformal, 114 f.

Referring expressions. *See* Expressions, referring

Referring paradox, xviii f., 139 f.; resolution of, 140–42, 147, 161, 176–79, 260 f.

Roscelin, 273

Rules: formal vs. nonformal, xvii, 122 f., 126 ff., 134-36, 155–57, 174–76, 189 f.; of projection, 97, 103 f., 127, 174, 189; designation, 114, 124 ff., 139, 155, 164, 169, 172, 176, 179, 259 f.; reference, 127, 134–36, 164, 176

ff., 259; of a framework, 163 ff., 174, 189

Russell, B., xv, 106–10, 146, 152, 158 n., 200, 203, 217, 223

Ryle, G., xii ff., 16, 79, 125, 176, 251, 263; double language theory, 38 ff., 244 ff.; on relation of linguistic to traditional problem, 63 ff., 237–39, 242

Sanction, linguistic, 141, 161–64, 173 f.

Sceptic: epistemological, 278–80; ontological, 278

Science and philosophy. *See* Philosophy and science

Sellars, R. W., 7 f., 13 f.

Sellars, W., 72 f., 127 n., 128 n.

Semantic system, 87, 90, 114, 165 f., 186, 271 f.

Sense-data and material objects, xi, xxi, 137, 171 f., 206–09, 243

Sentences, structure of, 95 f., 103 f.; representation of, 106 f. *See also* Pictures

Sheffer, R. M., stroke, 202

Smart, J. J. C., 16, 79, 125, 127, 128, 175, 178 f., 239; double language theory, 34 ff., 74, 77, 244 ff.; materialism, 55, 137, 193

Spinoza, B., 12

Stenius, E., 109 n.

Stevenson, J. T., 42 n.

Strawson, P. F., 78 n., 173 n.; on induction, 279

Structure of sentences. *See* Sentences, structure of

Synonymy, xx, 116 ff., 200 f., 212, 217, 222, 266; problems involved in, 210–16. *See also*

Analysis: MEANING; Entailment and logical implication;
Paraphrasing; Translation
Syntactical sentences, 57. *See
also* Pseudo-object sentences

Tarski, A., 107 n.
Taylor, R., 275 n.
Theory of definite description,
xv, 125, 152, 200, 203, 217,
223. *See also* Russell, B.
Theory of meaning. *See* Meaning, theory of
Theory of reference. *See* Reference, theory of
Translation, 18 ff., 33, 39, 42
ff., 58 ff., 73, 78, 128 ff.;
argument, 128 ff. *See also*
Analysis: MEANING; Para-
phrasing; Synonymy
Truth-value, 91 f., 116, 118–21,
274. *See also* Verifiability
criterion of meaning

Universals, problem of, xi, 137,
193; logicism and medieval
realism, 149–50, 272; major
medieval positions on, 272–
74
Urmson, J. O., 22 n., 103, 105,
109 n.

Verifiability criterion of meaning, 17 f., 19, 23, 92–94, 182
f., 274. *See also* Meaning,
theory of

Waismann, F., 214 n., 229, 231
Weitz, M., 228 n.
Williams, D. C., 7
Wittgenstein, L., 137, 174, 184,
189 f., 197, 214, 253 f., 269;
picture theory of meaning,
xvi f., 95 ff., 259, 261; objections to picture theory of
meaning, 103 f., 106 ff.